MARK, CANONIZER OF PAUL

MARK, CANONIZER OF PAUL

Tom Dykstra

OCABS PRESS
ST PAUL, MINNESOTA 55124
2012

MARK, CANONIZER OF PAUL

Copyright © 2012 by
Tom Dykstra

ISBN 1-60191-020-2

All rights reserved.

PRINTED IN THE UNITED STATES OF AMERICA

Mark, Canonizer of Paul

Copyright © 2012 by Tom Dykstra
All rights reserved.

ISBN 1-60191-020-2

Published by OCABS Press, St. Paul, Minnesota.
Printed in the United States of America.

On the cover: a thirteenth century image of Paul and Mark, from Cilician Armenian Gospel no. 9422.

Books are available through OCABS Press at special discounts for bulk purchases in the United States by academic institutions, churches, and other organizations. For more information please email OCABS Press at press@ocabs.org.

Abbreviations

Books of the Old Testament*

Gen	Genesis	Job	Job	Hab		Habakkuk
Ex	Exodus	Ps	Psalms	Zeph		Zephaniah
Lev	Leviticus	Prov	Proverbs	Hag		Haggai
Num	Numbers	Eccl	Ecclesiastes	Zech		Zechariah
Deut	Deuteronomy	Song	Song of Solomon	Mal		Malachi
Josh	Joshua	Is	Isaiah	Tob		Tobit
Judg	Judges	Jer	Jeremiah	Jdt		Judith
Ruth	Ruth	Lam	Lamentations	Wis		Wisdom
1 Sam	1 Samuel	Ezek	Ezekiel	Sir	Sirach	(Ecclesiasticus)
2 Sam	2 Samuel	Dan	Daniel	Bar		Baruch
1 Kg	1 Kings	Hos	Hosea	1 Esd		1 Esdras
2 Kg	2 Kings	Joel	Joel	2 Esd		2 Esdras
1 Chr	1 Chronicles	Am	Amos	1 Macc		1 Maccabees
2 Chr	2 Chronicles	Ob	Obadiah	2 Macc		2 Maccabees
Ezra	Ezra	Jon	Jonah	3 Macc		3 Maccabees
Neh	Nehemiah	Mic	Micah	4 Macc		4 Maccabees
Esth	Esther	Nah	Nahum			

Books of the New Testament

Mt	Matthew	Eph	Ephesians	Heb	Hebrews
Mk	Mark	Phil	Philippians	Jas	James
Lk	Luke	Col	Colossians	1 Pet	1 Peter
Jn	John	1 Thess	1 Thessalonians	2 Pet	2 Peter
Acts	Acts	2 Thess	2 Thessalonians	1 Jn	1 John
Rom	Romans	1 Tim	1 Timothy	2 Jn	2 John
1 Cor	1 Corinthians	2 Tim	2 Timothy	3 Jn	3 John
2 Cor	2 Corinthians	Titus	Titus	Jude	Jude
Gal	Galatians	Philem	Philemon	Rev	Revelation

*Following the larger canon known as the Septuagint.

Contents

Preface	*ix*
Introduction	*13*
Part I - Background	
1. Mark's Sources and Purpose	*23*
2. A Tale of Two Missions	*29*
3. The Chimera of Oral Tradition	*41*
The Modern Theory of Oral Tradition	*44*
New: Oral Tradition as a Recent Invention	*45*
Unfounded: Oral Tradition Theory's Flawed Origin	*48*
Unworkable: Oral Tradition Theory's Implausibility	*55*
Unnecessary: Alternatives to Oral Tradition	*62*
Unhelpful: Oral Tradition Theory's Impact on Biblical Interpretation	*64*
Part II - Pauline Themes in Mark	
4. Defending the Gentile Mission	*69*
A Gentile Christian Intended Audience	*69*
Jesus Visits Gentile Lands	*72*
Jesus Accepts Individual Gentiles As They Are	*77*
Jesus Unites Jews and Gentiles at the Communal Meal	*78*
Jesus Rejects Jewish Exclusivism	*82*
Jesus Rejects Jewish Legalism	*87*
The Parable of the Fig Tree	*90*
5. Presenting Jesus as the Crucified One	*93*
The Messianic Secret	*95*
The Irony of the Cross	*96*

6. Discrediting Jesus' Disciples and Family — 105

Jesus' Family — *106*
The Twelve — *109*
"One of the Twelve" — *116*
The Pillars — *118*
Peter — *119*

7. Alluding to Paul in the Main Parables and the Ending — 127

The Parable of the Sower — *127*
The Parable of the Wicked Husbandmen — *133*
The Apparently Inconclusive Ending — *136*

8. Appropriating Paul's Language and Example — 143

Pauline Language — *143*
Presenting John the Baptist as an Image of Paul — *147*
Modeling Jesus' Life after Paul's — *149*

Part III - The Genre of Mark

9 Why Genre Matters — 161

Biblical Scholarship on the Gospels' Genre — *164*
How Authors and Readers Actually Determine Genre — *167*
Applying Different Generic Criteria to the Gospels — *171*

10. Scripture as a Genre — 179

Fiction versus Nonfiction in Scriptural Historiography — *183*
History versus Myth in Scriptural Historiography — *189*

11. Mark as Scriptural Historiography — 201

Mimesis in Mark — *207*
Mimesis in the Other Gospels — *214*
A Broader View of Intertextuality in Mark — *219*

Part IV - The Historical Jesus in Mark

12. Conservatism and Curiosity	*223*
13. Historical Implausibilities	*229*
14. Historical Plausibilities	*235*
Conclusion	*241*
Bibliography	*241*

Preface

Frank Kermode was a scholar of literature, but he also wrote a book about the New Testament that became well known in the field of biblical scholarship. He prefaced that book with an acknowledgement that to write outside of his field was a risky business:

> The volume of scholarship is dismaying, and any outsider is bound to make mistakes. I am sure I have done so, in the teeth of good advice. . . . I have undertaken the studies here reported only because the importance of the subject, and the need of a secular approach, justify a measure of rashness. I think the gospels need to be talked about by critics of a quite unecclesiastical formation.[1]

Biblical studies is indeed a vast field, so much so that even those who live their life in it – let alone outsiders – are bound to make mistakes. But Kermode correctly saw the field's tendency to get stuck in groupthink, he saw how profoundly interpretations of the gospels affect peoples' lives, and he saw an opportunity to contribute a new interpretation that might have a positive impact. His attribution of the groupthink phenomenon to "ecclesiastical formation" was simplistic, however. Michael Goulder cites Kuhn's *Structure of Scientific Revolutions* to point out that even scientific communities get stuck in groupthink:

> . . . once a paradigm is accepted it shapes all scientific work: to be a scientist is to accept the paradigm. . . . The history of the subject is told in terms of the paradigm; its professors have made their reputations by assuming and extending it, and will not lightly abandon it. ... Shifts of paradigm do not come from professors;

---

[1] Frank Kermode, *The Genesis of Secrecy: On the Interpretation of Narrative* (Cambridge: Harvard UP, 2006), ix.

they come from young men, and from those on the margin of the subject."[2]

I have the advantage of being "on the margin of the subject," where Kermode was outside the margin. The latter jumped into the fray without having an education in biblical studies, without knowing Hebrew, with limited knowledge of Greek, and having "German so enfeebled that whenever possible I use translations."[3] My German needs work too, but I'm familiar with Greek and Hebrew, and the course of studies for my Master of Divinity degree gave me a background in biblical studies. I have built upon that background over the course of 25 years by my own research and by editing books and articles about biblical studies. If I fit Goulder's "margin of the subject" description it's because I don't make my living as a biblical scholar and my Ph.D. is in Russian history (a field which, by the way, turns out to have many parallels to that of biblical studies).[4]

Nevertheless, Goulder himself was by no means "on the margin," and that is not what is really needed to effect a revolution either in the hard sciences or the humanities. What is needed is exactly what Goulder exemplified: a determination to follow the lead of the text even when that takes you in

---

[2] Michael D. Goulder, *Luke: A New Paradigm* (Sheffield: Sheffield Academic Press, 1989), 4.

[3] Ibid., 4.

[4] My article "Metropolitan Ilarion of Kiev's use of Scripture in Defense of Russian Autocephaly" (*St. Vladimir's Theological Quarterly* 44[2000]:3-4:223-262) offers an interpretation of an 11th century Russian text that in many ways parallels the interpretation of Mark that I propose in this book. I developed that interpretation further in "*Slovo o zakone i blagodati mitropolita Ilariona kak tri iznachalno samostoiatelnych proizvedeniia.*" in *Rossica antiqua 2006: Issledovaniia i materialy*, Andrej Dvornichenko and Alexander Maiorov, eds. (St.-Petersburg: Izdatel'stvo St.-Peterburgskogo universiteta, 2006).

undesirable or uncomfortable directions. Goulder paid a personal price for his relentless academic honesty, and his memoir, *Five Stones and a Sling*, should be read by anyone interested in biblical studies.[5] On the other hand, what I have found is that those scholars who do exemplify this determination to follow the text no matter where it leads tend to also have a great sense of humor and are gracious, courteous people who have a positive attitude about life. This often comes out in person more than in their writing, but Goulder had a unique ability to weave a wonderful sense of humor into otherwise dry academic writing. I would like to do that but have a ways to go before I measure up to the Goulder standard. Meanwhile, I can and do borrow from him when it fits.

The present book offers a view of Mark that many may find goes in an undesirable or uncomfortable direction. But every step along the way is illustrated with facts from the text, so that the reader can make his or her own judgment as to whether the interpretations offered make sense or not. Any individual piece of evidence may not constitute a "smoking gun," but taken together, the evidence is about as strong as any we're likely to find in textual and historical inquiry into an ancient writing. Goulder found himself in the same position advocating a paradigm shift, and he commented on the situation with characteristic humor and humility:

> In the long run, there will be some who will not be persuaded however great the evidence; and of them it is written, 'Neither will they believe though one should rise from the dead.' But despite Kuhn, I retain an optimistic confidence in the integrity of my profession as a whole. If they are not persuaded, it will be either

---

[5] Michael D. Goulder, *Five Stones and a Sling: Memoirs of a Biblical Scholar* (Sheffield Phoenix Press Ltd., 2009).

because I have explained the position badly, or because I am wrong.[6]

I would like to thank Fr. Paul Tarazi, without whose support and encouragement the book would never have been written. His thorough reading and commenting on drafts of the book corrected many errors and deficiencies.

Thanks also to Fr. Christopher Salamy, Fr. Tim Perry, and Allen Bender for editorial support. Thanks to Bishop Vahan Hovhanessian for organizing the festschrift and SBL session that got me started on the subject matter that eventually became this book.[7] And special thanks to John Simon and those who collaborated with him to create audio recordings of the biblical texts in their original languages and make them freely available on the greeklatinaudio.com website. Mark's Gospel was written to be read out loud to a group, and there is no better way to get a deeper understanding of such a text than to listen to it. Some of my most valuable insights about the text of Mark came from listening repeatedly to the recordings provided by greeklatinaudio.com.[8]

---

[6] *Luke: A New Paradigm* (Sheffield: Sheffield Academic Press, 1989), 25-26.

[7] Earlier versions of some of the content of this book were published in "From Volkmar to Tarazi and Beyond: Mark as an Allegorical Presentation of the Pauline Gospel," forthcoming in vol. 2 of a 3 volume festschrift for Paul Nadim Tarazi; "The Gospels' Genre as Scriptural Historiography: Applying Lessons Learned from Ronald Reagan's Biography," *Journal of the Orthodox Center for the Advancement of Biblical Studies* (JOCABS), 4(2011):1:n.p.; and "'New, Unfounded, Unworkable, and Unnecessary': Thomas Brodie's Critique of Oral Tradition," JOCABS 3(2010):1:n.p.

[8] It is also, of course, important to be aware of textual variants in the manuscript tradition, which these recordings of necessity ignore.

Introduction

> Mark is remarkably uninterested in relating the teaching of Jesus. He often states that Jesus taught, but the reader seldom learns what that teaching is.
> Jesper Svartvik[1]

One of the most striking features of the second gospel is that it promises to present a "gospel" that consists of what Jesus taught, but it never delivers on the promise. The book opens by announcing that it is about "the gospel of Jesus Christ," and the narrative quickly clarifies that this gospel is what Jesus preached:

> The beginning of the gospel of Jesus Christ, the Son of God . . . (Mark 1:1)
>
> . . . after John was arrested, Jesus came into Galilee, preaching the gospel of God, and saying, "The time is fulfilled, and the kingdom of God is at hand; repent, and believe in the gospel." (1:14-15)

The word "gospel" is thus the key to the entire book. The word refers to teachings from the mouth of Jesus, and people must believe in it order to attain the kingdom of God – yet little of what Mark reports Jesus actually saying in the rest of the book is clearly identifiable as "the gospel" in this sense.

That Mark is not as interested as Matthew and Luke in what Jesus taught is well known,[2] but there is much more to this issue than just fewer sayings compared to the other synoptic[3] gospels.

---

[1] Jesper Svartvik, *Mark and Mission: Mk 7:1-23 in its Narrative and Historical Contexts* (Stockholm: Almqvist & Wiksell, 2000), 345.
[2] See, for example, Werner H. Kelber, *The Oral and the Written Gospel: The Hermeneutics of Speaking and Writing in the Synoptic Tradition, Mark, Paul, and Q* (Indiana UP, 1997), 100-1; Svartvik, *Mark and Mission*, 345.

After the statement in 1:15 that proclaims the absolute necessity for faith in the gospel, the text does not tell what the gospel is all about; instead, it jumps into a short story about Jesus calling the disciples (1:16-20). After that, Jesus is teaching again:

> . . . immediately on the sabbath he entered the synagogue and taught. And they were astonished at his teaching, for he taught them as one who had authority, and not as the scribes. (1:21-22)

But once again, the narrative continues after this with a healing story, without so much as dropping a hint about just what Jesus was saying that was so astonishing and authoritative. After the healing, people are amazed and say to each other, "What is this? A new teaching!" (v.27) – but no "teaching" has been related.

In 1:38, Jesus tells his disciples, "Let us go on to the next towns, that I may preach there also; for that is why I came out." This ratchets up the importance of the "preaching" theme by insisting that Jesus' whole reason for being is to preach the gospel. But again the narrative continues with healings and says nothing about what it is he taught.

In 2:2, while Jesus was in the crowded house where four men lower a paralytic through the roof, he "was preaching the word," but after that remark the story recounts the healing scene and offers not a word about the actual content of "the word" he was preaching.

In 6:2, Jesus "began to teach in the synagogue; and many who heard him were astonished, saying, 'Where did this man get all this? What is the wisdom given to him?'" But the story moves from here to the negative reactions of Jesus' kin, followed by still

---

[3] Matthew, Mark, and Luke are often called the synoptic gospels because large portions of their text are very similar or even word-for-word identical.

Introduction

more healings, and it never recounts the content of the teaching or the astonishing wisdom.

In 6:34, the text says that Jesus helped people by teaching them: "he saw a great throng, and he had compassion on them . . . and he began to teach them many things." But the next thing the reader encounters is Jesus' command to the disciples to send the crowd away, and not so much as one of the "many things" he taught is ever identified.

In 10:1, the narrative has crowds gathering around him again, and "as his custom was, he taught them." But what follows is a question-and-answer session with the Pharisees, and so yet another opportunity to recount what Jesus taught is lost.

There is no "sermon on the mount" or "sermon on the plain" in Mark. Jesus performs actions such as healings, feedings of multitudes, and the cleansing of the temple. He enters into disputes with opponents over legal observances such as Sabbath, food, and hand-washing regulations. He fields questions from his disciples and directs the answers only to them, on topics such as whether others can use Jesus' name to cast out demons, whether divorce is permitted, and whether there is resurrection from the dead. But only a few times does the text actually tell us what he was teaching and preaching to "the crowds," and those few times are exceptions that prove the rule.

In 4:1, Mark introduces the sower parable with the words, "Again he began to teach beside the sea . . . and he taught them many things in parables, and in his teaching he said to them . . ." This time, some words of Jesus do follow, *but they do not convey the content of the gospel.* They do not tell *what* people have to "believe in," they tell *what happens when people do or don't believe in (and obey) the gospel.* Jesus himself explains to his disciples that the parable is about how the gospel word grows or fails to grow depending on how people receive and respond to it:

> The sower sows the word. And these are the ones along the path, where the word is sown; when they hear, Satan immediately comes and takes away the word which is sown in them. And these in like manner are the ones sown upon rocky ground, who, when they hear the word, immediately receive it with joy; and they have no root in themselves, but endure for a while; then, when tribulation or persecution arises on account of the word, immediately they fall away. And others are the ones sown among thorns; they are those who hear the word, but the cares of the world, and the delight in riches, and the desire for other things, enter in and choke the word, and it proves unfruitful. But those that were sown upon the good soil are the ones who hear the word and accept it and bear fruit, thirtyfold and sixtyfold and a hundredfold. (4:14-20)

This text gives no hint about the *content* of that word. Nothing about just what it is that people are supposed to believe in and obey. The seed parables in 4:26-32 are similar but substitute "the kingdom of God" in place of "the word":

> The kingdom of God is as if a man should scatter seed upon the ground, and should sleep and rise night and day, and the seed should sprout and grow, he knows not how. The earth produces of itself, first the blade, then the ear, then the full grain in the ear. But when the grain is ripe, at once he puts in the sickle, because the harvest has come. . . . With what can we compare the kingdom of God, or what parable shall we use for it? It is like a grain of mustard seed, which, when sown upon the ground, is the smallest of all the seeds on earth; yet when it is sown it grows up and becomes the greatest of all shrubs, and puts forth large branches, so that the birds of the air can make nests in its shade. (4:26-32)

Introduction 17

It is following these remarks that Mark adds in 4:34, "with many such parables he spoke the word to them." "Such parables" do not tell the hearer the content of the gospel teaching.

The other half dozen cases where Jesus speaks parables or teachings of some sort to the crowds are similar.[4] They warn of consequences for failing to believe and obey the word – but they don't indicate *what* to believe or obey. This applies to the saying about putting one's lamp on a stand, with the accompanying warning that everything hidden will be manifest:

> Is a lamp brought in to be put under a bushel, or under a bed, and not on a stand? For there is nothing hid, except to be made manifest; nor is anything secret, except to come to light. If any man has ears to hear, let him hear. (4:21-23)

The saying about getting in return whatever measure one gives is similar:

> Take heed what you hear; the measure you give will be the measure you get, and still more will be given you. For to him who has will more be given; and from him who has not, even what he has will be taken away. (4:24-25)

And the same message is conveyed by the discourse about taking up one's cross, with its immediately following warning about the fast approaching kingdom of God:

> If any man would come after me, let him deny himself and take up his cross and follow me. For whoever would save his life will lose it; and whoever loses his life for my sake and the gospel's will save it. For what does it profit a man, to gain the whole world and

---

[4] The parable of the wicked husbandmen in 12:1-11 is addressed to the Jewish leadership rather than the crowds. And even that parable does not convey Jesus' teaching; it is about the Jewish leadership's negative reaction to him.

forfeit his life? For what can a man give in return for his life? For whoever is ashamed of me and of my words in this adulterous and sinful generation, of him will the Son of man also be ashamed, when he comes in the glory of his Father with the holy angels. ... Truly, I say to you, there are some standing here who will not taste death before they see that the kingdom of God has come with power. (8:34-9:1)

A few sayings do hint that "the teaching" addressed to the crowds had something to do with an exhortation to avoid treating other people badly. One is the remark about being defiled by what you say rather than what you eat, and another is the criticism of scribes' pretentious behavior:

Hear me, all of you, and understand: there is nothing outside a man which by going into him can defile him; but the things which come out of a man are what defile him. (7:14-15)

Beware of the scribes, who like to go about in long robes, and to have salutations in the market places and the best seats in the synagogues and the places of honor at feasts, who devour widows' houses and for a pretense make long prayers. They will receive the greater condemnation. (12:38-40)

But such hints are rare, and even they leave the hearer perplexed about just what Jesus was commanding people to "believe in." In any case, nothing Jesus ever says to the crowds comes close to qualifying as "new," "astonishing," or "authoritative."

What is especially interesting is that one of the characters in the story is perplexed in exactly the same way. When he poses a direct question to Jesus about what this new gospel teaching is that people are supposed to believe in, Jesus refuses to tell him. The man asks directly, "Good teacher, what must I do to inherit eternal life?" (10:17) This would have been the perfect opportunity for Mark to portray Jesus expounding the content of "the gospel," but instead he has Jesus answer, "You know the commandments ..."[5]

The modern reader of Mark who takes for granted the abundant sayings of Jesus in Luke and Matthew tends to skip right past this without giving it due attention. But the original hearers of Mark's narrative would hear the text stressing again and again that Jesus taught something new, authoritative, astonishing, and full of wisdom, while the expectation those promises raise would be disappointed at every turn. At the very point where that very question is posed directly to Jesus, an answer comes back that frustrates all of the hopes and expectations the hearer has amassed: *"You know the commandments."* In other words, Jesus himself answers by saying that he has nothing new to say. He can only refer his questioner to the Old Testament. What then is this "new" gospel that he's preaching all the time?

Jesus' questioner eventually is told to sell all he has and follow Jesus, but this takes the hearer right back to the "you must obey" theme, leaving the content of the gospel word that one is expected to obey conspicuous by its absence once again.

One must conclude that Mark's purpose in writing the Gospel could not have been to preserve any teaching or teachings that might have been new, unique, or special to Jesus. For Mark, what is uniquely significant about Jesus is not his teaching but his passion, crucifixion, and resurrection. And as for the latter,

---

[5] The complete answer is "Why do you call me good? No one is good but God alone. You know the commandments: 'Do not kill, Do not commit adultery, Do not steal, Do not bear false witness, Do not defraud, Honor your father and mother.'" (10:18-19)

the evangelist strongly downplays the resurrection by not even portraying it in his Gospel. As John Donahue rightly observes, "Martin Kähler's century-old description of the gospels as passion narratives with extended introductions aptly describes the Gospel of Mark."[6]

The conclusion that the evangelist had no interest in conveying any teachings that originated with Jesus begs a whole series of questions. Were Jesus' teachings absent from all of the sources available to Mark also? If so, why? If traditions about what Jesus taught were available, why did Mark ignore them? And why, then, did Mark write his Gospel? Maybe he saw the crucifixion and resurrection as most important, but then why did he emphasize the importance of Jesus' teaching, and why did he leave out an account of the resurrected Christ?

---

[6] John R. Donahue, "Windows and Mirrors: The Setting of Mark's Gospel," *CBQ* 57(1995):1-26; here: 9.

Part I

Background

1
Mark's Sources and Purpose

> With the development . . . of narrative-critical tools and an increasing sensitivity on the part of scholars to the nuances of narrative theology, Volkmar's original suggestion that Mark's Gospel is an allegorical presentation of Pauline teaching in the form of a narrative may be due, therefore, for a comeback.
>
> William Telford[1]

The traditional answers to questions about Mark's sources and his literary purpose are that Mark got the story by listening to the disciples and he wrote it in order to spread the good news about Jesus. But these answers sound simplistic for a text in which Jesus' only teaching is "You know the commandments" and which leaves his resurrection out of the story.

The explanation I offer in this book can be summarized as follows. Mark's primary purpose was to defend the vision of Christianity championed by Paul the Apostle against his "Judaizing" opponents. He undertook this defense because epistles written in the Apostle's name were no longer deemed adequate, possibly because Paul himself was no longer around to personally defend his authority. Mark didn't report any new teachings of Jesus because none were available to him: his main sources were the Old Testament, the Homeric epics, and Paul's epistles, not the disciples or oral tradition. And so he wrote a Gospel that implicitly validated the authority of Paul and his epistles.

---

[1] William R. Telford, *The Theology of the Gospel of Mark* (Cambridge: Cambridge UP, 1999), 169.

This approach to understanding Mark is not entirely new. In 1857 Gustav Volkmar published *Die Religion Jesu*, in which he argued that the Gospel of Mark was an allegorical presentation of Paul's teaching and Paul's life.² Volkmar was a member of the Tübingen School, one of a series of late nineteenth century German scholars based in Tübingen, Germany, who became known for historical-critical study of the gospels.³ At that time, questioning the historicity of the gospels was the avant-garde, or "cutting edge" of scholarship. Members of the Tübingen School were openly reviled by many if not most Christians at the time, with much the same vehemence that people who reject the historicity of the Holocaust are reviled today. This applied even to members of the school who rejected as unhistorical mainly the miraculous elements of the gospel stories, a position that would be regarded as conservative today. Volkmar went far beyond that, essentially denying the historicity of the entire thread of Mark's narrative. Even his Tübingen colleagues were not ready for quite that radical a viewpoint, and one of the most prominent of them went so far as to label the Volkmar thesis as "madness."⁴

In the end Volkmar's name sank into obscurity and his theory was all but forgotten, partly because he did a poor job backing up his interpretation with objective evidence from the text. As

---

² He developed his thesis further in *Marcus und die Synopse der Evangelien nach dem urkundlichen Text und das Geschichtliche vom Leben Jesu* (1876).
³ For more information about the Tübingen school, see Harris 1975.
⁴ David Friedrich Strauss: "Einen närrischen Kauz . . . habe ich in Volkmar . . . kennen gelernt; es ist Tollheit, was er vorbringt . . ." ("I have recognized in Volkmar a foolish fellow; it's madness that he proposes . . ."), cited in W. Schmithals, "Kritik der Formkritik," *ZTK* 77(1980):149-85; here: 180. For a similar evaluation, see Hajo Uden Meijboom, *A History and Critique of the Origin of the Marcan Hypothesis, 1835-1866. A contemporary Report Rediscovered, a Translation with Introduction and Notes* (Mercer UP, 1993), 83.

Quentin Quesnell puts it, Volkmar showed "unconcern for demonstrating that *his* meaning is *the* meaning, and not just one more pattern of which the text, in itself vague, is susceptible at the hands of an imaginative interpreter."[5] What sealed Volkmar's fate was the work of another scholar some 70 years later who did show a great deal of concern for demonstrating that *his* meaning was *the* meaning – and *his* meaning was the opposite of Volkmar's. In 1923 Martin Werner published a book in which he argued that Mark was not allegorical at all, and in fact not Pauline at all. Werner's arguments, backed by abundant and meticulously presented evidence, were received by so many biblical scholars as definitive that they delivered the coup de grâce to Volkmar's thesis.[6]

---

[5] Quentin Quesnell, *Mind of Mark* (Loyola Press, 1969), 41.
[6] Clifton Black expresses a view typical among modern scholars: ". . . Volkmar's assumptions concerning traces of Paulinism in Mark were weighed and found wanting seven decades ago by Martin Werner . . . Werner's assessment has since been refined but not overturned" ("Christ Crucified in Paul and in Mark: Reflections on an Intracanonical Conversation," in Eugene H. Lovering, Jr. and Jerry L. Sumney, eds., *Theology and Ethics in Paul and His Interpreters. Essays in Honor of Victor Paul Furnish* [Nashville: Abingdon Press, 1996], 184-206; here: 185). See also K. Romaniuk, "Le Problème des Paulinismes dans l'Évangile de Marc," *NTS* 23(1977):266-274; Vincent Taylor, *The Gospel According to St. Mark* (Grand Rapids: Baker Book House, 1981). Vincent Taylor calls the idea of a Pauline Mark a "wild and unsubstantiated hypothesis." (Cited in Sean P. Kealy, *A History of the Interpretation of the Gospel of Mark* (Lewiston: Edwin Mellen Press, 2007), 2:1:7. Benjamin W. Bacon (*The Gospel of Mark: Its Composition and Date* [New Haven: Yale UP, 1925]) provides a striking example of resistance to seeing a Pauline connection. He adduces a great mass of evidence suggestive of literary dependence on the Pauline epistles, yet ultimately rejects any direct connection. Svartvik cautions that Mark's Pauline focus does not necessarily imply a direct connection between the historical Paul and the actual author of Mark (*Mark and Mission*, 344-46). A few continued to evaluate Volkmar's work more positively. William Wrede asserted that "The sum total of what is false and impossible in his work is great in things both great and small ... [Yet] without a doubt Volkmar's book is the most perceptive and shrewd, and to my mind altogether the most important, that we possess on Mark" (cited in Joel Marcus, "Mark Interpreter of Paul," *NTS* 46[2000]:4:473-487; here: 473). See also Telford, *Theology of Mark*, 169.

Werner's reasoning has been called into question relatively recently,[7] and over the years many scholars have found Pauline themes in Mark.[8] Some have interpreted Mark as primarily allegorical,[9] and some have proposed that Mark created parts of

---

[7] See Marcus, "Mark, Interpreter of Paul."
[8] See M. E. Boismard and Paul Benoit, *Synopse des quatre Évangiles en français avec parallèles des Apocryphes et des Pères* (Paris: Cerf, 1972); J. C. Fenton, "Paul and Mark," in Dennis E. Nineham, ed., *Studies in the Gospels: Essays in Memory of R. H. Lightfoot* (Oxford: Basil Blackwell, 1955), 89-112; Michael Douglas Goulder, *St. Paul vs. St. Peter: A Tale of Two Missions* (Westminster John Knox Press, 1994); Marcus, "Mark, Interpreter of Paul"; Willi Marxsen, *Mark the Evangelist: Studies on the Redaction-History of the Gospel* (New York: Abingdon, 1968); John Painter, *Mark's Gospel: Worlds in Conflict* (London: Routledge, 1997); Svartvik, *Mark and Mission*. Marcus provides a long list of themes that are identical in Mark and Paul ("Mark, Interpreter of Paul," 475 and *Mark 1-8* [New Haven: Yale UP, 2002], 73-4) and his own list of scholars who sit on one or the other side of the fence ("Mark, Interpreter of Paul," 473-4). Svartvik (*Mark and Mission*, 345) asserts that "The Gospel of Mark may best be described as a narrative presentation of the Pauline Gospel."
[9] My use of the word "allegorical" in this context is not meant to be taken in a narrow technical sense but in a more general sense of expressing a message indirectly by means of symbolic language. As Svartvik (*Mark and Mission*, 212ff.), Alter (*Art of Biblical Narrative*, 21), and Meir Sternberg (*The Poetics of Biblical Narrative: Ideological Literature and the Drama of Reading* [Bloomington: Indiana UP, 1987], 56) assert, biblical literature in general does not conform to modern technical definitions of words such as "allegory," "parable," or even "fiction" or "nonfiction." For interpretations of Mark as allegorical in the sense I use the word here, see: Mary Ann Tolbert, *Sowing the Gospel: Mark's Work in Literary-Historical Perspective* (Augsburg Fortress, 1989), 24-26; Thomas L. Brodie, *The Birthing of the New Testament: The Intertextual Development of the New Testament Writings* (Sheffield: Sheffield Academic Press, 2004), 146ff.; Thomas L. Brodie, "Towards Tracing the Gospels' Literary Indebtedness to the Epistles," in Dennis R. MacDonald, ed., *Mimesis and Intertextuality in Antiquity and Christianity* (Harrisburg, PA: Trinity Press International, 2001), 104-116; Michael D. Goulder, *Five Stones and a Sling: Memoirs of a Biblical Scholar* (Sheffield Phoenix Press Ltd, 2009); Dennis R. MacDonald, *The Homeric Epics and the Gospel of Mark* (New Haven: Yale UP, 2000), 170ff.; Burton L. Mack, *A Myth of Innocence: Mark and Christian Origins* (Philadelphia: Fortress Press, 1991); Burton L. Mack, *The Christian Myth: Origins, Logic, and Legacy* (Continuum, 2003); K. Hanhart, "Son, Your Sins are Forgiven," in Frans Van Segbroeck et al., eds., *The Four Gospels 1992: Festschrift Frans Neirynck* (Leuven: Leuven University Press, 1992), 997-1016. Some assume that Mark had traditions about Jesus to work with but

Mark's Sources and Purpose

his narrative by borrowing from the Old Testament, the Homeric epics, and the Pauline epistles.[10] My goal in this book is mainly to present the evidence for a literary relationship between Mark and Paul's epistles. This intertextual relationship works both ways: Mark's Gospel borrows from the epistles, and it bolsters the authority of the epistles.

---

exercised complete freedom to change them however he wanted; see Theodore J. Weeden, *Mark: Traditions in Conflict* (Philadelphia: Fortress Press, 1971), 3, 16; Willi Marxsen, *Mark the Evangelist: Studies on the Redaction-History of the Gospel* (New York: Abingdon, 1968), 215; David B. Gowler, "The *Chreia*," in Amy-Jill Levine, Dale C. Allison, and John Dominic Crossan, eds., *The Historical Jesus in Context* (Princeton: Princeton UP, 2006), 132-148; here: 135; Austin Farrer, *St. Matthew and St. Mark* (London: Dacre, 1954), 15, 37; Werner H. Kelber, *The Passion in Mark. Studies on Mark 14-16* (Minneapolis: Fortress Press, 1976), 139; Daniel J. Harrington, *What are they Saying About Mark?* (New York: Paulist Press, 2004), 28.

[10] On the Old Testament connection, see Brodie, *Birthing*; on the Homeric epic connection, see MacDonald, *Homeric Epics*; and on the connection to Paul's epistles, see Paul Nadim Tarazi, *The New Testament Introduction. Paul and Mark* (Crestwood: SVS Press, 1999).

2
A Tale of Two Missions

The consensus among scholars is that Mark is the earliest of the four canonical gospels and was not written until after 65 A.D. This means the first communities of believers began and grew throughout their first three decades without a written "gospel." The only writings reflecting faith in Jesus as the Messiah and originating from this period are the letters Paul sent to the Gentile churches he had founded.[25] In these epistles the word "gospel" refers not to a written document but to Paul's teaching about the Messiahship (divine Sonship) of Jesus and its significance for both Gentiles and Jews. "The gospel" in this context is essentially a synonym for "the faith," as is most obvious in Galatians. The agreement reached among Christian leaders at Jerusalem and described in this letter (2:1-10) bears witness to the fact that the lack of interest in a written gospel evident in Paul's epistles is not unique to him: no one during this early period spoke of "a gospel" or "the gospel" as a written document and thus as a part of scripture. There was in fact no "New Testament" as we now know it, and more importantly, *there was no discernible sense that something was amiss because of that lack.* Indeed, our term "Old Testament" presumes there is a "New" counterpart, but such was not the case at this time. The Old Testament as scripture was considered complete and sufficient throughout those first 30 years.

Paul Tarazi[26]

One of the difficulties with many of the competing theories about why Mark wrote his Gospel is that they fail to explain why it took 30 years for someone to begin such a project.

---

[25] As Tarazi observes in a footnote at this point, the exception is Romans, which was written to a church not founded by him.
[26] Tarazi, *Paul and Mark*, 111-112.

The lack of interest in a written version of the gospel is all the more striking when one realizes that Paul's epistles bear witness to sharp divisions within the nascent Christian community over the content of the gospel. A written record of Jesus' words and actions could have been very useful to either side in these disputes over practical and theological matters, and yet it was 30 years before someone created such a record. How can this delay be explained?

The epistle to the Galatians was called forth specifically in response to one of these early divisions in the Christian community:

> I am astonished that you are so quickly deserting him who called you in the grace of Christ and turning to a different gospel – not that there is another gospel, but there are some who trouble you and want to pervert the gospel of Christ. But even if we, or an angel from heaven, should preach to you a gospel contrary to that which we preached to you, let him be accursed. As we have said before, so now I say again, If anyone is preaching to you a gospel contrary to that which you received, let him be accursed. (Gal 1:6-9)

The rest of the epistle clarifies that the competing "gospel" included a requirement that all who believe in Christ and join his community obey Jewish traditions such as circumcision and dietary restrictions.

Paul gives us some background to this conflict in Galatians 1:1-2:14. There we learn that he began his apostolic mission work independently from the other apostles, considering himself to be personally commissioned by the risen Lord himself. He was converting Gentiles to faith in Jesus Christ and was telling them they did not have to become Jews or follow Jewish traditions such as circumcision in order to become full members of the Christian community.

Paul continued to work independently as an apostle for fourteen years until the controversy arose. It began when certain Jewish Christians came to the Gentile communities Paul had established and told Paul's converts that they did in fact need to be circumcised and observe Jewish traditions. Paul vigorously opposed these "Judaizers" and took his case to the Christian leaders who were based in Jerusalem – the "so-called pillars" of the church: James, Peter, and John. He achieved an official agreement there: Paul was in charge of the mission to the Gentiles, and Peter was in charge of the mission to the Jews.

> ... when they saw that I had been entrusted with the gospel to the uncircumcised just as Peter had been entrusted with the gospel to the circumcised (for he who worked through Peter for the mission to the circumcised worked through me also for the Gentiles), and when they perceived the grace that was given to me, James and Cephas and John, who were reputed to be pillars, gave to me and Barnabas the right hand of fellowship, that we should go to the Gentiles and they to the circumcised ... (Gal 2:7-9)

The only condition placed on Paul was that he undertake a money collection among his relatively well-off Gentile congregations and bring it as an offering to the relatively poor congregations of Jerusalem.

According to Paul, he returned to his base in Antioch, where there was an integrated and harmonious mix of Jews and Gentiles, with this agreement vindicating him in hand. Shortly thereafter Peter joined him there and honored the agreement by deigning to "eat with the Gentiles."[27] In that culture, taking part

---

[27] Gal 2:12.

in table fellowship was a fundamental way of showing one's full membership in a community. By joining the Gentiles in this way, Peter showed that he considered Gentiles to be full and equal members of the community even if they did not observe the Jewish Law regarding matters such as circumcision.

Apparently the "pillars" remaining in Jerusalem had a different view of the agreement that had been hashed out with Paul than Paul himself did, because they did not allow this behavior to continue unchallenged. Paul reports that before long James sent some men from Jerusalem to tell Jews that they still had to observe Jewish traditions.

Peter complied by curtailing his table fellowship with Gentiles, and this incensed Paul, who saw Peter's actions as cowardly and traitorous. Paul tells us that he condemned Peter openly for this breach of trust:

> But when Cephas [that is, Peter] came to Antioch I opposed him to his face, because he stood condemned. For before certain men came from James, he ate with the Gentiles; but when they came he drew back and separated himself, fearing the circumcision party. And with him the rest of the Jews acted insincerely, so that even Barnabas was carried away by their insincerity. But when I saw that they were not straightforward about the truth of the gospel, I said to Cephas before them all, "If you, though a Jew, live like a Gentile and not like a Jew, how can you compel the Gentiles to live like Jews?" (Gal 2:11-14)

How could Peter's actions "compel the Gentiles to live like Jews"? Apparently, what Peter did intimated that if you were a Gentile it was not enough to believe in Christ. Until you adopted Jewish traditions such as circumcision and table fellowship rules, you were still in reality only a second-class

A Tale of Two Missions 33

citizen within the community – on your way to salvation perhaps, but having taken only the first of two requisite steps. (James and Peter might not have seen things this way, but we do not have their side of the story.)

Paul's decisive reaction did not put an end to the controversy. Emissaries of the "circumcision party" that Peter "feared" made their way later to Paul's churches in Galatia and managed to convince them too that they had to obey Jewish traditions. This continued challenge to Paul's gospel and his authority was all the more galling because he had gone to the trouble of hashing things out with the Jerusalem leaders. And so Paul penned the angry response that began "I am astonished that you are so quickly deserting him who called you in the grace of Christ and turning to a different gospel . . ."

Paul's conflict with the leaders of the Jewish mission persisted. Although the epistles may have been edited to create an image of unity among the apostles,[28] evidence of the split remains in places. In 1 Thessalonians Paul laments about how "the Jews" have been hindering his efforts:

> For you, brethren, became imitators of the churches of God in Christ Jesus which are in Judea; for you suffered the same things from your own countrymen as they did from the Jews, who killed both the Lord Jesus and the prophets, and drove us out, and displease God and oppose all men by hindering us from speaking to the Gentiles that they may be saved – so as always to fill up the measure of their sins. (1 Thess 2:14-16)

The ongoing severity of this as the main conflict that Paul and his Gentile congregations faced is reflected in the fact that most

---

[28] This is the thesis of David Trobisch (*Paul's Letter Collection: Tracing the Origins* [Minneapolis: Fortress Press, 1994]). See also David Trobisch, *First Edition*.

of Romans – the magnum opus within the Pauline corpus – addresses at great length the relationship between Jews and Christian Gentiles.

Taking all this into account, the phrase "disobedient people in Judea" at the end of Romans can be interpreted as an allusion to the party of James and to Peter for going along with them:[29]

> I appeal to you, brethren, by our Lord Jesus Christ and by the love of the Spirit, to strive together with me in your prayers to God on my behalf, that I may be delivered from the disobedient people[30] in Judea, and that my service for Jerusalem may be acceptable to the saints . . . (Rom 15:30-31)

In Paul's view, if James were to refuse the collection in order to disavow the agreement, that would constitute disobedience to the gospel. The warning against divisive people in Romans 16 may then have the same implied targets:[31]

> I urge you, brothers, to watch out for those who cause divisions and put obstacles in your way that are contrary to the teaching you have learned. Keep away from them. For such people are not serving our Lord Christ, but their own appetites. By smooth talk and flattery they deceive the minds of naïve people. Everyone has heard about your obedience, so I am full of joy over you; but I want you to be wise about what is good, and innocent about what is evil. (Rom 16:17-19)

Another example is in 1 Corinthians. In chapter 7 Paul praises his own ability to remain unmarried while allowing that marriage is acceptable for people who are "unable to control

---

[29] See Trobisch, *Paul's Letter Collection*, 90.
[30] Some English versions translate "unbelievers," which is misleading. The word ἀπειθούντων literally means the disobedient ones, not the unbelieving ones.
[31] Ibid.

themselves" (7:8-9); then just two chapters later he alludes to the married status of "the brothers of the Lord [James] and Cephas [Peter]" (9:3-6). The effect, and quite possibly the intent, of these two passages is to portray in a negative light the men who opposed Paul in Jerusalem and Antioch.

In *St. Paul vs. St. Peter: A Tale of Two Missions*, Michael Goulder argues that the differences between Paul's Gentile mission and Peter's Jewish mission went well beyond the question of whether Gentiles were required to observe Jewish traditions.[32] He sees a more fundamental disagreement: Peter's mission believed that the heavenly kingdom had already arrived and believers were already enjoying resurrected life, while Paul's stressed that the resurrection was yet to come and believers' present life was more like the crucifixion. Out of this fundamental divide developed other differences: Peter's mission stressed tongues and visions and gifts of the spirit, while Paul's stressed love and charity; Peter's mission stressed the need to give away all of one's possessions since the end had already come, while Paul's mission advised people to keep working and earning a living. As will be seen, some of these differences are reflected in the text of Mark's Gospel.

Those who are unfamiliar with biblical scholarship but have read the New Testament may find this theory surprising or consider it improbable because the book of Acts portrays a harmonious college of early Christian leaders all reaching out to Gentiles. Indeed, Acts has Peter initiating the mission himself at the direct command of God, with Paul picking up the torch and

---

[32] Goulder, *Paul vs. Peter*. As Goulder notes, a similar idea was first proposed by Ferdinand Baur in 1831, but scholars lost sight of it after problems with it were pointed out by W. Lütgert in 1908. Goulder addresses the difficulties cited by Lütgert in this book and other writings; see 194-95.

running with it later. However, this harmony between Paul and the other apostles directly contradicts what we read in Paul's own epistles, which bear evidence of a split between them.

If we approach the New Testament writings as historical sources, the epistles appear to be closer to what we would call primary sources than the gospels, which are secondary sources that were written much later.[33] Although the epistles have clearly been carefully edited,[34] some of them were apparently written by participants and eyewitnesses of the events that they depict, possibly within a relatively short time after those events took place. It is true that the author of Luke-Acts cites access to "eyewitnesses" (Luke 1:2), and the famous "we passages"[35] in Acts give the impression that the author was involved in the reported action. But the bulk of Acts is a secondary source whose author had a particular point to make in writing it. More specifically, the author of Acts went to great lengths to highlight the unity and harmony of all of the apostles.[36] In fact, many scholars interpret Acts as a tendentious attempt to portray a Christian unity after the fact that did not in reality exist.[37] There is, then, no convincing evidence to disprove Paul's accounts of a sharp divide between him and "Judaizing" Christians, and the "Two Missions" theory of Goulder has much to recommend it

---

[33] In historical research, primary sources are first-hand accounts by eyewitnesses or participants in the events recounted; secondary sources are compilations by people who have read or heard about the events second-hand. Primary sources are generally considered more reliable as historical sources, just as first-hand testimony is permitted in court while hearsay is not.
[34] See Trobisch, *Paul's Letter Collection*, especially 22-3, 44-47, 57-62, 75.
[35] Acts 16:10-17; 20:5-15; 21:1-18; 27:1-28:16.
[36] See Trobisch, *Paul's Letter Collection*, 90ff.; *First Edition*, 77ff.
[37] See, for example, Trobisch, *First Edition*, 45-63, 77ff. The presence in Acts of some accurate references to people and events outside the Christian community does not mean that its history of early Christianity is accurate.

in general even if support for some of the specifics is relatively weak.

And so it appears that Paul was engaged in a pitched battle to defend everything he had worked for against powerful opponents, including Jesus' brother James, the leader of the church in Jerusalem. In this battle both sides acknowledged the Old Testament as their scriptural authority, and both sides thought the Old Testament supported their side against the other. The Apostle fought the opponents who preached this "other gospel" with only two weapons: his personal authority and his rhetorical skill in support of his interpretation of the Old Testament.[38]

The content of "the gospel," then, was hotly contested, and one side of the struggle drew its support largely if not entirely from the person of Paul. Indeed, much of the Pauline corpus is devoted to defending the Pauline version of "the gospel" against aggressive proponents of competing versions. Yet we have no evidence that in the midst of this raging battle anyone thought a systematic literary exposition of their own version of the gospel was needed to resolve the matter. For three long decades no one saw the need for such a document either to defend their own view against opponents or to evangelize people yet unreached by any version of the gospel story.

What, then, could have prompted someone to undertake the composition of Mark at the specific time it was written so long after the history it recounts? One hypothesis that makes sense of the known facts is that the same group involved in creating the epistles simply added a new tactic – that of narrative – to their

---

[38] Gal 1:1-2:14 is largely devoted to asserting Paul's personal authority; for an example where he argues for his interpretation of the Old Testament, see 3:6-22; 4:22-31.

literary repertoire. The change in tactics may have been occasioned by the death of Paul and the realization that the effectiveness of his personal authority in the ongoing battle was diminishing. The primary intended audience would then be the same as for the epistles: established Christian communities in which the battle between competing gospels continued to rage. The primary purpose of the gospel narrative would then be to assert that Paul's gospel was correct, that Paul's interpretation of the significance of the person of Christ and his crucifixion and resurrection was the correct one, and that Paul's opponents were wrong even though they could boast of close personal connections to Jesus while Paul could not.

This would be a tall order. First of all, it would involve projecting (or "retrojecting") back to around 30 AD a dispute that did not actually arise until the 40s or 50s. The controversy about Law observance that we know from Paul's epistles could not have begun until Paul started converting Gentiles and allowing them to ignore circumcision and other Jewish traditions. So the author of a gospel narrative intended to support Paul's position would have to skillfully craft a story that was at once anachronistic and plausible.

Secondly, such a narrative would have to show Jesus disavowing the authority of his own closest associates, since it was precisely apostles whose "pillar" status was based on closeness to Jesus dating back before his resurrection who were opposing Paul.

To accomplish these tasks in a written narrative set in Jesus' day, the author would have to portray a Jesus who was misunderstood by his own closest associates, and who made clear that Jewish traditions were of relative rather than absolute value.

This literary Jesus would not need to present any new or unique teaching but would have to confirm the authority of the Old Testament. And the narrative would have to emphasize the crucifixion and de-emphasize the resurrection, because that is what Paul did in his epistles. The Apostle to the Gentiles did defend belief in Christ's resurrection against those who would deny it, but the core of his message was the crucified Christ: "For I decided to know nothing among you except Jesus Christ and him crucified." (1 Cor 2:2)[39]

The literary strategy laid out here is precisely what we find in the Gospel of Mark.

---

[39] See also 1 Cor 1:13, 23; Gal 2:20; 3:1; 5:24; 6:14

3
The Chimera of Oral Tradition

If the reason why Mark wrote his Gospel is less obvious than is commonly assumed, the question of where he found his sources raises even greater difficulties. How can a narrative written 30-plus years after the events that it records include such vivid detail, extensive verbatim conversations, and even the innermost thoughts and feelings of the participants in the drama? If this is all or mostly an accurate historical record, someone would have to have hired a stenographer to follow Jesus and his disciples around everywhere (not to mention a clairvoyant to pass on private thoughts of participants to the stenographer).

In fact, we have no evidence at all that anything about Jesus' life and sayings was written down during his lifetime or even shortly thereafter. The earliest writings we have that mention Jesus are the New Testament epistles attributed to Paul, but the Apostle records almost nothing of his Lord's life and sayings.[40] How is it that Mark's elaborate narrative appeared suddenly out of nowhere after three decades?

Some scholars postulate the existence of a written document they call Q which preserved a substantial series of Jesus' sayings, and which might have been written down before Mark.[41]

---

[40] For a complete list of everything in Paul's epistles that cites sayings of Jesus or can be interpreted as alluding to such sayings, see Nikolaus Walter, "Paul and the Early Christian Jesus-Tradition," in A. J. M. Wedderburn, ed., *Paul and Jesus: Collected Essays* (Sheffield: JSOT Press, 1989), 51-80.

[41] For an exposition of the Q theory, see James M. Robinson, *Jesus: According to the Earliest Witness* (Minneapolis: Fortress Press, 2007). For a proposed reconstruction of Q, see Paul Hoffmann, John S. Kloppenborg, and James M. Robinson, eds., *The Critical Edition of Q: A Synopsis Including the Gospels of Matthew and Luke, Mark, and*

According to this hypothesis, Matthew and Luke were each ignorant of the other's gospel but each used Mark and Q as their sources, and so Q can be reconstructed from areas where the text of Matthew and Luke is identical without a counterpart in Mark. But no physical remnants of Q have ever been found, no ancient writer clearly mentions the existence of such a document,[42] and even Q's advocates assume it was not written down until, as in the case of Mark, decades had elapsed after the words recorded were originally spoken.

Remnants of non-canonical gospels such as the Gospel of Thomas have survived, but none of the surviving manuscripts can be dated earlier than the second century. While a few scholars assign a first-century date to the original version of Thomas, here too even the most optimistic among them do not propose that the sayings were committed to papyrus at the time when the recorded words were spoken.[43]

The most plausible conclusion is that there were no written records of Jesus' life and sayings earlier than Mark, and the question remains: where did Mark get all the detailed information he preserved in his Gospel? The traditional answer to this conundrum was that the gospels were either written by

---

Thomas with English, German, and French Translations of Q and Thomas (Minneapolis: Fortress Press, 2000). And for arguments that nothing like Q ever existed, see Mark Goodacre, *The Case Against Q: Studies in Markan Priority and the Synoptic Problem* (Harrisburg: Trinity Press International, 2002) and Mark Goodacre and Nicholas Perrin, eds., *Questioning Q: A Multidimensional Critique* (Downers Grove: InterVarsity Press, 2004).

[42] Eusebius quotes a certain bishop Papias of Hierapolis as mentioning a compilation of sayings of Jesus that was used by Matthew, and some scholars take this to be a reference to Q. Most, however, interpret Papias' comments as referring to the canonical book of Matthew.

[43] For an introduction to the Gospel of Thomas, see Norman Perrin, *Thomas, The Other Gospel* (Louisville: Westminster John Knox Press, 2007).

The Chimera of Oral Tradition

"eyewitnesses" or by people who spoke to "eyewitnesses." The prescribed belief was that the evangelists were either writing from memory as disciples of the Lord (Matthew and John), or they relied upon the disciples' accounts told to them as they were composing their narratives (Mark and Luke). Eusebius, a fourth-century church historian, quotes the second century "bishop" Papias of Hierapolis in support of this view with respect to Mark:

> Mark, having become the interpreter of Peter, wrote down accurately, though not indeed in order, whatsoever he remembered of the things said or done by Christ. For he neither heard the Lord nor followed him, but afterward, as I said, he followed Peter, who adapted his teaching to the needs of his hearers, but with no intention of giving a connected account of the Lord's discourses.[44]

One of the Papias passages is also frequently cited to explain why so much time elapsed before someone wrote down the gospel story. In this view, "oral tradition" was valued even higher than a written record:

> If then, anyone came, who had been a follower of the elders, I questioned him in regard to the words of the elders — what Andrew or what Peter said, or what was said by Philip, or by Thomas, or by James, or by John, or by Matthew, or by any other of the disciples of the Lord, and what things Aristion and the Presbyter John, the disciples of the Lord, say. For I did not think that what was to be gotten from the books would profit me as much as what came from the living and abiding voice.[45]

---

[44] Eusebius, *Church History* 39:15 (*NPNF2* 1:172-3).
[45] Eusebius, *Church History* 39:4 (*NPNF2* 1:171).

At first glance this sounds like a reasonable explanation for the content of Mark, but in reality it isn't historically plausible. Memories even of eyewitnesses grow dim and lose detail after a day or two, let alone weeks, months, or 30-plus years. Scattered impressions and individual emotionally charged moments might remain, but this would hardly supply a long and detailed narrative with extensive verbatim dialogue. Such a narrative might be extrapolated from such memories, but it would be more the result of later reflection and extrapolation than an accurate historical record.

The Modern Theory of Oral Tradition

Within the last couple of centuries New Testament scholars recognized the problem and devised an alternative theory that seems to solve the problem. Mark's main source, they propose, is "oral tradition." What this implies is succinctly expressed by William Telford in his description of the Gospel of Mark:

> The Gospel is the compilation of a number of single, isolated, easily memorized traditions or pericopae (or small clusters of such pericopae) which circulated in oral form before being written down.[46]

Some scholars believe these traditions were often composed out of thin air to serve specific purposes in the life of a community. For example, if a dispute over dietary rules arose in a community, the community might make up a saying to settle the matter, like "there is nothing outside a man which by going into him can defile him; but the things which come out of a man are what defile him." (Mark 7:15) Others believe that the traditions originally resulted from people memorizing events and

---

[46] William R Telford, *The Theology of the Gospel of Mark* (Cambridge: Cambridge UP, 1999), 153.

conversations they participated in. Within this group of scholars are two sub-groups. Some who subscribe to the memorization scenario believe that the traditions changed radically as they were passed along from person to person, as in the childhood game where a phrase gets passed from child to child around a circle and comes out unrecognizable by the time it gets back to the originator. Others believe that people passing on oral traditions were careful to avoid changing anything in them and succeeded in doing so.

Still others question the very foundations of the idea of oral tradition itself. One of the most serious attacks on this theory comes from the pen of Thomas Brodie, who convincingly asserts that the idea of oral tradition as the source for the gospels is new (recently devised by modern scholarship, and thus at least questionable), unfounded (the arguments that created the hypothesis are weak), unworkable (the hypothesis doesn't explain the actual evidence in the text), and unnecessary (alternative explanations are simpler and more credible).[47]

Brodie's argument is worth a close examination because the modern theory of oral tradition offers the only real alternative to the view of Mark as a creative author who was reworking other literary sources such as Paul's epistles to create his narrative.

New: Oral Tradition as a Recent Invention

Christians have had some conception of "oral tradition" since the earliest centuries, but modern scholars invented an entirely new meaning for the term. The process of invention began in the early years of the twentieth century when Hermann Gunkel

---

[47] Brodie, *Birthing*, 50-62. My discussion of oral tradition here follows closely the structure of the chapter on the subject in Brodie's book.

devised a new method for analyzing the book of Genesis. Gunkel proposed that Genesis was a compilation of stories that were developed and passed on orally within communities for specific purposes in the life of the community. The reason why an individual story was composed, and thus the key to its intended message or meaning, was determined by its original *Sitz im Leben* (situation in life). A story's ultimate context in whatever literary work it eventually got written into was a secondary setting with less important or even misleading clues for the story's interpretation. The modern scholar began to pay less attention to literary context and tried instead to determine the original situation in life and thus the original meaning of each separate story. The methodology developed to do this was called *Gattungsgeschichte* (genre history), which in English has come to be known as form criticism. Form criticism deconstructs a written text into supposed originally independent parts, called pericopes or pericopae depending on how enamored one is of Latin plural word forms.[48]

Gunkel did not limit this approach to Genesis but rather considered ancient literature in general to be fundamentally different in this way from modern literature. For Gunkel, all ancient literature involved committing to writing stories that were invented and preserved orally as folk traditions. The creative genius came not from individual authors but impersonally from *communities*. Modern literature, on the other hand, was seen as fundamentally different insofar as it involves the genius of individual creativity. It is the product of *authors*. To make a long story short, this view made the leap from Old

---

[48] Ironically, the word pericope is from the Greek, and a transliteration of the Greek plural would have an *–ai* ending, but Western scholarship is so accustomed to Latin forms that the customary transliteration is *–ae*.

Testament to New Testament, took the world of biblical scholarship by storm, and remains today a commonly accepted paradigm among biblical scholars.[49]

The modern oral tradition and form criticism paradigm has perpetuated the conception of the evangelists as scribes or redactors rather than authors. Today scholars have developed other methodologies to interpret the gospels,[50] but the evangelist-as-compiler-rather-than-author paradigm persists. Redaction criticism, for instance, is founded on this paradigm insofar as it assumes the evangelists stitched together various independent pericopes into a single narrative. Even scholars who practice narrative criticism, in which each pericope's current literary context provides the primary clues to its interpretation, typically assume that the bulk of the narrative came ready-made to the evangelists through oral tradition.

Brodie laments that the new theory of oral tradition has even led scholars to downplay literary relationships among the New Testament texts. When parallels are seen between two texts, the parallels tend to be ascribed to a common source in oral tradition

---

[49] For a concise yet complete account of how the modern conception of oral tradition and form criticism developed, see Robert C. Culley, "Oral Tradition and Biblical Studies," *Oral Tradition* 1:1:30-65. The theory's status as a paradigm is shown by the way it is not only widely accepted but typically is treated as unquestionable. For example, well-known names in the field, such as James D. G. Dunn and Jerome Murphy-O'Connor, freely use phrases like "without doubt" and "certain conclusion" when discussing this conception of oral tradition. See James D. G. Dunn, "Altering the Default Setting: Re-envisaging the Early Transmission of the Jesus Tradition," *NTS* 49(2003):139-175 and Jerome Murphy-O'Connor, *Jesus and Paul: Parallel Lives* (Collegeville: Liturgical Press, 2007), 88. The article by Dunn was written specifically to assert that the author of Mark depended heavily on oral tradition.

[50] For a survey of various methodologies that have been applied to the gospels in recent scholarship, see Janice Capel Anderson and Stephen D. Moore, *Mark and Method: New Approaches in Biblical Studies* (Minneapolis: Fortress Press, 2008).

rather than to literary dependence.⁵¹ The ultimate consequence is that instead of the New Testament as a whole being viewed as a cohesive literary creation in which the books are all literarily interdependent, each book is interpreted as a standalone unit – just as each pericope within a gospel is interpreted as a standalone unit. Brodie argues that it's time to strip the false aura of venerability from the modern oral tradition theory and acknowledge that it is subject to re-thinking, as are all new theories. The first step in that re-thinking is to ask how strong the arguments were that established it so recently.

Unfounded: Oral Tradition Theory's Flawed Origin

Gunkel did not create the modern conception of oral tradition out of thin air but borrowed it from anthropological studies of pre-literate societies. His primary basis for attributing the biblical material to anthropological oral tradition was that he did not consider Genesis to be "history." In his view there were only two possible genres for an ancient work of narrative literature: saga or history. And since saga was by definition an oral production, the conclusion was clear:

> Are the accounts (*Erzälungen*) of Genesis stories or sagas (*Geschichte oder Sage*)? For the modern historian this question is no longer a question, yet it is important to make clear the grounds for this modern position. History writing (*Geschichtsschreibung*) is

---

[51] Brodie observes that "if two passages do not show fairly obvious parallelism they are either not compared, or their complex relationship, instead of being set in literary context, is usually accounted for on the basis of evidence which is missing and uncontrollable - oral tradition and lost documents." (Cited in MacDonald, *Homeric Epics*, 171.) An extreme example of this is Benjamin Bacon (*The Gospel of Mark*, 270-271), who chronicles a vast assortment of remarkably clear correspondences between passages in Mark and Paul's epistles, but then concludes there cannot have been literary borrowing because "the transfer of Pauline terms is too free for literary dependence. The relation is close, but still traditional and oral rather than literary."

The Chimera of Oral Tradition

no innate art of the human spirit, but has emerged in the course of human history, at a particular point of development (*an einem bestimmten Punkte der Entwicklung*). Uncultured peoples (*Die uncultivierten Völker*) do not write history.[52]

It is not difficult to see that this is an unreal dilemma: the conception of "history" among ancient people might well be different from the modern conception. Gunkel's reasoning amounts to an assertion that the mere fact that an ancient literary work contains things that we know cannot possibly be "historical" in our sense of the word means it must have been an oral production.[53] Proceeding on this flawed basis, Gunkel pointed out some similarities between the Genesis text and "sagas" from oral cultures, such as the inclusion within Genesis of apparently self-contained short stories. This assumes that the mere presence of short, apparently independent stories in an ancient literary work amounts to definitive proof that such stories originally circulated independently and orally. It also assumes that the culture that produced the sagas and the culture of Israel were fundamentally similar. These assumptions made sense to Gunkel because of his belief that cultures were essentially "cultured" or "uncultured." For Gunkel, the brevity of many of the stories found in Genesis substantiated his view of early Judaic society as "uncultured":

> [The brevity of the stories] corresponds to the art of the storyteller and the hearer's ability to absorb. The oldest storytellers were not able to set forth complex works of art . . . Rather, the old times (*die alte Zeit*) were satisfied with giving very small products (*ganz kleinen Produkten*) that would fill something less than half

---

[52] Cited in Brodie, *Birthing*, 54.
[53] The question of what constitutes "history" is addressed at greater length below in Part 3 on the genre of Mark.

an hour. And when the story was ended, the hearer's fantasy was fully satisfied and his ability to absorb exhausted.

In fact, this condescending European attitude toward ancient society as "uncultured" is itself not well founded, and the belief that people a few millennia ago had limited mental capacity is an unsubstantiated assumption. Gunkel found other similarities between saga and Genesis, but in such a large body of literature it is not difficult to find whatever one is looking for. As Brodie observes, this is what Gunkel did.

> And so the fateful path was taken: on the fortieth page of his commentary, Gunkel starts talking about the foundational role of oral tradition. And behind the oral tradition were, not authors, but communities.[54]

Shortly thereafter New Testament scholarship picked up the torch, and ultimately "The first half of the 20th c. surrendered to his influence."[55]

Today scholars are more inclined to recognize the complex literary artistry of books such as Genesis, so the original basis for ascribing its content to oral tradition seems fundamentally flawed. But more recently others have attempted to build on his foundation, citing additional reasons for believing a Gunkel-like anthropological oral tradition is behind the text of the gospels. Werner Kelber and Albert Lord argue that the gospels are influenced by oral culture and rhythms and that "some of the patterns of oral literature also occur in biblical texts such as the gospels."[56] But nearly all ancient literature bears evidence of oral forms, and this does not automatically mean the content had to

---

[54] Brodie, *Birthing*, 55.
[55] Ibid., 55.
[56] Ibid., 56.

The Chimera of Oral Tradition 51

come from oral tradition. Such patterns are evidence that the *form* of the text was influenced by oral culture, not that the *content* originated from oral tradition. Also, first-century religious texts such as the gospels were written for oral performance, and so oral speech patterns are to be expected. Indeed, making a text sound like oral speech is itself a literary convention:

> In other words, the patterns which Lord claims are oral, are in fact literary, and found in genuine literature. More of what Lord attributes to oral influence can be more fully accounted for by what R. Alter (1981: 51-52) calls 'literary conventions.' And the fact that the gospels largely consist of episodes fits into a literary pattern 'the cult of the episode.'[57]

In addition, patterns that appear to reflect oral culture can be found in literature from any period. A modern author as well as an ancient one may write with a view to oral delivery, as any speech-writer must. An author may intend to portray rustic, rural, life in a largely oral culture without being a part of that culture.

One pattern that scholars sometimes cite as suggestive of oral tradition is minor variations in the wording of the same story in separate texts.[58] But the same kinds of variations can occur in an exclusively literary environment.[59] An author may freely alter a

---

[57] Ibid., 56.
[58] Jerome Murphy O'Connor (*Jesus and Paul*, 88) offers a succinct expression of this view: "... identity in essentials and divergence in marginals points to one certain conclusion. We are dealing with a foundational narrative that not only began in oral tradition, but that continued to preserve its salient features."
[59] Numerous studies of ancient literature have shown that the ways in which ancient authors borrowed from literary texts were incredibly varied and included precisely this pattern. See Thomas L. Brodie, Dennis Ronald MacDonald, and Stanley E. Porter,

text that he borrows from, in ways that result in minor variations. Minor variations in similar stories may point to literary artifice as well as to oral tradition. Actually, in oral transmission those variations are random in nature, but in literary transmission one can often detect behind them the purposes of the author, and this is precisely what scholars can do very frequently in the gospel texts.

Birger Gerhardsson and James D. G. Dunn take a somewhat different tack in the quest to substantiate the oral tradition theory: their argument is that Jesus and his disciples taught orally and so it is to be expected that such would be the initial mode of transmission of the gospel materials. However, this argument is based on the portrayal of Jesus and the disciples in the gospels and so presupposes the gospels' essential historicity. The gospels do tell the story that way, but the degree to which that story or that aspect of the story is historically accurate is an open question. Historicity in this case is an assumption, not an argument:

> [Dunn] makes an impassioned plea for attention to oral tradition, but his case is based on a presumption: 'We simply cannot escape from a presumption of orality for the first stage of the Jesus tradition' (2003a: 157). Dunn does not discuss how ancient writers composed their texts. His leading example of a text allegedly shaped by oral tradition (Lk. 7.1-10; cf. Mt. 8.1-13; Jn 4.46-54) is in fact heavily dependent on the text of the Elijah-Elisha narrative.[60]

Dunn's argument is to some extent circular: he assumes that the gospels are historical, based in part on the reliability of oral

---

eds., *The Intertextuality of the Epistles: Explorations of Theory and Practice* (Sheffield: Sheffield Phoenix Press, 2006).
[60] Brodie, *Birthing*, 57.

The Chimera of Oral Tradition

tradition; and he assumes the reliability of oral tradition based in part on the historicity of the gospels.

Helmut Koester takes a different approach to defending the validity of oral tradition theory. His argument is based on data outside of the gospels: from some passages in Paul's epistles he supposes that the tradition was transmitted orally to Paul and thus was created and transmitted by a community:

> Christianity began as a religious movement that established its distinctive interior structures by the creation of a ritual and a story ... Paul ... received a tradition of an oral version ... (1 Cor. 11.23b). The organization of the new communities was accomplished ... by sayings ... transmitted in the oral tradition ... Writings that were later called 'gospels' came into existence as alternative forms of the continuing oral tradition ...[61]

However, the idea of the central role of "communities" in passing on the tradition is a questionable presupposition of form criticism methodology, and it is far from clear that Koester is correctly interpreting the Pauline passages in question. The key passages are 1 Corinthians 11:23 and 15:3:

> For I received (παρέδωκα) from the Lord what I also delivered (παρεδίδετο) to you, that the Lord Jesus on the night when he was betrayed took bread ...

> For I delivered (παρέδωκα) to you as of first importance what I also received (παρέλαβον), that Christ died for our sins in accordance with the scriptures ...

As Brodie cautions, these statements most likely do not refer to what modern scholars mean by the term oral tradition:

---

[61] Cited in Brodie, *Birthing*, 58.

> ... when Paul invokes tradition going back to the Lord, one cannot be sure whether this call is an appeal to a historical tradition related to Jesus and a community, or whether, as his language suggests, he is using and adapting the general Jewish idea about tradition going back to Moses and God. Paul's language is itself general; he gives no details about the source and workings of the tradition.[62]

In other words, Paul is asserting that he is firmly within authentic Jewish tradition; he does not explicitly say that he received the tradition orally.

Actually, if Paul did admit to receiving the tradition orally it would undermine virtually all of the arguments he so forcefully advanced in behalf of his own unique apostolic authority. Throughout his epistles he insists on his absolute authority as an apostle personally commissioned by the Lord to preach the gospel and determine for others what that gospel is and isn't; if he admitted to receiving the tradition orally from "the community," such a claim to authority would fall flat.

Brodie also points out that even if Paul did admit to being secondary to community-based oral tradition, the statement might not actually be literally true. The epistles are carefully crafted literary creations just as the gospels are, and their historical veracity is just as subject to questioning and verification:

> If the gospels are so suspect historically, then on what basis is one so sure of the historical reliability of a particular reading of an epistle? It is not only the gospels which are artistic, rhetorical.

---

[62] Ibid., 57. See also the discussion of 1 Cor 15:3 in Paul Nadim Tarazi, *1 Corinthians: A Commentary* (St. Paul, Minn.: OCABS Press, 2011), 263-65.

Evidence grows that, to some degree, something similar is true of the epistles.[63]

Ultimately, oral tradition theory can be seen as "unfounded" because the arguments that established it are only sufficiently forceful to convince those who are inclined to be convinced. But an unfounded theory may still be at least plausible, or to use Brodie's term, "workable." As it turns out, this theory does not meet that bar either.

Unworkable: Oral Tradition Theory's Implausibility

An "unworkable" theory may either be one that is couched in such vague terms that there is no way to test it against the evidence, or one that can be tested and fails the test. Oral tradition qualifies on both counts. Many conceptions of how oral tradition works are as vague as Rudolf Bultmann's blithe statement that in oral cultures "The literature . . . springs out [*entspringt*] of definite conditions and wants of life." As Brodie observes, "Bultmann never explained how this springing process works."[64] It has been said that a troop of monkeys armed with typewriters could produce the Encyclopedia Brittanica given enough time. If so, perhaps the "springing" explanation works for Genesis since one can extend the "springing" process almost indefinitely far back into the distant past. But it doesn't work quite as well for the New Testament, where the time frame is just thirty years or so.

Charles H. Dodd recognized that the theory didn't work so well for the New Testament due to the limited time-frame, so he rose to the challenge by changing the theory. He proposed that

---

[63] Ibid., 58.
[64] Ibid., 58.

oral tradition was not a process of "springing" as in the creation of new stories from scratch, but rather it was a process of passing on historical memories:

> The materials . . . were already in existence as an unarticulated wealth of recollections and reminiscences of the words and deeds of Jesus – mixed, it may be, with the reflections and interpretations of his followers.[65]

This change in the theory was not based on any evidence but was simply a conjecture intended to make the idea of oral tradition in the New Testament plausible. Besides the lack of evidence, the problem here is the allowance for "reflections and interpretations": add those up over 30 years and what you have at the end may have little to do with what you started with.

Martin Hengel took Dodd's idea and pushed it a bit further by denying the "reflections and interpretations" part: oral tradition involved no changes over time. This too was a case of conjecture without evidence. Gerhardsson followed with an attempt at backing this view up with indirect evidence. He suggested that Jesus engaged in meticulous methods of rabbinical teaching that guaranteed whatever he said and did would be firmly implanted in his disciples' memory, resulting in "fixed and permanent impressions." However, the gospels make no suggestion that Jesus used such methods, and the vast differences between versions of the same stories in different gospels point in a different direction. If the methods were so meticulous and the traditions so fixed, why did they end up so radically different in so many ways? Moreover, if anyone would have been aware of and used such methods, it would have been Paul. Yet we have direct evidence in Paul's epistles that even if they were tried, they

---

[65] Ibid., 58.

didn't work. He was constantly trying to correct followers who strayed from his teachings. The epistle to the Galatians bears witness to the development of "oral tradition" directly contradicting the gospel that Paul preached in Galatia, and the tradition in Galatia metamorphosed so drastically not over 30 years but within a very short time after he left:

> I am astonished that you are so quickly deserting him who called you in the grace of Christ and turning to a different gospel – not that there is another gospel, but there are some who trouble you and want to pervert the gospel of Christ. But even if we, or an angel from heaven, should preach to you a gospel contrary to that which we preached to you, let him be accursed. (Gal 1:6-8)

If Paul had to write the epistle to the Galatians specifically to correct "oral tradition" that had already gone drastically wrong within weeks or months of his presence there, how can anyone reasonably suppose that "oral tradition" remained reliable after 30 years?

Joseph Fitzmyer recognized some of the difficulties and tried to rescue the theory of oral tradition by revising it yet again. He envisioned a three-stage process: the first stage was the teaching of Jesus, the second stage was oral transmission which could involve "embellishment and modification," and finally in the third stage the evangelists took in the modified traditions and further modified them with their own "theological formulation." Besides the fact that, as we've seen in Galatians, "embellishment and modification" might involve drastic and fundamental changes, the literary unity of each of the gospels makes Fitzmyer's revision of the theory unworkable. If Fitzmyer's scenario were accurate, a gospel would be a patchwork quilt of ill-fitting individual pieces stitched together with all-too-visible seams between them. Fitzmyer's theory could be further revised to fit the evidence better by adding a "literary formulation" stage, but then precious little would remain of the original "oral tradition" after all the embellishment and modification and reformulation.

In her study of Mark, Mary Ann Tolbert discusses the difficulty in ascribing to oral tradition individual pericopes that all fit so perfectly into the literary fabric of the gospel:

> It is possible that these parables or some variation of them existed in Christian oral tradition prior to Mark. Yet they are so crucial to the organization of the Gospel and to the molding of so much other material that it is hard to believe the author did not shape them to fit his requirements. The interpretation of the parable of the Sower, with its point-by-point expansion and repetition of the parable, is especially likely to have come from the author's own hand.[66]

Tolbert concludes that recognizing the literary unity of Mark means that "*if* an oral tradition prior to Mark is to be discovered – and that may well be an impossibility," we will never be able to say with any certainty what parts he received versus what he changed or invented.[67]

Perhaps recognizing that endless revision to the oral tradition theory was a dead end, Werner Kelber came up with a radically new suggestion: Mark did not like and did not trust oral tradition precisely because of its changeability. The first evangelist wanted to put an end to oral tradition by establishing a fixed written tradition to take its place. As with the other theories devoid of direct evidence, it is easy to propose and just

---

[66] Tolbert, *Sowing the Gospel*, 306.
[67] Ibid., 307.

The Chimera of Oral Tradition

as easy for others to call the proposal a "house of cards."[68] Still others can come to the exact opposite conclusion: C. H. Giblin proposes that the whole purpose of Mark was to deflect the reader's attention away from any written gospel and toward oral tradition. This, he asserts, is the purpose of the apparently inconclusive ending of Mark which leaves hearers to seek the final resolution of the story in oral tradition.[69]

Some scholars try to salvage some form of oral tradition by scaling back the sweeping claims made for it by others. Thus, Pieter J. J. Botha finds the "dynamics of rumor" in "parts" of the gospels. But this pulls back from the idea of something fixed and reliable and pervasively behind the gospel content, so much so as to render the theory of little use. In addition, anything that relies for evidence on "parts" of a gospel is suspect: in such a large body of literature any carefully selected set of parts could correspond to any given theory, be it oral tradition or monkeys banging on typewriters:

> That is why so many diverse models – Bultmann, Dodd, Gerhardsson, Fitzmyer, Botha – can appear credible. The theories really do correspond to data. But not to all the data.[70]

Perhaps the greatest mismatch between data and theory is between the memorization-at-the-source scenario for oral tradition and the text of Mark. The story we actually read in the second gospel is one in which no one understood Jesus' significance during his earthly ministry. Throughout the story, the obtuse disciples fail Jesus in every way. They do not understand who he is or why he is there, and to a man they

---

[68] Quoting Halversen. ibid., 60.
[69] C. H. Giblin, "The Beginning of the Ongoing Gospel (Mk 1:2-16:8)," in Van Segbroeck, *The Four Gospels*, 975-986.
[70] Ibid., 59-60.

desert him in his hour of need at the beginning of his passion. If we assume some degree of historical veracity for the story as related in Mark, it is extraordinarily difficult to imagine these same disciples stopping and memorizing each dialogue as it happened – or even the gist of each dialogue – from the moment Jesus summoned them.

To get a feel for the implausibility of the memorization scenarios one must think seriously about the actual stories that are related in Mark and what must have happened if they occasioned the creation of "permanent and fixed impressions." Consider, for example, the story of the woman with a 12-year hemorrhage (5:25-34). According to the text, the disciples were not aware anything was happening until they heard Jesus tell a woman that her faith healed her. They then would have had to quickly memorize not only Jesus' words but the whole story recounted by the woman. Something like that would have to have been done on the spot by disciples who had no idea what was going on ("You see the crowd pressing around you, and yet you say, 'Who touched me?'"). Or consider the stories of Jesus disputing with his enemies in the temple: if this came from memorized-at-the-source oral tradition, these same obtuse disciples would have had to memorize not only Jesus' words but those of his opponents, some of which were spoken not even to Jesus but privately among the opponents themselves *about* Jesus (11:31-33; 12:14-15, 19-23). The source of the entire passion story becomes similarly incomprehensible, for the disciples would have had to find surrogate investigators for things they didn't personally witness, which means the entire story after Jesus' arrest. According to Mark, the moment Jesus was taken into custody "they all forsook him and fled" (14:50).

The Chimera of Oral Tradition

The disciples never get a clue in Mark; they might have come around after the story ends in 16:8, but how would they then remember so many details from the period when they were in a perpetual fog? The fact that much of the dialogue in Mark consists of Jesus castigating his disciples for being slow-witted, slothful, and even disobedient makes this even harder to believe. Did these slow-witted and slothful disciples make it a point to memorize even embarrassing stories about themselves and the very words with which Jesus castigated them?

"Then are you also without understanding?" (7:18)

"Do you not yet perceive or understand? Are your hearts hardened? Having eyes do you not see, and having ears do you not hear? And do you not remember? . . . Do you not yet understand?" (8:17-21)

"Get behind me, Satan! For you are not on the side of God, but of men." (8:33)

But when Jesus saw it he was indignant, and said to them, "Let the children come to me, do not hinder them; for to such belongs the kingdom of God." (10:14)

And he came and found them sleeping, and he said to Peter, "Simon, are you asleep? Could you not watch one hour?" . . . And he came the third time, and said to them, "Are you still sleeping and taking your rest?" (14:37-41)

For memorized-at-the-source oral tradition to be behind the earliest gospel, the disciples had to be perceptive and diligent and self-effacing in actual fact, yet take part in creating an oral tradition that inaccurately portrayed them as obtuse and slothful and self-aggrandizing.[71]

Unnecessary: Alternatives to Oral Tradition

As Brodie observes, showing that a theory is unfounded and unworkable may not be enough to cause its rejection:

> Even if a hypothesis is unclear in its foundation, and even if in practice there are serious difficulties with getting it to work, perhaps in some way it is still the only apparent response to a real need.[72]

This is indeed a pervasive feeling among scholars. Even a critical scholar such as Mark Goodacre, who has produced books that question the existence of Q, assumes that the only real alternative to explaining the synoptic problem is to rely more heavily on oral tradition.[73] Brodie lists several reasons why people tend to think this way, followed by explanations why those reasons are not as compelling in reality as they may seem.

First, much of the text in the gospels follows the rhythms of oral speech. But in fact writers often deliberately impart such rhythms to a text, and it would be especially appropriate for the evangelists to do that if the gospels were written for oral performance, as is likely.

Second, minor variations between similar stories in the gospels seem to correspond to the minor variations that occur in oral communication. But in fact myriad other reasons may give rise to numerous small differences between texts. Authors make use of earlier texts when composing their own in many ways other

---

[71] For an example of the latter theme, see Mark 10:35-45.
[72] Brodie, *Birthing*, 60.
[73] See Goodacre, *The Case Against Q*, 187-89; *The Synoptic Problem*, 62, 166-67.

The Chimera of Oral Tradition

than word-for-word copying, especially when their own literary strategy differs from that of their source. If textual variations resulted from oral communication, they should be relatively random, but in the gospels the variations frequently seem deliberate. Where Matthew borrows from Mark, the differences fit Matthew's different literary strategy.

Third, the gospel stories depict an oral culture: Jesus and his disciples go around speaking to crowds and individuals, off the cuff and naturally, without the artifice that goes into literary productions. It would be natural for such people to pass on their teachings orally. But in fact the portrayal of such an environment in a literary work does not necessarily mean the work arose in such an environment or that the depiction corresponds accurately to historical reality. The image of rusticity may be artifice.[74]

The fourth and fifth reasons why oral tradition is often deemed necessary are closely interrelated. On the one hand, the oral tradition paradigm is simply so entrenched in modern biblical scholarship that people assume there is no alternative. On the other hand, biblical scholars have increasingly concluded that the

---

[74] The gospels' literary heritage is from both Greco-Roman and Jewish culture, both of which to some extent idealize oral culture. A whole genre of Greco-Roman literature idealized pastoral simplicity of life, and first-century Jews idealized the concept of oral tradition which they traced back to Moses. On the other hand these same Jews were ambivalent toward writing, along with many other religious cultures then and now. They venerated the written word but were wary of its becoming a calcification of the past: temple priests acted as guardians of the Torah but were constantly corrected by prophets who spoke directly from Yahweh. Portraying an oral culture within a written document could be a way to incorporate this tension within a written document. (A specific example is Giblin's theory that the inconclusive ending of Mark was intended to impel the reader into oral tradition.) Also, many of the literary models for the gospels – such stories as the Elijah-Elisha cycle – tend to portray the same pastoral simplicity of the itinerant prophet.

gospels are not historically reliable, and those who find this disconcerting see the oral tradition paradigm as the last chance to plausibly set a limit to that trend. Oral tradition seems necessary to keep biblical scholarship from "dislodging the Gospel from its historical moorings."[75] But in fact, the same reasons why oral tradition is unfounded and unworkable make clear that oral tradition is no guarantor of historical accuracy.

When scholars first devised the very idea of oral tradition, it was deemed fundamentally a matter of communities making up stories to suit their purposes. By its very nature oral tradition of this sort would not be and was not considered a historical source. Only later when it was applied to the New Testament, did some scholars introduce the ideas of memorization-at-the-source and fixed transmission. Each of those ideas was introduced as an unsubstantiated assumption, no one has been able to propose plausible concrete scenarios for them, and they are especially problematic for the text of Mark.

Unhelpful: Oral Tradition Theory's Impact on Biblical Interpretation

The desire to attribute as much historical accuracy as possible to the gospels is understandable, but this desire has been unhelpful in the quest for understanding this literature, because it has helped to perpetuate a deeply flawed paradigm in modern biblical scholarship. Under the influence of the oral tradition and form criticism paradigm, scholars studying the gospels have ripped apart these carefully constructed literary masterpieces and examined pieces of them out of context as if that were the best way to understand the text.

---

[75] Frank Matera, quoted in Harrington, *What are they Saying About Mark*, 7.

The Chimera of Oral Tradition

Abandoning the flawed paradigm would open the way to appreciating the gospels as cohesive literary works in which each part was carefully and deliberately crafted and organized to serve the author's overall purposes. This would also open the way to appreciating the authors as literary craftsmen who came from and worked within a literary culture even as they wrote for oral presentation.

In the world of antiquity, and particularly the subculture of Christian and Jewish literate society, borrowing from and reworking earlier texts was standard operating procedure for authors. If eyewitness testimony and oral tradition both fail to explain the level of detail we actually find in the Gospel, two likely sources remain: the evangelist's own imagination and other writings that were available to him. Other scholars have persuasively argued for Mark's use of the Old Testament and Homeric epic.[76] This book argues for Mark's use also of Paul's epistles.

---

[76] Especially Brodie (*Birthing*) and MacDonald (*Homeric Epics*).

Part II

Pauline Themes in Mark

4
Defending the Gentile Mission

And the most problematic Markan case, the illogical journey described in 7:31, may reflect not geographical ignorance but a Markan desire to construct a tour of non-Jewish areas, in line with the Gentile theme of this section of the Gospel ...
Joel Marcus[77]

Biblical scholarship has long recognized that the second gospel is aimed at a Christian, mixed Gentile-Jewish audience, and that it promotes and defends Gentile Christianity.[78] And not only does the text reveal an interest in advancing the agenda of the Pauline Gentile mission, it also preserves evidence that Paul's epistles provided inspiration for how to go about attaining these ends. If what we might call the Pauline school was the driving force behind the Gentile mission, these facts suggest that the author of Mark was a member of that school.

A Gentile Christian Intended Audience

Among the evidence showing an interest in an audience composed of Gentiles is the fact that Mark feels compelled to explain Jewish customs and refers to the Jews in the third person:

> For the Pharisees, and all the Jews, do not eat unless they wash their hands, observing the tradition of the elders . . . and there are many other traditions which they observe . . . (7:3-4)[79]

---

[77] Joel Marcus, *Mark 1-8* (New Haven: Yale UP, 2002), 21.
[78] For a thorough analysis of the evidence, see Ernest Best, "Mark's Readers: A Profile," in Van Segbroeck et al., *The Four Gospels*, 839-858.
[79] See also 2:26 where Mark has Jesus explain to Jewish interlocutors (who would have known this) that only priests could eat "the bread of the Presence."

Also, Greek-speaking Jews would know some Aramaic, but Mark's audience is not even expected to be familiar with common Aramaic words and phrases. In each of the following examples, the italicized word is Aramaic:[80]

> Taking her by the hand he said to her, "*Talitha cumi*"; which means, "little girl, I say to you, arise." (5:41)
>
> ... looking up to heaven, he sighed, and said to him, "*Ephphatha*," that is, "Be opened." (7:34)
>
> *Bartimaeus*, a blind beggar, the son of Timaeus, was sitting by the roadside. (10:46)
>
> "*Abba*, Father, all things are possible to thee; remove this cup from me; yet not what I will, but what thou wilt." (14:36)
>
> And they brought him to the place called *Golgotha* (which means the place of a skull). (15:22)
>
> And at the ninth hour Jesus cried with a loud voice, "*Eloi, Eloi, lama sabachthani?*" which means, "My God, my God, why hast thou forsaken me?" (15:34)

On the other hand, while Aramaic is outside the expected audience's ken, some familiarity with Latin terms is presumed. Mark occasionally explains a Greek term by reference to a Latin term that he transliterates:[81]

> And a poor widow came, and put in two copper coins [λεπτὰ], which make a penny [κοδράντης, transliterating Latin *quadrans*]. (12:42)

---

[80] 3:17 might be another example. Best takes this a step further and argues that Mark's readers are also not expected to know Syriac. See Best, "Mark's Readers," 846-47.

[81] Best (ibid., 851) also points out the use of Roman military terminology.

And the soldiers led him away inside the palace [αὐλῆς]; that is, the *praetorium* [πραιτώριον, transliterating the Latin word] . . . (15:16)

Mark does assume that his audience accepts the authority of the scriptures we now call the Old Testament. But either his knowledge of scripture is weaker than one might expect of a Jewish author writing for Jews, or he doesn't expect his audience to notice errors. In 2:26 Mark cites an incident under King David "when Abiathar was high priest" although in the cited passage 1 Sam 21:1-7 it is actually Ahimelech who was high priest.[82] In 10:19 "the commandments" are listed as "Do not kill, Do not commit adultery, Do not steal, Do not bear false witness, Do not defraud, Honor your father and mother." This contains errors in both order and content. Both versions of the Ten Commandments actually have "Honor your father and mother" before "Do not kill," and neither has "Do not defraud" at all.[83] The most famous inaccuracy is the quotation in Mark 1:2 from "Isaiah the prophet" which is actually an amalgamation of texts from Isaiah and Malachi.

The Gospel of Mark is not just aimed at a Gentile Christian community, it advocates for such a community. It does this both directly and indirectly, using both clear literal language and relatively obscure symbolic language. One of the clearest statements of this interest is in the climactic scene where Jesus

---

[82] The parallel passages in Matthew and Luke avoid the error by omitting the reference to Abiathar altogether.
[83] In its place after "Do not bear false witness" is "Do not covet" in Ex 20:2-17 and Deut 5:6-21.

cleanses the temple, which concludes with a teaching of Jesus on this subject:

> And he taught, and said to them, "Is it not written, 'My house shall be called a house of prayer *for all the nations*'? But you have made it a den of robbers." (Mark 11:15-17)

The quotation comes from a passage in Isaiah which very clearly expresses the idea of inviting Gentiles to join with God's people:

> [Thus says the Lord:] "And the foreigners who join themselves to the Lord, to minister to him, to love the name of the Lord, and to be his servants, everyone who keeps the sabbath, and does not profane it, and holds fast my covenant – these I will bring to my holy mountain, and make them joyful in my house of prayer; their burnt offerings and their sacrifices will be accepted on my altar; for my house shall be called a house of prayer for all peoples. Thus says the Lord God, who gathers the outcasts of Israel, I will gather yet others to him besides those already gathered." (Isaiah 56:6-8; see also vv.1-5)

Once again, Jesus' "teaching" is nothing new but simply reiterates what is already clear in scripture. This teaching is repeated in Jesus' warnings about the impending end times in chapter 13, for he announces that "the gospel must first be preached to all nations" before the end times actually begin. The theme is unmistakable in these passages, but this is just the tip of the iceberg. The Gospel conveys its message by means of a story, and the story's focus on advancing the Gentile mission is woven into the very fabric of the story.

Jesus Visits Gentile Lands

One of the most prominent symbolic ways that Mark supports the Gentile mission is the way he uses geographical references. The contrast between Galilee and Jerusalem in particular is a

Defending the Gentile Mission

thread that runs through the entire Gospel from beginning to end.

Galilee was a region outside of Judea known for its mixed Jewish-Gentile population, and is explicitly associated with "the nations" (the Gentiles) in Isaiah 9:1:

> In the former time he brought into contempt the land of Zebulun and the land of Naphtali, but in the latter time he will make glorious the way of the sea, the land beyond the Jordan, Galilee of the nations. The people who walked in darkness have seen a great light; those who dwelt in a land of deep darkness, on them has light shined.

Matthew quotes portions of this passage (4:15-16); Mark does not mention it, but his use of Galilee to mean a land where Jews and Gentiles mix, as opposed to Judea and Jerusalem which represent exclusively Jewish territory, seems to presuppose knowledge of it.

In Mark, this land of the Gentiles is the site of Jesus' origin, his successful mission, and his destination after the resurrection. In contrast, Jerusalem – the very epitome of Jewishness – is the place that rejected and crucified him.[84] At the end of the book (16:7) the disciples are informed that if they wish to see the resurrected Lord they must follow him to the land symbolic of Jew-Gentile unity – Galilee.

Even Jesus' movement within Galilee emphasizes his intention to attend to both Jews and Gentiles. One of the most prominent

---

[84] Telford (*Theology of the Gospel of Mark*, 149) interprets Galilee as symbolizing a mixed Jewish-Gentile community and lists others who do so. See also Bas M. F. Van Iersel, *Mark: A Reader-Response Commentary* (Sheffield: Sheffield Academic Press, 1998), 77-80 and Kealy, *History of Interpretation*, 2: 1: 228.

recurring themes within the first half of the Gospel is Jesus' frequent trips across the Sea of Galilee. What he is doing in these trips is going alternately to predominantly Gentile and predominantly Jewish areas.[85] Consequently, the Sea of Galilee appears to represent a microcosm of the Mediterranean Sea: by leading his disciples back and forth Jesus repeatedly calls on them to follow him from Judea to the Roman Empire at large.[86] It has frequently been suggested that Mark invented the term "Sea of Galilee" for what is actually not that large a lake, precisely in order to help his readers pick up the allusion to the Mediterranean Sea. (The lake is only 13 miles long by 7 miles wide, and the term "Sea of Galilee" is not attested in any work of literature earlier than Mark.)

In one of the crossings over the "sea" from Jewish land to Gentile land, the disciples are stuck in a storm, Jesus walks out to them, and as Mark puts it, "he meant to pass by them" (6:48). Why would Jesus walk out on the water toward the boat, but with the intention of just walking right past it? This enigmatic statement may suggest their reluctance to follow where he wanted to lead them. In other words, Jesus "meant to pass by them" because their fear kept them from making progress. The allusion is to Paul's opponents' fear of the consequences of accepting Gentiles as equals, which impelled them to impose Law observance on all Christians, which if successful would have kept most Gentiles far out of reach of the Gospel.[87] By the same token, Jesus' action of calming the storm in the same passage represents an assurance for Paul's Judaizing opponents that their

---

[85] See Marcus, *Mark 1-8*, 447 and Svartvik, *Mark and Mission*, 300.
[86] See Hanhart, "Son, Your Sins are Forgiven," 1015-16; Tarazi, *Paul and Mark*, 179.
[87] See Bas M.F Van Iersel, "Kai ethelen parelthein autous. Another Look at Mk 6:48d," in Van Segbroeck et al., *The Four Gospels*, 1065-76.

fears about the Gentile mission are groundless and all will be well in the end because Jesus has everything under control.

Mark also goes out of his way to portray Jesus visiting Gentile areas. In 7:24, Jesus visits "the region of Tyre and Sidon." The evangelist could hardly have picked a better pair of place names to emphasize the non-Jewish character of Jesus' destination; these were not just gentile cities but were cities with which Jews had a history of animosity.[88] When he leaves the region in 7:31, Mark names both cities again to remind us of what kind of area he was in, then recounts a singularly strange journey of Jesus back to Jewish lands. From "the region of Tyre," Jesus goes "through Sidon" (20 miles north along the coast) "to the sea of Galilee" (the opposite direction from Tyre, about 30 miles southeast) "through the region of the Decapolis" (beyond his destination Galilee by at least 10 miles and extending for about 40 miles farther). A modern U.S. equivalent would be to recount a journey from Los Angeles to Kansas City, first going through Seattle and then going through Miami. The starting point, ending point, and lands Jesus went "through" along the way are illustrated in the map on the following page.[89]

---

[88] See Josephus, *Ag. Ap.* 1:70; *J. W.* 2:478; Isa 23:1-4, 12; Jer 25:22; 47:4; Ezek 26-28; Joel 3:4-8; Amos 1:9-10; Zech 9:2-4. See also Roger David Aus, *Feeding the Five Thousand: Studies in the Judaic Background of Mark 6:30-44 par. and John 6:1-15* (Lanham, Maryland: University Press of America, 2010).

[89] Map courtesy of www.openbible.info and Google Maps.

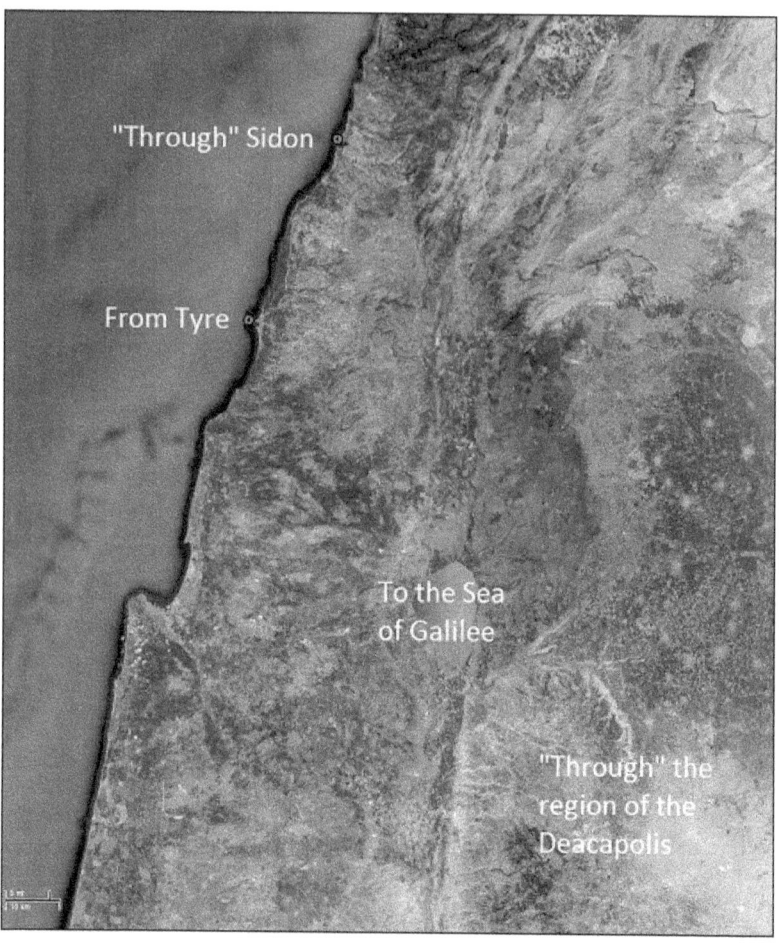

That Mark has in mind the intention to portray Jesus visiting Gentile lands is made clear by the fact that Mark uses his brief time there to highlight an encounter with a Gentile Syro-Phoenician woman.[90] It is as though the Gentile woman's faith, which convinces Jesus to heal her son although his ministry is like "bread" intended "first" for the Jews, convinces him to refocus his ministry for a longer time on Gentiles.

---

[90] See Marcus, *Mark 1-8*, 21.

Jesus Accepts Individual Gentiles As They Are

Jesus does not just travel to Gentile lands, he heals Gentile inhabitants of those lands just as he heals Jews, most notably the Gerasene demoniac (5:1-20) and the Syro-Phoenician woman (7:25-30). In doing so he makes no demands that they obey Jewish customs or traditions. For a narrative set in a pre-Pauline time, this represents as clearly as possible the Pauline principle that Gentiles who become Christians remain Gentiles and are not bound to adopt Jewish customs.

Mark employs a number of cues to make sure his readers understand that the Gerasene demoniac is a Gentile. He is found on the Gentile side of the Sea of Galilee, he dwells "among the tombs" (an unclean area for Jews), the name "Legion" attributed to the demons in possession of him has Roman connotations, the herd of swine clearly indicates this is not a story about Jews, and when the man goes off to proclaim his healing among "his friends," it is to the Gentile land of the Decapolis that he goes. In this story Jesus takes the initiative to heal the man, and the only requirement placed upon him as a result is that he go and proclaim to his "friends" what was done for him.

Mark also goes out of his way to emphasize the Gentile status of the Syro-Phoenician woman (7:24-30). She comes to Jesus as a resident of the Gentile land of Tyre and Sidon, and the text states unequivocally that "the woman was a Greek, a Syro-Phoenician by birth." The word Greek (Ἑλληνίς) here obviously does not identify her as "Greek" in the ethnic sense; the word Syro-Phoenician identifies her ethnicity. "Greek," then, in this context means "Gentile" or non-Jew, which corresponds to

Paul's unique use of that word in Galatians and Colossians.[91] The story is famous for Jesus' derogatory reference to Gentiles as "dogs":

> Now the woman was a Greek, a Syrophoenician by birth. And she begged him to cast the demon out of her daughter. And he said to her, "Let the children first be fed, for it is not right to take the children's bread and throw it to the dogs. (7:26-27)

Although this sounds like initial reluctance, in fact the story is quintessentially Pauline, for it is the Gentile's faith that saves her child insofar as it induces her to seek Jesus out and make her humble reply to his first response. Nothing beyond that is required of her:

> But she answered him, "Yes, Lord; yet even the dogs under the table eat the children's crumbs." And he said to her, "For this saying you may go your way; the demon has left your daughter." And she went home, and found the child lying in bed, and the demon gone. (7:28-30)

In contrast to these stories of Gentile healings, Mark includes one story in which Jesus heals a Jew and follows it up by commanding him to fulfill the requirements of the Law that result from the healing. In 1:40-44 he advises a healed leper to "show yourself to the priest, and offer for your cleansing what Moses commanded."

Jesus Unites Jews and Gentiles at the Communal Meal

One of the strongest indications of an interest in justifying or defending the Gentile mission is the pair of stories about Jesus feeding the multitudes (the five thousand in 6:34-45 and the

---

[91] See Svartvik, *Mark and Mission*, 297-8 on the correspondence between Mark's use of "Greek" to mean Gentiles and Paul's in Gal 2:3; 3:28; and Col 3:11.

four thousand in 8:1-10). Mark himself stresses their importance by appending to the second story an extended digression that culminates in Jesus expressing exasperation with his disciples for misunderstanding the significance of both of the feedings:

> Now they had forgotten to bring bread; and they had only one loaf with them in the boat. And he cautioned them, saying, "Take heed, beware of the leaven of the Pharisees and the leaven of Herod." And they discussed it with one another, saying, "We have no bread." And being aware of it, Jesus said to them, "Why do you discuss the fact that you have no bread? Do you not yet perceive or understand? Are your hearts hardened? Having eyes do you not see, and having ears do you not hear? And do you not remember? When I broke the five loaves for the five thousand, how many baskets full of broken pieces did you take up?" They said to him, "Twelve." "And the seven for the four thousand, how many baskets full of broken pieces did you take up?" And they said to him, "Seven." And he said to them, "Do you not yet understand?" (8:14-21)

Among many proposed interpretations of the feeding passages and this denouement,[92] the one that best explains the symbolism and fits the Gentile mission emphasis in the rest of Mark is that the intention is to portray Jesus prodding his disciples toward the Pauline goal of an inclusive, unified Jewish-Gentile community. More specifically, this pair of stories symbolizes a progression from an exclusively Jewish community at first, followed by a mixed Gentile-Jewish group which is the divinely-appointed goal.[93]

---

[92] Svartvik lists other interpretations (*Mark and Mission*, 295-6); see also Camille Focant, "Les Doublets dans la Section des Pains," in Van Segbroeck et al., *The Four Gospels*, 1039-63; here: 1057-58.
[93] For a thorough review of the evidence, see Focant, "Les Doublets." See also John Drury, "Understanding the Bread: Disruption and Aggregation, Secrecy and

The symbolism leading up to and surrounding the first feeding suggests a Jewish milieu. The location is not far from the region of "his own country" (6:1, 6), and all the people who find him in that place are from the villages of his own country (6:33). The numbers five and twelve are prominent: five loaves (6:38, 43), five thousand men (6:44), and twelve baskets of broken pieces (6:43). The number five calls to mind the number of books of the Torah, and the number twelve symbolizes the twelve tribes of Israel (see 5:25, 42). It is precisely these numbers that Jesus emphasizes when he intimates that the disciples should have paid attention to the symbolism of the numbers: "'When I broke the five loaves for the five thousand, how many baskets full of broken pieces did you take up?' They said to him, 'Twelve.'" (8:19)

In contrast, the second feeding comes after the encounter with the Gentile Syro-Phoenician woman (7:25-30), which in turn is followed by a long journey through Gentile territory (7:31). Especially considering that immediate history, the comment that "some of them have come a long way" (8:3) suggests a mixed group and leaves the hearer with a very different impression from the first episode, in which "they ran there on foot from all the towns" of Jesus' home country. The number symbolism is also quite different. Here the salient numbers are four and seven: four thousand people (8:9); seven loaves (8:5, 6), and seven baskets taken up at the end (8:8). The number four alludes to the ends

---

Revelation in Mark's Gospel," in J. P. Rosenblatt and J. C. Sitterson, eds., *"Not in Heaven:" Coherence and Complexity in Biblical Narrative* (Bloomington: Indiana UP, 1991), 98-119; Austin Farrer, *St. Matthew and St. Mark* (London: Dacre, 1954), 65; Frank Kermode, *The Genesis of Secrecy: On the Interpretation of Narrative* (Cambridge: Harvard UP, 2006), 36; Marcus, *Mark 1-8*, 407; G. Rau, *Das Markusevangelium: Komposition und Intention der ersten Darstellung christlicher Mission* (ANRW, 1985); Svartvik, *Mark and Mission*, 297ff.; John Painter, *Mark's Gospel: Worlds in Conflict* (London: Routledge, 1997), 118-9; Aus, *Feeding the Five Thousand*.

Defending the Gentile Mission

of the earth, symbolism which is confirmed even within the text of Mark, for in 13:27 Jesus says, "And then he will . . . gather his elect from the four winds, from the ends of the earth to the ends of heaven." The number seven represents divine completeness, calling to mind scriptural texts such as the Genesis story of seven days of creation. And once again, it is precisely these numbers that Jesus highlights when he castigates his disciples for their hardness of heart: "'And the seven for the four thousand, how many baskets full of broken pieces did you take up?' And they said to him, 'Seven.'"

In addition to setting the stage and using number symbolism, Mark may also have left subtle clues in the wording of the stories. The word for "basket" is different in each case; κοφίνους in the first feeding story may reflect a Jewish context, while σπυρίδας in the second feeding reflects a Gentile milieu.[94] Farrer notes that the word χορτασθῆναι ("were filled") appears in both feedings and on the lips of the Gentile Syro-Phoenician woman.[95] In other words, the Jews want to be filled and are, then a single Gentile wants also to be filled and Jesus acquiesces, and after that Jesus shows that Gentiles en masse can and should also be filled.

It is also significant that Mark uses "Greek" in the Pauline sense to mean "Gentile" in only one place, in the text leading up to the second feeding; while the text leading up to the first feeding has the only place where he uses the word "Jews" (7:3).[96]

---

[94] See Marcus, *Mark 1-8*, 407; Svartvik, *Mark and Mission*, 299.
[95] Farrer, *Matthew and Mark*, 63.
[96] Svartvik, *Mark and Mission*, 297-8. This is the only place where Mark uses the word "Greek."

There may also be another connection to Pauline epistles here. In both feedings the language that describes how many remnants were taken up is very unusual in Greek. The awkward phrases are typically translated into normal-sounding English: "twelve baskets full of broken pieces" in the first feeding story (6:43) and "the broken pieces left over, seven baskets full" (8:8) in the second feeding story. The Greek in the first case is κλάσματα δώδεκα κοφίνων πληρώματα (literally, "pieces twelve of baskets fullnesses") and in the second case is περισσεύματα κλασμάτων ἑπτὰ σπυρίδας (literally, "surpluses of pieces seven baskets"). Why "fullnesses of baskets" (κοφίνων πληρώματα) instead of "full baskets"? And why "surpluses of pieces" (περισσεύματα κλασμάτων) instead of "surplus pieces"? These odd constructions make sense if the Pauline literature was Mark's inspiration. In Romans 11:12, the word πλήρωμα (fullness) refers to the Jews:

> Now if their trespass means riches for the world, and if their failure means riches for the Gentiles, how much more will their fullness (πλήρωμα) mean!

And in 2 Corinthians 8:13-14, the word περίσσευμα (surplus) describes the process by which Jews and Gentiles supply each other's needs:

> I do not mean that others should be eased and you burdened, but that as a matter of equality your surplus (περίσσευμα) at the present time should supply their want, so that their surplus (περίσσευμα) may supply your want, that there may be equality.

Jesus Rejects Jewish Exclusivism

The feeding stories are not symbols of the Eucharist. No wine is distributed. The emphasis is entirely – and very heavily so – on bread. In both instances, the story mainly revolves around how many loaves of bread are distributed, and how many baskets of crumbs are taken up. Between them the crumbs appear again in the story of the Syro-Phoenician woman who induces Jesus to proclaim that crumbs can be given to Gentiles. After the feeding episodes Jesus warns his disciples against the "leaven of the Pharisees and the leaven of Herod," and the perpetually confused disciples have no idea what he means and only know that "We have no bread." Of everything they saw at the feedings, Jesus reminds them only about the numbers of loaves and baskets of crumbs.

In a heavily symbolic tight-knit series of stories that revolves around bread, understanding what the bread is all about would be one of the main keys to understanding the gospel of Mark as a whole. Some scholars have proposed that bread here is a symbol for the teaching of the Torah.[97] In that case what Mark is saying is that the gospel of Jesus is essentially the act of sharing the Torah with the Gentiles, giving the Gentiles an opportunity to opt in to the community that the Torah created. In a word, Jesus breaks down any basis for Jewish exclusivism.

Another attack on the idea and practice of Jewish exclusivism can be seen in Jesus' association with people who are ostensibly Jews but are viewed as outsiders by Jewish officialdom. In 2:15-17, the evangelist emphasizes that Jesus was eating with "tax collectors and sinners" by repeating that phrase three times in quick succession, following up with yet a fourth instance of "sinners":

> And as he sat at table in his house, many *tax collectors and sinners* were sitting with Jesus and his disciples; for there were many who followed him. And the scribes of the Pharisees, when they saw that he was eating with *sinners and tax collectors*, said to his disciples,

---

[97] See, for example, Aus, *Feeding the Five Thousand*, 5-6.

"Why does he eat with *tax collectors and sinners*?" And when Jesus heard it, he said to them, "Those who are well have no need of a physician, but those who are sick; I came not to call the righteous, but *sinners*."

Repetition in an ancient literary work indicates emphasis, and the word "sinners" in particular connotes not so much evil-doing as outsider status typical of Gentiles. This is how Paul uses the word in Galatians 2:15, where it simply indicates the way Jews see Gentiles: "We ourselves, who are Jews by birth and not Gentile sinners. . . ." For anyone familiar with the usage of "sinner" reflected in Galatians, this episode in Mark clearly parallels Paul's defense of table fellowship with "Gentile sinners" against the Jerusalem apostles' attempts to put a stop to it.

Another part of the Gospel narrative that fits the pattern of allegorically supporting inclusiveness for Gentiles is in 9:36 through 10:16. At the start of this section, Jesus instructs his disciples to accept children, at the end of it he rebukes them for continuing to shoo away children in direct disobedience to his command, and in between he warns of dire consequences for "whoever causes one of these little ones who believe in me to sin" (9:42) and states categorically that "he who is not against is for us" (9:40).[98] Children, like "tax collectors and sinners," and like Gentiles, are social outsiders, and Jesus welcomes them. This is yet another scenario in which the actions of Jesus on the one hand and his disciples on the other hand parallel Paul's acceptance of Gentiles on the one hand and the Jerusalem

---

[98] See Tarazi, *Paul and Mark*, 194-8; Tolbert, *Sowing the Gospel*, 210. Tarazi suggests that children act especially effectively as symbols of Gentiles because both were forbidden to speak or teach in Jewish religious gatherings.

apostles' policies effectively rejecting them on the other hand.[99] As I will show later when I focus on Mark's treatment of the disciples, the narrative here closely follows Paul's own presentation of his Gentile converts as his "children" and his own indignation against those who were hindering their acceptance of his gospel (1 Thess 2:10-16).

The flip side of positive encounters with Gentiles is negative encounters with Jews, of which the Gospel is full. Some of these encounters carry fairly clear echoes of Pauline epistles. For example, in Mark 8:11-12 the Pharisees seek a sign from heaven. In response Jesus sighs "deeply in his spirit," warns that "no sign shall be given to this generation," and shortly thereafter warns his disciples against "the leaven of the Pharisees and the leaven of Herod" (8:15). This language corresponds to what Paul says in 1 Cor 1:22: "For Jews demand signs and Greeks seek wisdom, but we preach Christ crucified, a stumbling block to Jews and folly to Gentiles."

Tarazi points to yet another place where Mark adopts a Pauline theme in order to combat Jewish exclusivism. In Mark 10:2-12 some Pharisees ask Jesus if it's legal for a man to divorce his wife, and Jesus responds in no uncertain terms that it should not be done, even if it is legal:

> And Pharisees came up and in order to test him asked, "Is it lawful for a man to divorce his wife?" He answered them, "What did Moses command you?" They said, "Moses allowed a man to write a certificate of divorce, and to put her away." But Jesus said to them, "For your hardness of heart he wrote you this commandment. But from the beginning of creation, 'God made

---

[99] Another example: the remark "My son, your sins are forgiven" in Mark 2:5-9 may be seen as an invitation to the Jewish church to treat Gentiles as equals (see Hanhart, "Son, Your Sins are Forgiven," 997-1016).

them male and female.' 'For this reason a man shall leave his father and mother and be joined to his wife, and the two shall become one flesh.' So they are no longer two but one flesh. What therefore God has joined together, let not man put asunder." (Mark 10:2-9)

His disciples are dismayed at this apparently unworkable demand and ask him about it, apparently seeking a way around it, but his response doesn't allay their fears:

> "Whoever divorces his wife and marries another, commits adultery against her; and if she divorces her husband and marries another, she commits adultery." (Mark 10:11-12)

How does this fit in a section of Mark focused on exhorting the disciples to receive and accept "children" or "little ones," or anyone who was "not following" them? In other words, how is this related to Paul's Gentile mission? It is related because there was a history in Judaism of Jews being advised to put away Gentile spouses (see Ezra 10:1-5, 44), and this could have been extrapolated by Gentiles newly converting to Christianity into a belief that they could or should divorce their unbelieving spouses. Paul explicitly opposed this idea in 1 Corinthians:

> If any woman has a husband who is an unbeliever, and he consents to live with her, she should not divorce him. For the unbelieving husband is consecrated through his wife, and the unbelieving wife is consecrated through her husband. Otherwise, your children would be unclean, but as it is they are holy. But if the unbelieving partner desires to separate, let it be so; in such a case the brother or sister is not bound. For God has called us to peace. Wife, how do you know whether you will save your husband? Husband, how do you know whether you will save your wife? (1 Cor 7:13-16)

Defending the Gentile Mission

Tarazi points out that what is unique about Jesus' words in Mark is the same as what is unique about Paul's words in 1 Corinthians:

> Both the Deuteronomic ruling quoted in [Mark 10] v.4 (Deut 24:1-3) and the Ezra passage speak only of a man divorcing his wife, but Jesus' reply concerns the woman as well as the man. This two-sided approach – addressing man and woman separately and on an equal footing – occurs nowhere else either in the Old Testament or the New Testament except in 1 Cor ch.7.[100]

Jesus Rejects Jewish Legalism

The only way Gentiles would enter the church en masse would be if they were not subject to the dictates of the Jewish law, especially circumcision. Mark could not make such a blatant anachronism as to portray Jesus addressing circumcision directly. Circumcision did not become an issue until after Paul established Gentile communities and Paul's opponents demanded that members of those communities be circumcised, so it would be obvious to Mark's audience that a circumcision controversy would not fit in a narrative about Jesus.[101] But one way to reach the same goal of showing that circumcision should not be considered necessary would be to assert that the essence of the Law consists in loving God and one's neighbor, and the rest of it is of relative, not absolute value.

Thus we have the dialogue where Jesus proclaims that to love God and neighbor are the greatest commandments. A scribe the

---

[100] Tarazi, *Paul and Mark*, 197.
[101] Marcus is one of many scholars who cites the lack of reference to circumcision as evidence that Mark is not a Paulinist (*Mark 1-8*, 74). Others recognize that this is based on a false presupposition; Painter, for example, recognizes the constraint I point out here that prevents such reference (*Mark's Gospel*, 118-9).

narrator identifies as "wise" approves that proclamation, and Jesus responds that "You are not far from the kingdom of God" (12:29-34). The earliest record we have of this understanding of the Law comes from the pen of Paul, who stated that "the whole law is fulfilled in one word, 'You shall love your neighbor as yourself'" (Gal 5:14). Romans 13:8-9 expresses the same view. In both those Pauline contexts, love of the neighbor also leads eventually to the "kingdom of God" (Gal 5:21; Rom 14:17), as it does in Mark.[102] And the apostle made both of these assertions in literary contexts associated with the defense of his Gentile mission.

The ongoing disputes between Jesus and the Jewish authorities about observance of specific requirements of the Law also serve to relativize all Jewish laws and regulations besides love for others.[103] This is clearest in the passage where Jesus openly abrogates all Jewish dietary regulations by saying what matters is not what you eat but how you treat other people by what you say (7:14-19).[104] The attitude and the very words placed on Jesus' lips by Mark in this passage reflect what Paul asserted in Rom 14:20: "Do not, for the sake of food, destroy the work of God. Everything is indeed clean, but it is wrong for anyone to make others fall by what he eats . . ." The Gospel and epistle texts are closer in Greek than in English since the same three words

---

[102] Thanks to Fr. Paul Tarazi for pointing this out to me.

[103] K. Romaniuk argues that Mark is not Pauline because Mark does not abrogate the Law altogether ("Le Problème des Paulinismes," 268). However, even Paul did not do that – he argued that the Law was irrelevant for Gentiles, but not necessarily for Jews. Relativizing external observances has essentially the same effect.

[104] Svartvik's dissertation focuses on this passage and concludes that the purpose of v.14 (the "parable" itself) was to emphasize the importance of speaking with care, not to annul food regulations. But he sees v.19 (the interpretation) as a polemical interpretation added precisely to attack the food regulations. See Svartvik, *Mark and Mission*, 346, 411.

Defending the Gentile Mission

appear in each, in exactly the reverse order: καθαρίζων πάντα τὰ βρώματα in Mark 7:19 and βρώματος ... πάντα ... καθαρά in Rom 14:20.[105]

Another passage in which a dispute about Law observance contains evidence suggestive of a direct connection to Romans is Mark 3:1-5. Jesus encounters a man with a withered hand in a synagogue on the Sabbath and the authorities watch him to see if he will heal the man. He asks them, "Is it lawful on the Sabbath to do good or to do harm, to save life or to kill." When they remain silent, Jesus looks at them "with anger, grieved (μετ' ὀργῆς, συλλυπούμενος) at their hardness (πωρώσει) of heart." These words, especially the strange combination of "grief" and "anger," can best be explained as inspired by Paul's comments on the same theme in Romans. In chapter 9, Paul expresses his "grief" (λύπη; v.2) about the Jews' rejection of Christ because it leads to God's "anger" (ὀργὴν; v.22).[106] And within the same context in Romans, the word "hardness" (πώρωσις; 11:25) describes the Jews' refusal to have faith in Jesus.

In these and other ways, throughout the Gospel Mark demolishes the arguments of Paul's opponents who want to force Gentiles to observe the Jewish Law. He does that by making clear that "new wine" (Gentiles) must go in "new wineskins" (a

---

[105] This is frequently noted; see, for example, Van Iersel, *Mark: A Reader-Response Commentary*, 53. Marcus argues that Paul himself may have borrowed the saying from somewhere else, and "The parallel, therefore, may merely mean that Paul [sic; Mark is meant here] moved in the same circles that Paul did, namely those of Gentile Christians who did not feel themselves bound by the Jewish Law." ("Mark, Interpreter of Paul," 455) This is speculation without evidence backing it, and it assumes that such circles could be disconnected from the Pauline tradition.

[106] The two verses in Romans are directly related: in the former, Paul regrets that most Jews have rejected Jesus, and in the latter he identifies them as "vessels of wrath" that God has endured in order to "show his wrath and make known his power."

new approach to the Law), as he puts it in 2:21-22. And yet at the same time, Mark doesn't engage in wholesale rejection of cultic requirements of Jewish Law for Jews: as Paul advised, Gentiles remain Gentiles while Jews remain Jews. Accordingly, when Mark depicts Jesus healing a Jew, he shows Jesus advising the man to fulfill the Jewish requirement of presenting himself to the priests (Mark 1:44), while the Gentile he heals is simply advised to proclaim his salvation among "his friends" (5:19).

The Parable of the Fig Tree

The evangelist had no choice but to go about his task of supporting Paul's approach to Law observance with great subtlety, for he was projecting into the past issues that did not actually arise until later. This explains why he had to resort to extensive use of parables in his Gospel. Of special note with respect to the theme of Jews and Gentiles is the parable of the fig tree. This parable is actually wrapped around the temple cleansing episode, which as I observed earlier contains one of the clearest expressions of Mark's interest in the Gentile mission. It begins before the temple cleansing episode:

> On the following day, when they came from Bethany, he was hungry. And seeing in the distance a fig tree in leaf, he went to see if he could find anything on it. When he came to it, he found nothing but leaves, for it was not the season for figs. And he said to it, "May no one ever eat fruit from you again." And his disciples heard it. (Mark 11:12-14)

And it ends after the temple cleansing episode:

> And when evening came they went out of the city. As they passed by in the morning, they saw the fig tree withered away to its roots. And Peter remembered and said to him, "Master, look! The fig tree which you cursed has withered." And Jesus answered them,

Defending the Gentile Mission

"Have faith in God. Truly, I say to you, whoever says to this mountain, 'Be taken up and cast into the sea,' and does not doubt in his heart, but believes that what he says will come to pass, it will be done for him." (Mark 11:19-23)

Considering the symbolism of the sea of Galilee in the rest of Mark and the location of this text surrounding the temple cleansing episode, it is no great leap to see the "mountain" as an allusion to the temple mount and the sea as the Roman sea.[107] This view of the temple and its fate, as expressed metaphorically in the fig tree parable and literally in the Isaiah quotation that concludes the temple cleansing, perfectly represents the understanding behind the Pauline mission. The physical temple in Jerusalem was of no importance to Paul; it had in a sense "withered away to its roots," being replaced by the "Jerusalem above" (Gal 4:25-26). This Jerusalem above was available to all, including the Gentiles, wherever they lived; thus "the house of prayer for all the nations" was metaphorically thrown into the Roman sea.

---

[107] See the discussion in Tarazi, *Paul and Mark*, 204-205.

5
Presenting Jesus as the Crucified One

Alas for the vanity of all human endeavour! We strive and strain, and would die for our convictions; and when we have won the battle, those who follow us totally misunderstand what we have maintained, and in reading and sermon inculcate in our name the teaching of our opponents!
Michael Goulder[108]

Another theme unique to Paul is his emphasis on the cross, or more specifically on the crucified Christ over the resurrected Christ. From the accounts of opposition to him and his message in his letters, it appears that this emphasis was controversial; Marcus goes so far as to suggest Paul may have been its sole advocate.[109]

Paul's epistles record the Apostle's battles not only with so-called Judaizers but also with those from his own communities who wanted a resurrection experience in the present rather than the suffering symbolized by the cross.[110] Accordingly, he consistently plays down the resurrection and emphasizes the crucifixion. In 1 Corinthians, the purpose of the Eucharist is to "proclaim the Lord's death until he comes," and the verse that recalls the words of institution does not even mention the resurrection.[111] Chapter 15 of the same epistle, which defends belief in the resurrection, concludes with a remark that makes it

---

[108] Goulder, *Paul vs. Peter*, 172.
[109] Marcus, "Mark, Interpreter of Paul," 481.
[110] Goulder addresses this issue at length (*Paul versus Peter*, 84-88), and it is the main subject of Theodore J. Weeden, *Mark: Traditions in Conflict* (Philadelphia: Fortress Press, 1971).
[111] 1 Cor 11:26.

clear that in Paul's mind the entire digression was forced upon him due to his fear that denying the resurrection altogether would result in people not having incentive to do good. In Romans, one is "buried with Christ" in order to "live to God" (live a virtuous life) but "living with" the resurrected Christ is strictly a hope for the future (Rom 6:3-8; see also 2 Cor 13:4). [112]

Paul was so extraordinarily careful to avoid letting anyone think of resurrection as present reality rather than as a promise of something future to hope for, that he avoids even mentioning the very idea of resurrection using the past tense. The fact that the Christian Easter ceremony so heavily stresses the resurrection as something already accomplished is what Goulder laments in the superscription to this chapter.

Mark's story of Jesus with its heavy emphasis on passion and crucifixion portrays the same view: today life involves weakness, pain, disgrace, mockery, and even the feeling of being forsaken by God. Resurrection is not yet.[113] As Focant observes, even on the cross itself, Mark's Jesus prevents the hearer from anticipating the resurrection too quickly. Jesus' cry of "My God, My God, why have you forsaken me" is the first part of a psalm that eventually winds up proclaiming victory, but Mark must have a reason for reporting only its cry of despair.[114] As in Paul, the only image of Christ one is left with after reading this "passion story with an extended introduction" is that of a Jesus

---

[112] See also Galatians where the resurrection is mentioned in passing, then the rest of the epistle is about the crucified Christ. See Goulder, *Paul vs. Peter*, 172.

[113] So Marcus, "Mark, Interpreter of Paul," 481; Goulder, *Paul vs. Peter*, 87; Weeden, *Mark: Traditions in Conflict*, 126, 137.

[114] Psalm 22. Camille Focant makes this point in *Marc, un évangile étonnant: recueil d'essais* (Leuven: Leuven University Press, 2006), 16.

broken and crucified – no image of a resurrected Christ to be found in the book.

It is precisely this context that can make sense of a conundrum that has plagued biblical scholars for more than a century: what is the meaning or purpose of the "messianic secret" in Mark?

The Messianic Secret

In the Gospel of Mark, Jesus goes around preaching to everyone who will listen, in some cases to thousands at a time, and yet paradoxically, almost every time he heals someone he warns them not to make his identity known to anyone. He gives his disciples the same command immediately after the Transfiguration (9:9). Many explanations for this have been advanced, all of which are problematic in one way or another.[115] It is the context of Paul's struggle to keep focus on the cross and crucifixion that best makes sense of the commands to secrecy. All of these commands are issued before Christ's passion. Mark's

---

[115] Wrede says the secrecy theme was invented by Mark to explain why Jesus was not recognized as the messiah in his lifetime. However, Mark appears to have been written not to convert non-believers but for Christians. Others suggest the purpose was to portray a rejection of personal glory – the humility of Christ (Tolbert, *Sowing the Gospel*, 227-28). However, Jesus did acknowledge his exalted status during his trial. Some propose that Mark wanted to send a message to Rome that Jesus was no insurrectionist (Tolbert, *Sowing the Gospel*, 228). But then he wrapped it in such obscure language that virtually no one could decode the message. Some interpret the secrecy as "a literary device that makes clear to the reader of the importance of what he's reading" (Adela Yarbro Collins, *Mark: A Commentary* [Minneapolis: Fortress Press, 2007], 171-2). But that too would be an inscrutable code that obscures what exactly is being emphasized. Others suggest that secrecy bought Jesus time to complete his ministry, because his claim to be the messiah prompted the authorities to destroy him. (Dennis R. MacDonald, "Secrecy and Recognitions in the Odyssey and Mark: Where Wrede Went Wrong," in Ronald F. Hock et al., eds., *Ancient Fiction and Early Christian Narrative* [Atlanta: Scholars Press, 1998], 139-153; here: 142; Tolbert, *Sowing the Gospel*, 229). However, Mark explicitly identifies Jesus' public disputes with Jewish leaders about the Law as prompting the conspiracy against him. (3:6)

point is that the weakness of the crucifixion is what seals Christ's identity for all of his followers, not the power revealed in miracles and healings. Christ himself does not claim to be the messiah who will come in glory in the future, until he is in the midst of suffering his passion. Or, to put it another way, the message of Christ must be kept secret until it can be properly understood, until the true basis of his Messiahship is revealed.[116]

The Irony of the Cross

Paul's gospel that focuses so single-mindedly on something as awful as the cross and crucifixion can only be "good news" because the message of the cross is essentially one of irony: when others see the crucifixion as a defeat, Paul knows it to be a victory; when others see suffering as cause for sadness, Paul sees it as something to rejoice in and give thanks for. Irony of this sort pervades Paul's epistles because at the core of his gospel is the message that insiders see a reality that is the opposite of the way outsiders see it. "For the word of the cross is folly to those who are perishing, but to us who are being saved it is the power of God."[117] One can hardly read any given chapter of Paul's epistles without running across some expression of this irony.

In a similar manner, irony pervades Mark's Gospel.[118] Frequently, irony is evident without recourse to special knowledge from outside the text. For example, the disciples want

---

[116] Tarazi, *Paul and Mark*, 193. See also Elizabeth Struthers Malbon, "Narrative Criticism. How Does the Story Mean?" in Anderson and Moore, *Mark and Method*, 29-57; here: 46. Kealy notes that Perrin offers this interpretation (*History of Interpretation*, 2: 2: 379).

[117] 1 Cor 1:18; see the entire context, 1:18-24. See also Rom 1:22; 1 Cor 1:25-29; 2:6-8; 2 Cor 6:8-10, 12:9-10.

[118] On Mark's use of irony, see J. Camery-Hoggatt, *Irony in Mark's Gospel: Text and Subtext* (Cambridge: Cambridge UP, 1992), 192-231; Mack, *Myth of Innocence*, 335-39.

Presenting Jesus as the Crucified One

to sit on the right and left in Jesus' glory, while those who do turn out to be on his right and left are the thieves at the crucifixion.[119]

Other instances of irony are intertextual and function as irony only for those who know another text that is alluded to. An example of this is Jesus' cry from the cross, "My God, My God, why have you forsaken me?" A reader familiar with the Old Testament will know that that psalm begins with defeat but ends in a proclamation of victory.[120]

Various explanations have been offered for why Mark relies so heavily on irony.[121] But considering all the other evidence of Pauline themes, it can hardly be a coincidence that both Paul and Mark not only made it central to their text, but also employed it mainly to convey the paradoxical message of the cross.

In addition, a direct link to Paul is visible in instances of intertextual irony that are apparent only to those who have read both Mark's Gospel and Paul's epistles.[122] Consider the parallels

---

[119] Tolbert, *Sowing the Gospel*, 31-2. Stephen Smith provides a number of examples of intra-textual irony (*A Lion with Wings: A Narrative-Critical Approach to Mark's Gospel* [Sheffield: Sheffield Academic Press, 1996], 220).

[120] See Smith, *Lion*, 230. MacDonald points out ironic parallels between Homer's Odysseus and Mark's Jesus, and suggests that Homer's use of irony may have contributed to the importance of irony for Mark ("Secrecy," 140-53).

[121] Camery-Hoggatt sees it as a "community building device." (This phrase is from Smith, *Lion*, 209; he is summarizing Camery-Hoggatt, *Irony*, 180-1). The idea is that people gain a sense of community because they share insider knowledge that outsiders do not know. However, as Smith observes, this would not work reliably because some in the community might not get the irony.

[122] With justification, Smith asks, ". . . can we be confident that we have discovered all the irony it is possible to discover in this Gospel?" (*Lion*, 217) The assumption that Mark did not know Paul's epistles has helped prevent links to those epistles from being found.

between Jesus' rebuke of Peter in Mark and Paul's rebuke of Peter in its context in Galatians.

> And he began to teach them that the Son of man must suffer many things, and be rejected by the elders and the chief priests and the scribes, and be killed, and after three days rise again. And he said this plainly. And Peter took him, and began to rebuke him. But turning and seeing his disciples, he rebuked Peter, and said, "Get behind me, Satan! For you are not on the side of God, but of men." (Mark 8:31-33)

> But when Cephas came to Antioch I opposed him to his face, because he stood condemned. For before certain men came from James, he ate with the Gentiles; but when they came he drew back and separated himself, fearing the circumcision party. And with him the rest of the Jews acted insincerely, so that even Barnabas was carried away by their insincerity. But when I saw that they were not straightforward about the truth of the gospel, I said to Cephas before them all, "If you, though a Jew, live like a Gentile and not like a Jew, how can you compel the Gentiles to live like Jews?" (Gal 2:11-14)

In both texts, Peter by his actions or words is denying the cross. In Mark he tells Jesus to avoid the cross, and in Galatians the ultimate aim of the "circumcision party" whose side Peter takes is to deny the cross. Paul states this explicitly in the concluding chapters of Galatians:

> But if I, brethren, still preach circumcision, why am I still persecuted? In that case the stumbling block of the cross has been removed. (Gal 5:11)

> It is those who want to make a good showing in the flesh that would compel you to be circumcised, and only in order that they may not be persecuted for the cross of Christ. (Gal 6:12)

Presenting Jesus as the Crucified One 99

In both texts, the impetus to deny the cross comes from a desire to please "man" rather than God. This theme is stated explicitly in Galatians in the prologue to the episode of Paul's conflict with Peter:[123]

> But even if we, or an angel from heaven, should preach to you a gospel contrary to that which we preached to you, let him be accursed (*anathema*). As we have said before, so now I say again, If anyone is preaching to you a gospel contrary to that which you received, let him be accursed (*anathema*). Am I now seeking the favor of men, or of God? Or am I trying to please men? If I were still pleasing men, I should not be a servant of Christ. (1:9-10)

The "pleasing man rather than God" idea is also implicit in Galatians when Paul attributes Peter's actions to fear of what the "men from James" would think (Gal 2:12).

In both texts, Peter's actions result in a stern rebuke. Jesus calling Peter "Satan" in Mark corresponds to Paul calling him "condemned," and also recalls the anathema pronounced upon all who preach "another gospel" that denies the cross.

In both texts the rebuke is deliberately done in public ("turning and seeing his disciples" in Mark, and "before them all" in Galatians).

For anyone who reads both of these texts, the irony is that what Paul's enemies accuse him of ("Am I now seeking the favor of men, or of God?"), Jesus turns around and applies to Peter ("You are not thinking of the things of God but of the things of man"). In other words, in the conflict between Paul and Peter, Jesus himself pronounces Paul right and Peter wrong. Paul's view of matters in Galatians is confirmed as clearly as possible in a

---

[123] The same theme also occurs in 1 Thess 2:4.

narrative that relates events supposed to have taken place decades before Galatians was written.

That Mark had Paul in mind when writing this passage is also indicated by some other instances of Pauline terminology that Tarazi points out. Both are in Jesus' exposition of what it means to take up the cross, following his rebuke of Peter. The first saying is about the irony that taking up the cross involves both gain and loss:

> For whoever would save his life will lose it; and whoever loses his life for my sake and the gospel's will save it. For what does it profit a man, to gain (κερδῆσαι) the whole world and forfeit (ζημιωθῆναι) his life? For what can a man give in return for his life? (Mark 8:35-37)

Tarazi sees a link to Philippians here in the words κερδῆσαι and ζημιωθῆναι, which occur elsewhere in the New Testament only in that epistle, where they have the same meaning:

> But whatever gain (κέρδη) I had, I counted as loss (ζημίαν) for the sake of Christ. Indeed I count everything as loss (ζημίαν) because of the surpassing worth of knowing Christ Jesus my Lord. For his sake I have suffered the loss (ἐζημιώθην) of all things, and count them as refuse, in order that I may gain (κερδήσω) Christ . . . (Phil 3:7-8)

The second connection to Paul in the text following the rebuke of Peter is in the way Mark uses the words "shame" and "glory":

> "For whoever is *ashamed* of me and of my words in this adulterous and sinful generation, of him will the Son of man also be *ashamed*, when he comes in the *glory* of his Father with the holy angels." (Mark 8:38)

Presenting Jesus as the Crucified One

The idea that "shame" denotes a negative verdict on judgment day, in contrast to boasting and "glory," which denote a positive verdict, is typically Pauline.[124]

Similarly Pauline language opens the discourse before the exchange of rebukes between Peter and Jesus:

> And he began to teach them that the Son of man must suffer many things, and be rejected by the elders and the chief priests and the scribes, and be killed, and after three days rise again. And he said this plainly (καὶ παρρησίᾳ τὸν λόγον ἐλάλει). (8:31-32).

The phrase καὶ παρρησίᾳ τὸν λόγον ἐλάλει literally means "and he was speaking the word plainly." As Tarazi points out, "speaking the word" is a Pauline phrase, and the word παρρησίᾳ may also be translated "boldly" and is the opposite of shame. παρρησίᾳ "occurs in Paul only four times, all four in conjunction not only with the gospel but with suffering for its sake."[125]

Another case of intertextual irony that reflects positively on Paul for anyone who reads both Mark and Paul's epistles can be found in Jesus' response to the disciples' quarrel over who was the greatest:

> . . . they had discussed with one another who was the greatest. . . . and he said to them, "If anyone would be first, he must be last of all and servant of all." (Mark 9:34-35)

---

[124] On glory and boasting (the opposite of shame), see Rom 2:5-10; 5:1-11; 11:13-15; 1 Cor 9:15-27; 15:29-34; 2 Cor 1:12-14; 5:11-15; Gal 6:4-5; Phil 2:16; 1 Thess 2:19-20. On shame in the sense of a negative verdict on judgment day, see Rom 1:16; 5:5; 9:33; 10:1; 1 Cor 1:27; 2 Cor 10:8; Phil 1:20; 2 Tim 1:12, 15. See also Tarazi, *Paul and Mark*, 187-90.
[125] Tarazi, *Paul and Mark*, 188.

". . . whoever would be great among you must be your servant, and whoever would be first among you must be slave of all." (Mark 10:43-44)[126]

It is obviously ironic that to be first one must be last. But there is also another level of irony here, because Paul calls himself the last of the apostles and slave of all:[127]

Last of all . . . he appeared also to me. For I am the least of the apostles. (1 Cor 15:8-9)

For though I am free from all men, I have made myself a slave to all, that I might win the more. (1 Cor 9:19)

For anyone who hears both Paul's words and Jesus' words, the implications are clear: the disciples want to be greatest but miss the whole point of the cross; Paul calls himself last and understands and accepts the cross and thus is in reality the greatest apostle.[128]

This irony that comes from juxtaposing these texts was probably intended by the evangelist. The two Gospel passages parallel the one in the epistle in more ways than just the "first-last" dichotomy and the additional phrase "of all" appended to "last" and "slave" (though these are already quite distinctive). In each instance in the Gospel, a temporal adjective (first or last) alternates with one that indicates importance (least or greatest): the disciples discuss who is *greatest*, and Jesus tells them whoever wants to be *first* must be *last* before adding that such a person must be *servant/slave* of all. If the disciples were discussing "who

---

[126] See Tarazi, *Paul and Mark*, 194, 200.
[127] The Greek behind the word translated "slave" is the same in each case: the noun δοῦλος in Mark 10:44 and the verb ἐδούλωσα in 1 Corinthians 9:19. The word translated "servant" in Mark 9:35 and 10:43 is διάκονος, which has a similar meaning.
[128] See Tarazi, *Paul and Mark*, 194.

is the greatest," it would have been more natural and direct for Jesus to address the question in the terms in which it was asked, by answering, "If any would be greatest, he must be least." Instead he shifts at first to "If any would be first, he must be last of all." This curious juxtaposition occurs in both Markan verses and in 1 Corinthians, where Jesus' appearance "last" to Paul makes him the "least" of the disciples.

That Mark has Paul in mind here is also suggested by a link to Galatians in Mark 10:42, where the disciples' desire to rule is likened to that of secular grandees:

> "You know that *those who are supposed to* (δοκοῦντες) rule over the Gentiles lord it over them, and their great men exercise authority over them. But it shall not be so among you; but whoever would be great among you must be your servant, and whoever would be first among you must be slave of all. . . ." (Mark 10:42-43)

The italicized phrase here translates the same word as the italicized phrase in these Galatians verses:

> And from those *who were reputed to be* (τῶν δοκούντων) something – what they were makes no difference to me; God shows no partiality – those, I say, who were *of repute* (οἱ δοκοῦντες) added nothing to me . . . and when they perceived the grace that was given to me, James and Cephas and John, *who were reputed to be* (οἱ δοκοῦντες) pillars, gave to me and Barnabas the right hand of fellowship, that we should go to the Gentiles and they to the circumcised . . . (Gal 2:6, 9)

In both texts the idea is that people commonly considered to be in charge actually aren't, because God is ultimately in charge. The most likely reason why Mark borrowed this word from Galatians at this point in the Gospel is to use Paul's ironic expression to strengthen the ironic element in his own text. The phrase "those who are supposed to" or "those who are reputed to" implies that what they are supposed or reputed to be is not what they really are. The apostles who were the intimates of Jesus during his earthly ministry are supposed or reputed to be the authoritative "first among the apostles," but in reality it is the "last of all" and "slave of all" Paul who is the authoritative Apostle, the one who finally understood Jesus and the significance of his crucifixion correctly.

6
Discrediting Jesus' Disciples and Family

> ... *when* the women appear, *how* they are described, and their identity *as women* all depict a group similar to but *much better than* the Twelve. They are not surrogates but superiors. The Twelve revealed themselves fully as rocky ground by their responses when active persecution started in Jerusalem ...
> Mary Ann Tolbert[129]

One of the particularly ironic aspects of the Markan story is that those closest to Jesus, both his relatives and his hand-picked associates, misunderstand and even oppose him. Not just once, but repeatedly, constantly, throughout the story from beginning to end. His family thinks he's gone mad. His disciples don't understand him no matter how many times he tries to explain, and they even disobey him. At the start of his passion when he needs their support the most, everyone close to him abandons him. Mark directs his readers' attention to this kind of behavior on the part of Jesus' mother and siblings as a group, on the part of the twelve as a group, on the part of Peter, James, and John as a smaller group, on the part of Peter especially as an individual, and also on the part of Judas.

Many scholars have recognized that Mark's attempt to discredit all these people makes sense in the context of Paul's ongoing conflict with those who were "apostles before him" (Gal 1:17), especially the Jerusalem leadership of the "so-called pillars," Peter, James the brother of Jesus, and John.[130]

---

[129] Tolbert, *Sowing the Gospel* 292.
[130] Gal 2:1-14. On the ongoing conflict between Paul and the other apostles, see Goulder, *Paul vs. Peter*; Weeden, *Mark: Traditions in Conflict*; John Dominic

Jesus' Family

In Mark 3:21, 31-35 Jesus' family hears what he has been up to, and they jump to the conclusion that he has gone mad. They come intending simply to take custody of him, not to talk to him to find out the truth of the matter:

> And when his family heard it, they went out to seize him, for people were saying, "He is beside himself." . . . And his mother and his brothers came; and standing outside they sent to him and called him. And a crowd was sitting about him; and they said to him, "Your mother and your brothers are outside, asking for you." And he replied, "Who are my mother and my brothers?" And looking around on those who sat about him, he said, "Here are my mother and my brothers! Whoever does the will of God is my brother, and sister, and mother."

The actions of Jesus' "mother and brothers" reflect negatively on them, since they react so negatively to hearsay. And their actions are even worse than that: it is not just that they believe hearsay without hearing out their son and brother, but the hearsay doesn't even report anything evil about him, it just reports his healings and exorcisms. This fits perfectly with the theme of the embedded story between when Jesus' family starts out on their travels to seize him and when they arrive:

> And the scribes who came down from Jerusalem said, "He is possessed by Beelzebul, and by the prince of demons he casts out the demons." And he called them to him, and said to them in parables, "How can Satan cast out Satan? If a kingdom is divided against itself, that kingdom cannot stand. And if a house is divided

---

Crossan, "Mark and the Relatives of Jesus," *NovT* 15(1973):81-113; Kelber, *Passion in Mark*; Kelber, *Mark's Story of Jesus* (Philadelphia: Fortress Press, 1979); Tarazi, *Paul and Mark*; Telford, *Theology of Mark*; Trobisch, *First Edition*; Focant, *Marc, un évangile étonnant*, 152.

against itself, that house will not be able to stand. And if Satan has risen up against himself and is divided, he cannot stand, but is coming to an end. But no one can enter a strong man's house and plunder his goods, unless he first binds the strong man; then indeed he may plunder his house. "Truly, I say to you, all sins will be forgiven the sons of men, and whatever blasphemies they utter; but whoever blasphemes against the Holy Spirit never has forgiveness, but is guilty of an eternal sin" – for they had said, "He has an unclean spirit." (Mark 3:21-30)

The hearer of this story-within-a-story can readily see the connection: Jesus' mother and brothers are very much like these scribes, for they assume he is mad because they hear he is healing people and driving out demons.

As Goulder observes, ". . . it would be a simple hypothesis to explain the anti-family tendency if Mark were a Pauline Christian embattled against the Jerusalem church's hegemony."[131] But more specifically, Jesus' response to the arrival of relatives seeking to take him away recalls Paul's statement about God not being a respecter of persons in Galatians. In Galatians that theme is important to Paul in asserting his authority vis-à-vis the other apostles, and here that very point is made as strongly as possible: even a close familial relationship doesn't matter to Jesus, even a mother-son relationship doesn't matter, all that matters is doing God's will. To emphasize the theme, Mark repeats it in 6:1-6 where he recounts that the residents of Jesus' home town also refuse to accept him:

> He went away from there and came to his own country . . . And on the sabbath he began to teach in the synagogue; and many who heard him were astonished, saying, "Where did this man get all

---

[131] Michael D. Goulder, "A Pauline in a Jacobite Church," in Van Segbroeck et al., *Four Gospels*, 859-76; here: 860.

this? What is the wisdom given to him? What mighty works are wrought by his hands! Is not this the carpenter, the son of Mary and brother of James and Joses and Judas and Simon, and are not his sisters here with us?" And they took offense at him. And Jesus said to them, "A prophet is not without honor, except in his own country, and among his own kin, and in his own house." And he could do no mighty work there,[132] except that he laid his hands upon a few sick people and healed them. And he marveled because of their unbelief.

This too functions to back up Paul's argument, for the logical conclusion is clear: no close relationship with Jesus during his earthly ministry, not even that of a relative such as "James the Lord's brother" (Gal 1:19), would automatically endow anyone with authority over the messianic community established in his name.[133]

The evangelist may also have added some more subtle prods in the same direction. Just prior to the statement about a prophet being without honor "among his own kin," one of Jesus' brothers is identified as "Judas." The only other Judas in Mark is the betrayer; even if this Judas is not explicitly called a betrayer or named Iscariot, the name carries negative connotations in the second gospel.

Also of interest, then, is how Mark identifies one of the women who come to the tomb after the crucifixion but flee in fear instead of responding positively to news of the resurrection. In 15:47 she is "Mary the mother of Joses," in 16:1 she is "Mary

---

[132] Matthew and Luke apparently deemed the statement that "he could do no mighty work there" too scandalous to report; the former changes it to "he *did not* do many works there," and the latter omits it altogether.

[133] See Tarazi, *Paul and Mark*, 154-6; Michael D. Goulder, "Those Outside (Mk. 4.10-12)," *NovT* 33:289-302; here: 297-300; Goulder, "A Pauline in a Jacobite Church," Goulder, *Paul vs. Peter*, 10-14. See also Marcus, *Mark 1-8*, 269ff.

Discrediting Jesus' Disciples and Family

the mother of James," and in 15:40 "Mary the mother of James the younger and of Joses" was looking on from afar at the crucifixion. The only other Mary in the entire Gospel besides Mary Magdalene is introduced in 6:3: "Is not this the carpenter, the son of Mary and brother of James and Joses . . ." For those with ears to hear, the allusion to Mary the mother of Jesus is not difficult to catch, nor is the intended message, which Mark has been driving home elsewhere in the Gospel as well: do not look to Jesus' close relatives as the best examples of people who understand and follow him. In the context of Galatians, this reinforces the impression that even the fact that James is "the Lord's brother" does not confer any special authority on him which would give him an edge in his conflict with Paul. James will only be a true "brother of the Lord" if he decides to adopt Paul's view of the gospel, in which case he will be doing the will of God.

The Twelve

Paul's conflict was with "apostles before me"[134] as well as with the brother of Jesus, and so Mark's representation of the twelve as missing the point of the gospel and even opposing Jesus could only strengthen Paul's position.[135] Actually, criticism of the disciples would apply as well to James the Lord's brother insofar as the disciples can be taken as representative of the entire Jerusalem leadership in general and thus James in particular.[136]

---

[134] Gal 1:17. See also 1 Cor 9:5; 2 Cor 11:12-13.
[135] For a list of scholars who see in Mark a polemic against the disciples, see Kealy, *History of Interpretation*, 2: 1: 106; 2: 2: 367. Weeden calls it a "devastating attack" (*Mark: Traditions in Conflict*, 25-51). See also Telford, *Theology of Mark*, 160. Scholars who see the disciples as positive characters in Mark rely on assumptions from outside the text; for an example, see Ernest Best, "The Role of the Disciples in Mark," *NTS* 23(1977):377-401.
[136] Crossan makes this point ("Mark and the Relatives of Jesus," 110-13).

As Werner Kelber points out, the attack on the other apostles' credibility so pervades the text that it can even be seen as the main theme of the entire book of Mark.[137]

Mark uses many means both subtle and not so subtle to call into question the disciples' credentials as leaders. The disciples stubbornly misunderstand and lack faith in Jesus, even after he carefully explains things to them. He frequently loses patience with them and castigates them for their obtuseness:

> . . . he was in the stern, asleep on the cushion; and they woke him and said to him, "Teacher, do you not care if we perish?" And he awoke and rebuked the wind, and said to the sea, "Peace! Be still!" And the wind ceased, and there was a great calm. He said to them, "Why are you afraid? Have you no faith?" (4:40)
>
> And he cautioned them, saying, "Take heed, beware of the leaven of the Pharisees and the leaven of Herod." And they discussed it with one another, saying, "We have no bread." And being aware of it, Jesus said to them, "Why do you discuss the fact that you have no bread? Do you not yet perceive or understand? Are your hearts hardened? Having eyes do you not see, and having ears do you not hear? And do you not remember? When I broke the five loaves for the five thousand, how many baskets full of broken pieces did you take up?" They said to him, "Twelve." "And the seven for the four thousand, how many baskets full of broken pieces did you take up?" And they said to him, "Seven." And he said to them, "Do you not yet understand?" (8:15-21)
>
> . . . he was teaching his disciples, saying to them, "The Son of man will be delivered into the hands of men, and they will kill him; and when he is killed, after three days he will rise." But they did

---

[137] Werner H. Kelber, *Mark's Story of Jesus* (Philadelphia: Fortress Press, 1979), 88.

not understand the saying, and they were afraid to ask him. (9:31-32) [138]

Their misunderstanding runs so deep that they do the exact opposite of what he tells them to do, and Jesus has to correct them for that:

> And he took a child, and put him in the midst of them; and taking him in his arms, he said to them, "Whoever receives one such child in my name receives me; and whoever receives me, receives not me but him who sent me." (9:36-37)

> And they were bringing children to him, that he might touch them; and the disciples rebuked them. But when Jesus saw it *he was indignant*, and said to them, "Let the children come to me, *do not hinder them*; for to such belongs the kingdom of God. . . ." (10:13-14)

As I pointed out earlier, the symbolism here represents Paul inviting the Gentiles into Jesus' community, while the requirement of Law observance insisted on by Jewish Christian leaders effectively barred the door to entry by Gentiles. The language here remarkably parallels a similar scenario that plays out in Paul's first epistle to the Thessalonians. There the Apostle likens his Gentile converts to children:

> You are witnesses, and God also, how holy and righteous and blameless was our behavior to you believers; for you know how, *like a father with his children*, we exhorted each one of you and encouraged you and charged you to lead a life worthy of God, who calls you into his own kingdom and glory. (1 Thess 2:10-12)

---

[138] See also 6:35-37; 9:10, 38-39.

Following this text is one that decries "the Jews'" act of "hindering" these children from hearing Paul's voice, which in turn inspired God's "wrath":

> For you, brethren, became imitators of the churches of God in Christ Jesus which are in Judea; for you suffered the same things from your own countrymen as they did from the Jews, who killed both the Lord Jesus and the prophets, and drove us out, and displease God and oppose all men *by hindering us from speaking to the Gentiles* that they may be saved – so as always to fill up the measure of their sins. But *God's wrath* has come upon them at last! (1 Thess 2:14-16)

Both contexts speak of anger stirred up by attempts to hinder the reception of children.[139]

As Robert Fowler observes, the reader of Mark has to be amazed at how obtuse the disciples are.[140] Stephen Smith points out the parallel between 8:18 and 4:11-12, which suggests that the disciples' behavior identifies them as the "outsiders" who are destined not to repent and be forgiven:

> "Having eyes do you not see, and having ears do you not hear?" (8:18)

> And when he was alone, those who were about him with the twelve asked him concerning the parables. And he said to them,

---

[139] See the discussion in Tarazi, *Paul and Mark*, 197-198. Mark kept the same Greek word for hinder (μὴ κωλύετε in Mark vs. κωλυόντων in 1 Thess) but adapted the words for children and anger to the new context. The Greek word παιδία used by Mark fits better the idea of children in general than does τέκνα used by Paul to evoke a father and his own children. Likewise, the Greek word ἠγανάκτησεν ("he was indignant") fits Mark's narrative situation better than ὀργή (wrath).

[140] Robert Fowler, "Reader-Response Criticism. Figuring Mark's Reader," in Janice Capel Anderson and Stephen D. Moore, *Mark and Method: New Approaches in Biblical Studies* (Minneapolis: Fortress Press, 2008), 59-93; here: 78.

> "To you has been given the secret of the kingdom of God, but for those outside everything is in parables; so that they may indeed see but not perceive, and may indeed hear but not understand; lest they should turn again, and be forgiven." (Mark 4:10-12)[141]

And the disciples' failings go far beyond just misunderstanding. They also seek glory and honor for themselves and quarrel among themselves about it, and Jesus has to correct that:

> And they came to Capernaum; and when he was in the house he asked them, "What were you discussing on the way?" But they were silent; for on the way they had discussed with one another who was the greatest. And he sat down and called the twelve; and he said to them, "If anyone would be first, he must be last of all and servant of all." (Mark 9:33-35)

> And James and John, the sons of Zebedee, came forward to him, and said to him, "Teacher, we want you to do for us whatever we ask of you." And he said to them, "What do you want me to do for you?" And they said to him, "Grant us to sit, one at your right hand and one at your left, in your glory." But Jesus said to them, "You do not know what you are asking. . . And when the ten heard it, they began to be indignant at James and John. And Jesus called them to him and said to them, "You know that those who are supposed to rule over the Gentiles lord it over them, and their great men exercise authority over them. But it shall not be so among you; but whoever would be great among you must be your servant, and whoever would be first among you must be slave of all. . . ." (Mark 10:35-44)

They prove unable or unwilling to do something as basic as pray,[142] and Jesus laments their slothfulness:

---

[141] Smith, *Lion*, 214-23.
[142] As Tolbert puts it, "Prayer in Mark is consistently outside the disciples' range of understanding or participation" (*Sowing*, 189).

And when he had entered the house, his disciples asked him privately, "Why could we not cast it out?" And he said to them, "This kind cannot be driven out by anything but prayer." (9:28-29; the implication is that prayer is something they didn't or couldn't do.)

And they went to a place which was called Gethsemane; and he said to his disciples, "Sit here, while I pray." And he took with him Peter and James and John, and began to be greatly distressed and troubled. And he said to them, "My soul is very sorrowful, even to death; remain here, and watch." . . . And he came and found them sleeping, and he said to Peter, "Simon, are you asleep? Could you not watch one hour? Watch and pray that you may not enter into temptation; the spirit indeed is willing, but the flesh is weak." And again he went away and prayed, saying the same words. And again he came and found them sleeping, for their eyes were very heavy; and they did not know what to answer him. And he came the third time, and said to them, "Are you still sleeping and taking your rest? It is enough; the hour has come; the Son of man is betrayed into the hands of sinners. . . ." (14:32-42)

In Jesus' voyages to bring his message to Gentile lands on the other side of the Sea of Galilee, their fear and reluctance makes them the very image of the sower parable's rocky soil. In fact, it is right after the sower parable equates fear of tribulation with rocky soil that the disciples show themselves fearful in the face of a storm:

And a great storm of wind arose, and the waves beat into the boat, so that the boat was already filling. But he was in the stern, asleep on the cushion; and they woke him and said to him, "Teacher, do you not care if we perish?" And he awoke and rebuked the wind, and said to the sea, "Peace! Be still!" And the wind ceased, and there was a great calm. He said to them, "Why are you afraid? Have you no faith?" (Mark 6:37-40)

Discrediting Jesus' Disciples and Family

The metaphorical message here is that, sure, opening up the community to Gentiles will result in some hard times, but Jesus is more than a match for those hard times and will carry his community through them safely. The disciples learn nothing from this, for they are fearful again during the next voyage to Gentile territory, so much so that Jesus almost decides to just bypass them altogether and leave them behind:

> And he saw that *they were making headway painfully*, for the wind was against them. And about the fourth watch of the night he came to them, walking on the sea. *He meant to pass by them*, but when they saw him walking on the sea they thought it was a ghost, and cried out; for *they all saw him, and were terrified*. But immediately he spoke to them and said, "Take heart, it is I; have no fear." And he got into the boat with them and the wind ceased. And they were *utterly astounded*, for they *did not understand about the loaves, but their hearts were hardened*. (Mark 6:48-52)

Again, the metaphorical message is not difficult to discern: Jesus is trying to get his disciples to follow his lead to Gentile lands, but they are reluctant and fearful. The first to overcome that fear and reluctance will be Paul, not one of the twelve.

Finally, when Jesus needs his disciples the most, to a man they desert him: "And they all forsook him and fled." (14:50).[143] Some scholars try to rescue the disciples' reputation by pointing out that they are not uniformly negative – at the start they do respond positively to Jesus.[144] However, their initial enthusiasm and eventual abandonment of Jesus out of fear fits perfectly the pattern of "rocky ground" in the parable of the sower.

---

[143] Tolbert suggests that the fact Joseph of Arimathea who buries Jesus is a member of the council that condemned him highlights the disciples' shameful flight (*Sowing*, 293).
[144] See the discussion in Svartvik, *Mark and Mission*, 315.

Mark was written after a conflict had developed between Paul and the Jerusalem Christian leadership under the leadership of the "pillars" Peter, James, and John. For the Gospel's original readers, the picture of obtuse, glory-seeking, slothful disciples couldn't help but bolster the authority of the one Apostle who was not so characterized.

"One of the Twelve"

The evangelist even foresaw the possibility that a reader might miss the point and suppose that, after all, even if the disciples made some mistakes early on, Jesus chose them to be leaders, and so they should be obeyed as such. In other words, maybe the mere status of being an apostle, one of the original twelve, should be recognized as a badge of authority. Mark attacks that belief as well.

In 3:19 where Jesus appoints Judas one of the twelve, Mark identifies him by indicating his surname Iscariot and adding that he was destined to betray Jesus. The next reference to a Judas (outside of the list of Jesus' brothers) is in the betrayal scene. In 14:10 he is "Judas Iscariot, one of the twelve," and in v.43 he is "Judas . . . one of the twelve." The phrase "one of the twelve" is superfluous in the first instance since the name Iscariot clearly identifies the person. It is even more so in the second instance since the Judas in question has already been identified. And it is even more superfluous at the last supper where Jesus is with the twelve and announces that "It is one of the twelve" who would betray him (14:20), since he already said "one of you will betray me" (14:18). However, Mark does not write superfluous words, and he emphasizes points by repeating them.[145]

The most straightforward interpretation is that the evangelist wanted to place extra heavy emphasis on the fact that Judas was one of the twelve; or, in other words, he wanted to leave no possibility that his hearers would miss the point that one of the twelve betrayed Jesus. The reader must naturally infer that mere membership in the ranks of "the twelve" – or, in the context of a Pauline epistle, mere status as one of "the apostles before me" – should not automatically confer authority on anyone. This impression is enhanced by the fact that in Mark no motivation is explicitly ascribed to Judas, which would otherwise make the treacherous deed more of a personal deviation than a point about his status as one of the twelve. It appears as though Judas exists in the story only in order to make the point that one of the twelve betrayed Jesus.

The Judas story also shows that in the end it is not only Jesus' opponents in the Jewish leadership who cause his demise, it is treachery from within his own ranks – or to rephrase that in the terms of Mark's own day and Paul's perspective, the real traitors are among the Christian Jewish leadership, not the non-Christian Jews.[146] The name Judas ("Jew") corresponds so well to Paul's view that his opponents were traitors to the cross of Christ by being zealots for Jewish traditions, that it is reasonable to suppose Mark deliberately named the betrayer Judas for that reason.

---

[145] Alter, *Art of Biblical Narrative*, 179-180: "... when a relational epithet is attached to a character ... the narrator is generally telling us something substantive without recourse to explicit commentary." See also p.179 on repetition for emphasis.
[146] Smith points out this aspect of the story (*Lion*, 225.1).

The Pillars

Mark also pays special attention to a sub-group of apostles: Peter James, and John, whose names coincidentally match those of the Jerusalem church leaders that Paul calls "those reputed to be pillars" in Galatians 2:9. This triumvirate forms an inner circle among the disciples. They are the only ones to whom Jesus assigns surnames[147] and they accompany Jesus to places the others cannot,[148] but they fall just as far short of their high calling as the other nine. They misunderstand the Transfiguration:

> And Peter said to Jesus, "Master, it is well that we are here; let us make three booths, one for you and one for Moses and one for Elijah." For he did not know what to say, for they were exceedingly afraid. . . . And as they were coming down the mountain, he charged them to tell no one what they had seen, until the Son of man should have risen from the dead. So they kept the matter to themselves, questioning what the rising from the dead meant. (Mark 9:5-10)

James and John selfishly seek glory for themselves by asking to become co-rulers with Jesus:

> And they said to him, "Grant us to sit, one at your right hand and one at your left, in your glory." . . . And when the ten heard it, they began to be indignant at James and John. (Mark 10:37-41)

And all three fail to even stay awake while Jesus prays, let alone pray with him:

> And he took with him Peter and James and John, and began to be greatly distressed and troubled. And he said to them, "My soul is

---

[147] Mark 3:16-17.
[148] Mark 5:37; 9:2; 13:3; 14:33.

very sorrowful, even to death; remain here, and watch." . . . And he came and found them sleeping, and he said to Peter, "Simon, are you asleep? Could you not watch one hour? Watch and pray that you may not enter into temptation; the spirit indeed is willing, but the flesh is weak." And again he went away and prayed, saying the same words. And again he came and found them sleeping, for their eyes were very heavy; and they did not know what to answer him. And he came the third time, and said to them, "Are you still sleeping and taking your rest? It is enough; the hour has come; the Son of man is betrayed into the hands of sinners." (Mark 14:32-41)

As I pointed out in the chapter on irony, the connection between these three and Paul's epistle to the Galatians is not only in their identical names but in the unusual phrase "those reputed to be" (οἱ δοκοῦντες), which in Galatians refers to their status as church leaders and in Mark refers to the Gentile leaders they are compared to.[149]

Peter

The self-serving request to rule with Jesus comes from James and John without Peter, but Mark takes full advantage of every other opportunity to highlight the hypocrisy of the man Paul condemned for hypocrisy (Gal 2:11-14).[150] Earlier I highlighted the irony in the story of Peter's denial of the cross. But that story does much more to make Peter look bad than just ironically

---

[149] See Tarazi, *Paul and Mark*, 201. Tarazi also points out other ways in which Mark may have used subtle means to disparage James and John in particular (143). He suggests the name Zebedee ascribed to their father has negative associations, and the word μισθωτός (they were found in a boat with "hirelings") has negative connotations, as can be seen from John 10:12-13.

[150] Besides the major episodes noted here, Mark uses more subtle means to ascribe negative characteristics to Peter. In Mark 1:36 where Simon "pursued" Jesus, the word κατεδίωξεν connotes pursuit in the sense of pursuing one's enemies, as in Ps 18:37.

asserting that Peter rather than Paul was the one who was seeking to please man rather than God.

Even the apparently positive aspect of the interaction between Peter and Jesus – Peter's confession of faith in Jesus as the Messiah – is marred by his omitting the "son of God" title. In Matthew, Peter proclaims 'You are the Christ, the Son of the living God" (Matt 16:16) but the latter half of the confession is conspicuously absent in Mark. This can hardly be merely an oversight in a gospel that signals the importance of the "son of God" title by featuring it prominently in the prologue: "The beginning of the gospel of Jesus Christ, the Son of God." (1:1) Outside of the prologue the title appears only twice: in 3:11 "unclean spirits" in a Gentile land recognize Jesus, and in a climactic recognition scene in 15:39 a Gentile Roman centurion proclaims Jesus to be the son of God. The dramatic tearing of the temple curtain sets the stage for the centurion's moment of enlightenment, the importance of which in Mark's Gospel can hardly be overemphasized:[151]

> And the curtain of the temple was torn in two, from top to bottom. And when the centurion, who stood facing him, saw that he thus breathed his last, he said, "Truly this man was the Son of God!" (15:38-39)

The revelation that passed Peter by because he didn't want to accept Jesus' suffering and death is granted to a lowly Gentile after Jesus' experience of suffering and death is completed. This is a climactic point in the story in part because the secrecy motif comes to its ultimate end here: with the image of the crucified

---

[151] See Tolbert, *Sowing*, 288. On the temple curtain scene as preparing the way for this recognition scene, see Marcus, *Mark 1-8*, 481.

Christ before the reader's eyes, the key to Jesus' true identity is revealed.

Unlike the parallel in Matthew, the Markan text says nothing positive at all about Peter's incomplete recognition of Jesus' identity. In Matthew Jesus responds with high praise for Peter's perspicacity:

> And Jesus answered him, "Blessed are you, Simon Bar-Jona! For flesh and blood has not revealed this to you, but my Father who is in heaven. And I tell you, you are Peter, and on this rock I will build my church, and the powers of death shall not prevail against it. I will give you the keys of the kingdom of heaven, and whatever you bind on earth shall be bound in heaven, and whatever you loose on earth shall be loosed in heaven." (Matt 16:17-19)

Mark has nothing like this: the next statement after Peter's chopped confession is "And he charged them to tell no one about him."

Mark also has nothing that would soften the impact of the remarkable statement that Peter "began to rebuke" his Lord and master. By putting the words "God forbid, Lord" in Peter's mouth, Matthew softens the word "rebuke"; without that, it stands out as yet another indication of Peter's arrogance.

At the end of the scene that presents Peter denying Jesus' cross is a statement that sets the stage for Peter denying his own cross later in the story. No one summarizes this point better than Michael Goulder:

> There is a worse matter, which is often not noticed. Jesus goes on immediately in Mark: "If any man would come after me, let him deny himself and take up his cross and follow me. For whoever would save his life shall lose it . . ." Can you think of anyone in

the Gospel story who wanted to *save his life*, who refused to *come after Jesus* and *take up his cross*, who did not *deny himself* but denied Jesus? Well, so could St. Mark.[152]

What Goulder overlooks is that the original readers of Mark would also have been familiar with the epistles, and what applies to Peter "in the Gospel story" applies also to Peter in the epistle to the Galatians. As presented by Paul in that epistle, Peter acts out of fear of the "men from James" and his actions have the effect of denying Jesus and denying the cross. In any case, Goulder rightly concludes that the original readers of the episode in Mark chapter 8 would find in it a clear warning against trusting Peter's judgment over Paul's.

The evangelist develops his warning about Peter's unreliability further in the passion story. In a double ironic twist, Peter denies knowing Jesus shortly after vowing not to do that, and he does so at the very moment when Jesus himself finally acknowledges openly his true identity.

Mark stresses the enormity of Peter's failure by portraying Peter's attitude as extreme self-confidence bordering on arrogance:

> Peter said to him, "Even though they all fall away, I will not." And Jesus said to him, "Truly, I say to you, this very night, before the cock crows twice, you will deny me three times." But he said vehemently, "If I must die with you, I will not deny you." And they all said the same. (Mk 14:29-31)

Later, Mark heightens the irony of the failure by juxtaposing Peter's denial with Jesus' revelation of his own identity. Notice how the repeated mentions of the "high priest" create a link

---

[152] Goulder, *Paul vs. Peter*, 18. Author's italics.

between Jesus' destination and Peter's destination, and between the question "are you the Christ" and the assertion "you were with Jesus":

> And they led Jesus to *the high priest*; and all the chief priests and the elders and the scribes were assembled. And Peter had followed him at a distance, right into the courtyard of *the high priest* . . . Again *the high priest* asked him, "Are you the Christ, the Son of the Blessed?" And Jesus said, "I am; and you will see the Son of man seated at the right hand of Power, and coming with the clouds of heaven." . . . And as Peter was below in the courtyard, one of the maids of *the high priest* came; and seeing Peter warming himself, she looked at him, and said, "You also were with the Nazarene, Jesus." But he denied it . . . (14:53-54, 61-62, 66-68)

As Mary Ann Tolbert explains, Peter's denial is "almost an exact antitype of the recognition scene," and the importance of that recognition scene and its antitype can hardly be overestimated:

> To anyone familiar with the conventions of recognition scenes in the ancient world, such a denial of correct identification would rule out any final happy reunion. The recognition sequence in Mark, like those of the ancient novels, is carefully plotted over a series of days and uses time references to tie the events together.[153]

Mark also uses geographical references to tie events together. He follows up the reference to the Galilean village of Nazareth in Peter's first denial with an explicit reference to Galilee in his third denial:

---

[153] Tolbert, *Sowing the Gospel*, 75. See also Frank Kermode, *The Genesis of Secrecy: On the Interpretation of Narrative* (Cambridge: Harvard UP, 2006), 114; Smith, *Lion*, 225-26.

And after a little while again the bystanders said to Peter, "Certainly you are one of them; for you are a Galilean." But he began to invoke a curse on himself and to swear, "I do not know this man of whom you speak." (14:70-71)

If Galilee symbolizes an integrated community of Jews and Gentiles in Mark, mentioning it in the denial story may be intended to call to mind Peter's behavior in Antioch where (in Paul's view) Peter betrayed the united Jewish-Gentile community (Gal 2:11-14).[154] Irony in Mark is not likely to be coincidental, and it is certainly ironic that the man Paul called "condemned" for effectively denying the cross in Galatians (2:11) here invokes a curse on himself while doing the same thing. The Mark versus Galatians irony works from another angle as well: Peter "invokes a curse" (ἀναθεματίζειν in 14:71) on himself, and in fact it actually applies because he is lying; while Paul "invokes a curse" on himself in Galatians if he should be found to deny the cross (ἀνάθεμα ἔστω in 1:8 and 9), and it actually does not apply because he is the one apostle who does not deny the cross.[155]

Goulder highlights Mark's "merciless treatment of Peter on Passover night" by contrasting it with the "whitewashing given by the kindly Luke."[156] In Luke, Peter asserts his faithfulness without hubris, and his failure is due to the supernatural influence of the devil.

> "Simon, Simon, behold, Satan demanded to have you, that he might sift you like wheat, but I have prayed for you that your faith may not fail; and when you have turned again, strengthen your

---

[154] Tarazi, *Paul and Mark*, 222.
[155] Ibid., 223.
[156] Goulder, *Paul vs. Peter*, 18

brethren." And he said to him, "Lord, I am ready to go with you to prison and to death." (Luke 22:31-33)

The avowal that "I am ready to go with you to prison and to death" doesn't evince the speaker's arrogance as does "Even though they all fall away, I will not." And the Lucan Peter is rehabilitated and lives up to his word in the end, for in Acts he is rehabilitated and eventually goes to prison as a follower of Jesus. The Markan Peter fails repeatedly for no other reason than his own arrogance and timidity, and he never redeems himself.[157]

---

[157] Tarazi (*Paul and Mark*, 141-45) points out additional, more subtle, ways in which the Markan text reflects negatively on Peter. In 1:16 Simon and Andrew are doing something "in the sea," and the word for what they are doing is ἀμφιβάλλοντας. The word is generally translated "casting a net," but the word for "net" is missing, and another meaning of the word ἀμφιβάλλοντας is "vacillating." The direct object may have been deliberately omitted in order to evoke the alternative meaning. Also, 1:36 is generally translated "Simon and those with him pursued" Jesus, but the word behind "pursued" is κατεδίωξεν, which usually connotes pursuing with intent to do harm, or persecuting.

7
Alluding to Paul in the Main Parables and the Ending

> . . . the parables are designed to show in concise format the general principles organizing the story as a whole. . . . The pervasive tendency of form criticism to remove these parables from their Gospel contexts, separate them from one another, and try to fit them into the historical ministry of Jesus has in the past and continues in the present to obscure what Mark is doing with them.
> Mary Ann Tolbert[158]

If the author of Mark intended to make discrediting Peter and the disciples a central part of his Gospel story, evidence of that should be detectable in the two main parables around which the entire book of Mark revolves: the sower parable and the wicked husbandmen parable.[159] And the ending of the book should confirm rather than undo what the rest of the book was building toward. Such evidence is detectable, and the ending fits the theme perfectly.

The Parable of the Sower

Mark himself explicitly identifies the sower parable as the key to everything: "Do you not understand this parable? How then will you understand all the parables?" (4:13) Considering that Paul used seeds and sowing and plant growth as his central

---

[158] Tolbert, *Sowing the Gospel*, 125, 149-50.
[159] Tolbert argues that the sower parable is central to the entire book (*Sowing*, 122). The sower parable is about Jesus' task and is the key especially to the first part of the book; the wicked husbandman parable is about Jesus' identity and is the key to the passion narrative.

metaphor for spiritual progress,[160] it can hardly be a coincidence that a text written many years later to support Paul's Gentile mission and apostolic authority would adopt the same metaphor for its central parable.[161] The direction of the borrowing from Paul to Mark rather than from Jesus to Paul to Mark is suggested by the fact that Paul never once attributes his seed and sowing metaphor to Jesus. And some of the language may have come directly from a Pauline source. The words αὐξανόμενα (increasing) and καρποφοροῦσιν (bear fruit) also appear in a similar context in Colossians. Compare Mark 4:8, 20 with Col 1:6 and 10:[162]

> And other seeds fell into good soil and brought forth grain, growing up and increasing (αὐξανόμενα) and yielding thirtyfold and sixtyfold and a hundredfold. . . . But those that were sown upon the good soil are the ones who hear the word and accept it and bear fruit (καρποφοροῦσιν), thirtyfold and sixtyfold and a hundredfold." (Mark 4:8, 20)

> Of this you have heard before in the word of the truth, the gospel which has come to you, as indeed in the whole world it is bearing fruit and growing (καρποφορούμενον καὶ αὐξανόμενον) . . . we have not ceased to pray for you, asking that you may be filled with the knowledge of his will in all spiritual wisdom and understanding to lead a life worthy of the Lord, fully pleasing to him, bearing fruit and increasing (καρποφοροῦντες καὶ αὐξανόμενοι) in every good work in the knowledge of God.. . . (Col 1:5-6, 9-10)

---

[160] He found the metaphor in the Old Testament, but he uses it far more frequently.

[161] Sowing, seeds, planting, growing plants, reaping or harvesting: Rom 1:13; Gal 6:7-9; 1 Cor 3:6-7; 9:7, 11; 15:36-38, 42-44; 2 Cor 9:6-11; Col 1:6; 2 Tim 2:6. Fruit (Mark 4:20): Rom 15:28; 1 Cor 14:14; Gal 5:22; Eph 5:9-11; Phil 1:11, 22; 4:17; Col 1:10; Tit 3:14. Roots: Rom 11:16-18. For more parallels, see Tarazi, *Paul and Mark*, 156-62.

[162] Elsewhere in the New Testament the word only appears in the Lucan parallel to Mark 4:20 (Luke 8:15). An adjectival form appears in Acts 14:17.

In both contexts the words refer at first to the increasing numbers of converts to the gospel, and in the second instance to the increase in good deeds done by those who obey the gospel. If such a parallel is a coincidence, it is truly an amazing one.[163]

In addition, the parable itself is an integral part of a persistent effort throughout the Gospel to discredit Peter and the disciples. In Greek it is all but impossible to miss the allusion to Peter (Πέτρος) in the remarks about "rocky ground" (τὸ πετρῶδες), especially since Jesus assigns the name "Peter" to Simon shortly before the parable. Other parallels make it clear that the rest of the disciples are rocky along with Peter. Compare the interpretation of rocky ground with Jesus' announcement that Peter and the rest of the disciples would abandon him:

> And these in like manner are the ones sown upon rocky ground, who, when they hear the word, immediately receive it with joy; and they have no root in themselves, but endure for a while; then, when tribulation or persecution arises on account of the word, immediately they fall away (σκανδαλίζονται). (Mark 4:16-17)

> And Jesus said to them, "You will all fall away (σκανδαλισθήσεσθε); for it is written, 'I will strike the shepherd, and the sheep will be scattered.' But after I am raised up, I will go before you to Galilee." Peter said to him, "Even though they all fall away (σκανδαλισθήσονται), I will not." And Jesus said to him, "Truly, I say to you, this very night, before the cock crows twice, you will deny me three times." But he said vehemently, "If I must die with you, I will not deny you." And they all said the same. (Mark 14:27-31)

> And they all forsook him, and fled. (Mark 14:50)

---

[163] See Tarazi, *Paul and Mark*, 159.

The evangelist has described rockiness and then portrayed Peter and the other disciples as the very epitome of rockiness by recounting their initial enthusiasm followed by prompt flight at the first sign of persecution. To make sure the correspondence won't be missed, he has taken care to describe the effect of rocky ground and the disciples' shameful behavior with same verb σκανδαλίζω (fall away). And he has made sure that no one might think any of these original disciples were any different, for Jesus predicts "you will *all* fall away," and like Peter "they *all* said the same" avowal that they wouldn't, but in short order "they *all* forsook him and fled." All are motivated to abandon Jesus by fear, which behavior in Mark represents the opposite of faith and the foundation of "rockiness." Taking all this together, it seems more than plausible that Mark crafted the sower parable himself, inspired by Paul's extensive use of the metaphor of sowing; and he deliberately chose the term "rocky soil" as an ironic allusion to Peter the "rock."[164]

The preface to Jesus' interpretation of the parable contains yet another key to understanding it:

> And he said to them, "To you has been given the secret of the kingdom of God, but for those outside everything is in parables; so that they may indeed see but not perceive, and may indeed hear but not understand; lest they should turn again, and be forgiven." (Mark 4:11-12)

This text has been a stumbling block for interpreters from the beginning. It appears to say that Jesus' purpose in speaking is to keep people from understanding and being forgiven, and

---

[164] On the correspondences between rocky soil and Peter and the disciples, see Tolbert, *Sowing the Gospel*, 127, 145-46, 154, 164-75, 212.

Alluding to Paul in the Main Parables and the Ending   131

scholars have struggled with that meaning for centuries.[165] Tolbert offers a fairly typical way of making the text more acceptable: she suggests it means that the way people respond determines whether they are "outside" or not: by definition if one hears and understands, one is an insider, and vice versa.[166] However, that is not what the text says.

An interpretation that does make sense of the hard saying without twisting it around to make it say something else comes from comparing it to Paul's epistle to the Romans. In Romans, Paul is grappling with the fact that the Jews have rejected Jesus while the Gentiles are accepting him. In Romans he asserts that this is part of God's plan: the Jews were offered the gospel first but were foreordained to reject it, so that the Gentiles could accept it, which would in turn make the Jews jealous so that in the end some of the Jews as well as Gentiles would be "saved":

> What then? Israel failed to obtain what it sought. The elect obtained it, but the rest were hardened, as it is written, "God gave them a spirit of stupor, *eyes that should not see and ears that should not hear*, down to this very day." And David says, "Let their table become a snare and a trap, a pitfall and a retribution for them; let their eyes be darkened so that they cannot see, and bend their backs forever." So I ask, have they stumbled so as to fall? By no means! But through their trespass salvation has come to the Gentiles, so as to make Israel jealous. Now if their trespass means riches for the world, and if their failure means riches for the Gentiles, how much more will their full inclusion mean! Now I am speaking to you Gentiles. Inasmuch then as I am an apostle to

---

[165] For comprehensive coverage of interpretations that have been offered, see R. H. Gundry, *Mark: A commentary on his Apology for the Cross* (Grand Rapids: Eerdmans, 1993), 195-204.
[166] Tolbert, *Sowing*, 160.

the Gentiles, I magnify my ministry in order to make my fellow Jews jealous, and thus save some of them. (Rom 11:7-14)

These eyes that don't see and ears that don't hear parallel the seeing but not perceiving and hearing but not understanding of Mark 4:12. The parallel is even stronger than is immediately apparent: the Old Testament text typically seen as behind Mark 4:12 is Isaiah 6:9, but the order there is "hearing" followed by "seeing," while the order in Mark is the reverse – which corresponds to what we have in Rom 11:8.[167] What Mark 4:11-12 implies, then, is that Jesus speaks to the Jews in parables so that they won't get the message, so that the Gentiles eventually will get the message first, which in the long run will inspire in at least some of the Jews sufficient envy to impel them join the repentant throng entering into salvation.

This interpretation makes sense of Mark's statement that Jesus only spoke in parables to the crowds ("he did not speak to them without a parable"; 4:34). It also helps make sense of Mark's statement that this exclusively parabolic talk is only "for those outside" (ἐκείνοις δὲ τοῖς ἔξω). In 3:31-32 – just before the sower parable begins – it is Jesus' relatives who stand "outside" (ἔξω).[168] It is Jesus' relatives in particular, and by extension the Jews, who are destined not to understand.[169] This interpretation based on the connection to Romans fits perfectly with the fact that Jesus' relatives are standing "outside" because they do not understand Jesus, having come to cart him away as a madman.

---

[167] Romaniuk acknowledges Romans as a source but does not specify details ("Le Problème des Paulinismes," 274).

[168] For a thorough examination of the connection between these passages, see Goulder, "Those Outside."

[169] John R. Donahue (*The Gospel in Parable: Metaphor, Narrative, and Theology in the Synoptic Gospels* [Philadelphia: Fortress Press, 1988], 44) refers also to 14:68-71 and suggests that "outside" is where those scandalized by the cross are found.

The Parable of the Wicked Husbandmen

The second major parable in Mark is the story of the wicked husbandmen. Its importance is evident in that it introduces the passion story, which itself is the denouement of the entire book. That the parable is about Jesus being rejected and killed is clear enough, in part because the term "beloved son" occurs only here and in 1:11 and 9:7, where God himself speaks the words:

> . . . and a voice came from heaven, "Thou art my beloved Son; with thee I am well pleased." (Mark 1:11)

> And a cloud overshadowed them, and a voice came out of the cloud, "This is my beloved Son; listen to him." (Mark 9:7)

> He had still one other, a beloved son; finally he sent him to them, saying, 'They will respect my son.' (Mark 12:6)

The parable is sometimes interpreted as being about the Jews rejecting Jesus and being replaced by the Gentiles.[170] However, the parable differentiates between the vineyard, which in Old Testament scripture symbolizes Israel, and the wicked group tending the vineyard, which would then symbolize Israel's leaders. The vine tending group that will be brought in to replace the wicked group is likewise not the vineyard itself but those who will tend it.

> A man planted a vineyard . . . When the time came, he sent a servant to the tenants, to get from them some of the fruit of the vineyard. And they took him and beat him, and sent him away empty-handed. . . . He had still one other, a beloved son; finally he sent him to them, saying, "They will respect my son." But those tenants said to one another, "This is the heir; come, let us kill him, and the inheritance will be ours." And they took him and

---

[170] From as early as John Chrysostom.

killed him, and cast him out of the vineyard. What will the owner of the vineyard do? He will come and destroy the tenants, and give the vineyard to others. . . . (Mark 12:1-11)

When read in the light of Old Testament symbolism, the parable is about the behavior of the leadership of God's community and a changing of the guard at that level, not about Jews or Gentiles generally. The parable condemns the behavior of one set of leaders and foretells a changing of the guard to a different set.

To make the theme of leadership and authority clear, Mark puts the controversy about the authority of John the Baptist and Jesus (11:27-33) immediately before the parable, has Jesus address the parable to "the chief priests, the scribes, and the elders" *in the Jerusalem temple* (11:27), and immediately after the parable tells us that these listeners "perceived that he had told the parable against them" (12:12). Therefore, the immediate context establishes that the parable is about Jesus, his rejection by the Jerusalem Jewish leadership of his day, and the impending establishment of a whole new leadership for "God's vineyard."

Aaron Milavec has pointed out a sticking point in this otherwise straightforward interpretation. He observes that nowhere else in the Old Testament or any contemporary Jewish literature is the messiah ever called the heir (κληρονόμος), and so he concludes that, "it is doubtful that Mark's hearers would have associated 'the son' with the expected Messiah."[171] However, precisely this anomaly is what points out a Pauline connection in

---

[171] "A Fresh Analysis of the Parable of the Wicked Husbandmen in the Light of Jewish-Catholic Dialogue," in *Parable and Story in Judaism and Christianity* (New York: Paulist Press, 1989), 81-120, 100.

this parable, for that link between "inheritance" and the messiah can be found nowhere else but in Galatians:

> Now the promises were made to Abraham and to his offspring. It does not say, "And to offsprings," referring to many; but referring to one, "And to your offspring," *which is Christ.* . . . For if *the inheritance* (κληρονομία) is by the law, it is no longer by promise . . . (3:16-18)

In the context of Galatians, the "inheritance" is the content of the promises, and if Christ along with Abraham is the recipient of the promises, then the "heir" is Christ.[172] Actually, as Tarazi points out, the phrase "beloved son" also provides evidence of a literary link to Galatians:

> The impression that Galatians was a source for Mark is strengthened by another phrase Mark uses at this point: "My beloved Son" (*ho huios mou ho agapetos*). This appears three times, exclusively in reference to Isaac, in the entire Old Testament (LXX Gen 22:2, 12, 16), all in the story about God's command that Abraham sacrifice him. It can hardly be a coincidence that in Galatians Paul discusses Isaac, presenting him as the image of true sonship to God and of innocent suffering (4:28-29). Since Paul viewed himself as a son of Abraham and of God after the manner of Isaac, and since this sonship to God was both made possible and put into effect through the agency of Christ (4:4-7), Mark presented the sonship of Jesus, the unique Son of God, in the same terms. The scene was thus set for the suffering of this unique son, which is a – if not the – central theme of Mark's gospel.[173]

---

[172] Paul develops the inheritance theme further in 4:1-7. There are, of course other indications that Jesus is meant, such as the quotations from Ps 118 at the end of the parable. See Timothy C. Gray, *The Temple in the Gospel of Mark: A Study in Its Narrative Role* (Grand Rapids: Baker Book House, 2010), 46-93.

[173] *Paul and Mark*, 138-39.

The message conveyed by the symbolism of the wicked husbandmen parable can be carried a step further in a direction that Mark may have intended. If in Jesus' day a whole corps of disobedient leaders based in Jerusalem needed to be replaced by new ones, it is no great leap to conclude that if Christian leaders based in Jerusalem in Paul's day (such as James the Lord's brother) also disobey, they too will need to be replaced. In the latter case, "disobedience" would mean opposition to the Pauline interpretation of the gospel, and the replacement leaders would be the Pauline school.

The Apparently Inconclusive Ending

> The effect, of course, is a startling, and to many an offensive, suggestion that the disciples never received the angel's message, thus never met the resurrected Lord, and, consequently never were commissioned with apostolic rank after their apostasy. . . . I conclude that Mark is assiduously involved in a vendetta against the disciples. He is intent on totally discrediting them. He paints them as obtuse, obdurate, recalcitrant men who at first are unperceptive of Jesus' Messiahship, then oppose its style and character, and finally totally reject it. As the coup de grace, Mark closes his Gospel without rehabilitating the disciples.
> Theodore Weeden[174]

A well-designed narrative ends in a way that fits with its main themes, ties up any remaining loose ends, and helps it achieve its main purposes.[175] People who believe that Mark's purpose is

---

[174] Weeden, *Mark: Traditions in Conflict*, 50.
[175] As Marxsen (*Mark the Evangelist*, 208-9) puts it, the ending must express "the inner goal of the entire Gospel."

Alluding to Paul in the Main Parables and the Ending 137

evangelistic naturally find its original ending disconcerting, for the oldest manuscripts end abruptly:

> And when the sabbath was past, Mary Magdalene, and Mary the mother of James, and Salome, bought spices, so that they might go and anoint him. . . . And entering the tomb, they saw a young man sitting on the right side, dressed in a white robe; and they were amazed. And he said to them, "Do not be amazed; you seek Jesus of Nazareth, who was crucified. He has risen, he is not here; see the place where they laid him. But go, tell his disciples and Peter that he is going before you to Galilee; there you will see him, as he told you." And they went out and fled from the tomb; for trembling and astonishment had come upon them; and they said nothing to any one, for they were afraid. (Mark 16:1-8)

Many English Bibles print a section labeled as verses 9-20 after this, with a note explaining that this only appears in later manuscripts. Some also print another, shorter alternate ending, with a similar note. Only in these later additions do the resurrected Jesus and the restored disciples appear. The original ending of the earliest gospel has no resurrection appearance, no bestowal of the spirit on the disciples, and no "great commission" directing the disciples to spread the word. Some who find this difficult to accept have suggested that the original ending somehow got lost, or that one or other of the alternate endings was original.[176]

However, the Gospel's ending as it appears in the earliest manuscripts fits the themes and purposes of Mark as I have explained them here. Throughout the Gospel, Mark consistently follows the Pauline theme of emphasizing the cross over the

---

[176] A vast literature on the subject has arisen. For an introduction to some of the main issues by scholars who have reached contradictory conclusions, see David Alan Black, ed., *Perspectives on the Ending of Mark: Four Views* (B & H Academic, 2008).

resurrection; a sharp focus on the resurrection at the end could have undone what the rest of the text was trying to do with its focus on the crucifixion. A mere hint at the resurrection fits perfectly with the "Christ crucified" theme.

Another theme the Gospel returns to again and again is the question of authority.[177] More specifically, Mark is interested in demonstrating the disciples' lack of leadership character and their failure to earn a right to the authority offered to them. Omitting any final restoration of these men fits perfectly with the portrayal of the disciples as "rocky ground."[178] Just as the final and resonant image of Christ in Mark is that of the crucified Christ, the final and resonant image of the disciples is that of apostate failures. As Tolbert puts it, "The saga of Peter and the disciples ends, as did that of the rich man (10:17-22), in grieving failure."[179]

At the same time, an ending may introduce something new, and this one does. The failure is not necessarily final: the text gives Peter and the others an opportunity to respond *outside the text of Mark* to the invitation to follow Jesus to Galilee. Galilee in Mark symbolizes the integrated Jewish-Gentile community. So the implication is that Christian leaders in Mark's day who "follow Jesus to Galilee" are those who endorse Paul's view of a united Jewish-Gentile community. If Peter or any of the other men Paul calls "the apostles before me" accept Paul's view of the gospel, they will have shown their faithfulness to Jesus. Those

---

[177] Tolbert (*Sowing*, 136) points out that even the healings are ultimately about authority.

[178] A few who call attention to this include Tolbert, *Sowing the Gospel*, 302; Weeden, *Mark: Traditions in Conflict*, 44, 50; Brenda Deen Schildgen, *Power and Prejudice: The Reception of the Gospel of Mark* (Detroit: Wayne State UP, 1999), 21-2; Telford, *Theology of Mark*, 150.

[179] Tolbert, *Sowing the Gospel*, 218.

Alluding to Paul in the Main Parables and the Ending

who oppose Paul are refusing to "follow Jesus to Galilee" and in so doing have forfeited their apostolic authority.

Mark's original audience within the Pauline communities may not have known which of "the twelve" ultimately proved faithful and which didn't, but they did know who followed this blueprint perfectly: Paul himself. Without explicitly mentioning Paul, the ending of Mark reveals that the Apostle to the Gentiles – who called himself the least of the apostles because Jesus appeared to him last (1 Cor 15:8-9), and who had to defend his authority vis-à-vis those apostles[180] – was in reality the first and greatest and most authoritative. It was Paul who first "followed Jesus to Galilee" by establishing the kinds of inclusive communities that Galilee symbolizes in the Gospel of Mark.[181]

Some might object that this interpretation is a weak "argument from silence." However, in reality it is more than that. It is based in part on the evidence that Mark knew well at least some of the Pauline corpus, which means his audience also was familiar with Paul and his claims to apostolic authority. More specifically, Mark knew 1 Corinthians, with its explicit mention of resurrection appearances of Jesus – which means Mark knew about such traditions but deliberately omitted them. An alternative explanation of Mark's ending would have to account

---

[180] As discussed earlier; see 1 Cor 9:5; 2 Cor 11:5, 12-13; 12:11; Gal 1:17-19.

[181] Tolbert points out that if the disciples are rocky soil and the women are rocky soil, then as a matter of fact, everyone in the Gospel who is actually named is rocky soil. She asks: if the women fail, who else is there? Her answer is that the readers themselves must follow Jesus on their own (*Sowing*, 295). However, this does not fit a book that is about church leadership, or a husbandmen parable that is about leaders of the flock. It is more likely that Mark's Gospel is mainly intended to call upon readers to choose carefully which church leaders they will follow, rather than to encourage them to act as though each individual is a separate leader with no need for actual leaders.

for such deliberate omission, and none of the proposed alternatives do that.

What the ending of Mark would make clear is that no apostle, neither Paul nor any of the others, was the first to see the resurrected Lord at the tomb or anywhere near Jerusalem.[182] No resurrection sighting whether by Paul or Peter or James or John could thus bestow the Lord's authority more effectively than any other. Moreover, for a resurrection appearance to be valid it would have to happen "in Galilee," that is, by an apostle who was committed to the combined Jewish-Gentile messianic community.[183] In this way the "last" and "least" of the apostles truly became the "first" and the "greatest."

In addition, the ending at 16:8 effectively brings the reader full circle back to the beginning. David Aune suggests that the Greek word ἀρχή (as in "the *beginning* of the gospel" in 1:1) is a technical term meaning that a "complete examination of a historical phenomenon must be based on its origins."[184] When the hearer of Mark first hears ἀρχή in 1:1 at the start of the book, it can be taken as a reference to the beginning of the book itself. But then upon hearing the book a second time, it becomes clear that the word applies to the entire literary work as a unit. This impression would be enhanced by the fact that the hearer gets to the end without ever having heard any sayings or teachings that

---

[182] See Giblin, "The Beginning of the Ongoing Gospel," 978.

[183] See Telford, *Theology of Mark*, 149-151. This interpretation addresses Werner's argument that Mark is not Pauline because 1 Cor 15 lists resurrection witnesses that Mark does not. Mark's text does not preclude later appearances; he just ensures that if they happen, they are no more authoritative than Paul's, and if they don't happen "in Galilee," that is, if they are not interpreted as pro-Gentile, they are invalid. (Werner 1923, 178)

[184] Cited in Adela Yarbro Collins, *Is Mark's Gospel a Life of Jesus? A Question of Genre* (Marquette UP, 1990), 28-29.

Alluding to Paul in the Main Parables and the Ending 141

are actually identifiable as "the gospel" anywhere in the text. The natural conclusion is that the book as a whole is about the origin of "the gospel."[185] The way Mark uses the title "son of God" contributes to this impression. The phrase occurs only in 1:1, 3:11, and 15:39. In the opening it states what the whole book is about, and at the end the Centurion becomes the first human being to recognize Jesus as the son of God.

Given the Pauline emphases throughout Mark and Paul's own unique use of the word "gospel,"[186] the entire book of Mark then comes to be seen as a narrative presentation of how Paul's gospel came into being. It functions, then, to solidly establish the authority of the one apostle who proved to be good soil rather than rocky soil.[187] As for the actual content of the gospel, Mark points beyond itself to the teaching of that "last" yet "greatest" apostle preserved in the epistles written in his name.

---

[185] Van Iersel, *Mark: A Reader-Response Commentary*, 90. See Giblin, "The Beginning of the Ongoing Gospel."

[186] See especially Phil 4:15, where Paul uses the very same phrase "beginning of the Gospel" (*arkhe tou euangeliou*) that Mark uses in 1:1.

[187] As Kealy observes, only Mark and Paul use the noun "gospel" frequently (Matthew uses it only from his source): seven times in Mark, four in Matthew, none in Luke, John, or Acts; and sixty in Paul. Mark normally uses it absolutely (except 1:1 and 1:14), which is another indication of Pauline origin. Jesus Christ and the Gospel are equivalent in Mark: the gospel "is not the message which Jesus proclaimed but 'the form in which Jesus is made present. Jesus is the content of the Gospel in the sense that he is preached'" (*History of Interpretation*, 2: 1: 230).

8
Appropriating Paul's Language and Example

If Mark was trying to defend the Gentile mission and validate the authority of the Pauline literary corpus, and if in doing so he developed themes from the epistles into narrative episodes, you would expect to find not more than just "narrativization" of broad Pauline themes. You would also expect to find traces of Pauline language and echoes of Pauline autobiographical narrative. Such expectations are not disappointed – Mark has both in abundance.

Pauline Language

Ironically, one of the cornerstones of Martin Werner's arguments against considering Mark to be Pauline is that Mark's language is not Pauline. Werner cites a table of statistics where he lists individual Greek words and the number of times each word appears in Paul's epistles versus how frequently it appears in Mark's Gospel. Here are some examples from his list: ἀγάπη (love) – 52 times in Paul, none in Mark; δικαιοσύνη (righteousness) – 51 times in Paul, none in Mark; δόξα (glory) – 60 times in Paul, 3 in Mark; νόμος (law) – 115 times in Paul, none in Mark; and χάρις (grace) – 74 times in Paul, none in Mark.[188]

Statistics such as these are not helpful in analyzing literary relationships. In the first place, just counting instances is misleading because the volume of text in the Pauline epistles far

---

[188] Werner, *Der Einfluss*, 207-8.

exceeds that of Mark. Percentages would have been a better comparison than numbers, and adjusting the figures to a proportion of total text would make these differences less impressive. Even more important, though, is the fact that this is simply not a valid way to establish or disprove a literary relationship. The author of Mark might have grown up with a very different vocabulary than did Paul, and if so much or most of what he wrote would reflect his own vocabulary rather than Paul's. This would remain true even if Mark relied heavily on Paul's epistles for ideas and thematic content. Even if Mark frequently copied words and phrases from Paul, much of Paul's wording and text would remain foreign to Mark.

In addition, the genre and purpose of a work affects its language. For Paul, ἀγάπη (love) and δικαιοσύνη (righteousness) were at the heart of his gospel and he had to repeat them frequently. If Mark's purpose were to elucidate the content of Paul's gospel, it would have been hard to avoid such words. But as I showed in the Introduction to this book, Mark is not interested in delivering an exposition of the gospel. And if his purpose led him in a different direction – such as to validate Paul's authority – he had no need to repeat the discussions of ἀγάπη in 1 Corinthians 13 or δικαιοσύνη in Romans. If he was successful in validating Paul's authority, the hearers of his Gospel would go to Paul's epistles themselves and would find these ideas at the heart of "the gospel" there.

On the other hand, if Mark was using Paul's epistles as his inspiration and source, you would expect to find distinctive usages of terms in scattered instances where the borrowing was relatively more direct. And that is precisely what we see. I have pointed out some instances already, where in developing a Pauline theme Mark used distinctive Pauline language. Examples

Appropriating Paul's Language and Example

are the combination of "grief" and "anger" with respect to the Jews' rejection of Paul's gospel, which links Mark 3:1-5 to Romans 9-11; the expression "making all foods clean," which links Mark 7:19 to Rom 14:20;[189] the reference to Jews seeking "signs," which links Mark 8:11-12 to 1 Cor 1:22;[190] the phrase "those supposed to be" in reference to community leaders whose leadership is to be taken with a grain of salt, which links Mark 10:42-43 to Gal 2:6-9;[191] the words "gain" and "loss" in reference to the gospel versus worldly goods, which links Mark 8:35 to Phil 3:7-8;[192] the words "shame" and "glory" in reference to judgment day, which link Mark 8:38 to typical Pauline usage;[193] "children" as a metaphor for Gentiles linked to anger about hindrances to their reception, which links Mark 9:36-10:14 to 1 Thess 2:10-12;[194] the words αὐξανόμενα (increasing) and καρποφοροῦσιν (bear fruit), which link Mark 4:8 and 20 to Col 1:6 and 10;[195] and the phrase "beloved son," which links Mark 1:11, 9:7, and 12:6 to Gal 4:28-29.[196]

M. E. Boismard and Paul Benoit discovered other instances of typically Pauline language in Mark, by comparing passages in Mark with parallels in the other synoptic gospels. One example is Mark 4:11 and parallels (the beginning of the explanation of the sower parable). In the quotations below, the differences are italicized:

---

[189] See also chapter 4.
[190] See **Jesus Rejects Jewish Exclusivism** in chapter 4.
[191] See **The Irony of the Cross** in chapter 5.
[192] See **The Irony of the Cross** in chapter 5.
[193] See **The Irony of the Cross** in chapter 5.
[194] See **The Twelve** in chapter 6.
[195] See **The Parable of the Sower** in chapter 7.
[196] See **The Parable of the Wicked Husbandmen** in chapter 7.

> And he said to them, "To you has been given *the secret* (μυστήριον) of the kingdom of God, but *for those outside everything* is in parables; (Mark 4:11)

> And he answered them, "To you it has been given to know *the secrets* (μυστήρια) of the kingdom of heaven, but *to them it* has not been given. . . . This is why I speak *to them* in parables . . . (Matt 13:11, 13a)

> he said, "To you it has been given to know *the secrets* (μυστήρια) of the kingdom of God; but *for others they* are in parables . . . (Luke 8:10)

In Mark μυστήριον ("secret") is singular, as it is most of the time in Paul (18 singular versus 3 plural), τὰ πάντα ("everything" in Mark 4:11) reflects Pauline usage (29 times in Paul, only 3 times elsewhere),[197] and "those outside" (τοῖς ἔξω or πρὸς τοὺς ἔξω) occurs elsewhere only in Paul.[198] In the Pauline texts, "those outside" refers to people who are outside the Pauline Christian community, which fits the interpretation I offered earlier in this book, according to which that phrase alludes to Jews who reject Christ.

Another example Boismard cites is Mark 1:14b-15 and its parallel in Matthew 4:17. In the quotations below, the italicized words are unique in Mark and are distinctively Pauline:

> Jesus came into Galilee, preaching *the gospel of God*, and saying, *"The time is fulfilled*, and the kingdom of God is at hand; repent, and *believe in the gospel*." (Mark 1:14b-15)

> From that time Jesus began to preach, saying, "Repent, for the kingdom of heaven is at hand." (Matt 4:17)

---

[197] In Acts 17:25 it appears in a speech of Paul; it also appears in Heb 2:10; Rev 4:11.
[198] 1 Thess 4:12; 1 Cor 5:12-13; Col 4:5.

Appropriating Paul's Language and Example 147

The phrase "gospel of God" appears five times in Paul and once in 2 Peter;[199] phrases like "the time is fulfilled" appear only in Paul;[200] and phrases like "believe in the gospel" appear only in Paul.[201] In Mark 1:14, the term "gospel of God" is the ending part of an inclusio in the Gospel's prologue, beginning with "gospel of Christ" in verse 1:

> The beginning of *the gospel of Jesus Christ, the Son of God*. . . . Jesus came into Galilee, preaching *the gospel of God*, and saying, "The time is fulfilled, and the kingdom of God is at hand; repent, and believe in *the gospel*." (Mark 1:1, 14b-15)

"The gospel of Christ" is another unique Paulinism, occurring only in Paul and nowhere else in the New Testament.[202]

In fact, it is around the word "gospel" – a distinctively Pauline expression – that the entire book of Mark revolves. As I explained in the Introduction, the whole book points to "the gospel" as the message its hearers must believe and obey, and the book as a whole tells the story of "the beginning of the gospel," yet the book offers no distinctive gospel teaching other than the narrative image of the crucified Christ. For the teachings at the heart of the gospel the hearer of Mark must go elsewhere – to Paul's epistles.[203]

Presenting John the Baptist as an Image of Paul

It is not difficult to see that there are some parallels between John the Baptist and Jesus in Mark, on the one hand, and Paul the Apostle and Jesus, on the other hand. John preached

---

[199] Rom 1:1; 15:16; 1 Thess 2:2, 8, 9; 2 Pet 4:17.
[200] Gal 4:4; Eph 1:10.
[201] Eph 1:13 ("you have believed in him"); cf. Phil 1:27; Rom 1:16; 10:16
[202] Rom 15:19; 1 Cor 9:12; 2 Cor 2:12; 9:13; 10:14; Gal 1:7; Phil 1:27; 1 Thess 3:2.
[203] See Tarazi, *Paul and Mark*, 115-19; 140.

(κηρύσσω) a Jesus who was to come after him. Paul preached (κηρύσσω) a resurrected Jesus who was to come in judgment after him.²⁰⁴ John preached repentance and baptism as a preparation for meeting the coming Lord; Paul preached repentance and baptism as preparation for meeting the coming Lord.²⁰⁵ John's work as a baptizer began "in the wilderness," which implies that it was a non-Jewish land; Paul's was commissioned by God as the apostle to the Gentiles and began his apostolic work in the wilderness of Arabia, a non-Jewish land.²⁰⁶ John proclaims he is "not worthy" of Jesus in exactly the same way that Paul proclaims he is "not worthy" of Jesus:

> And he preached, saying, "After me comes he who is mightier than I, the thong of whose sandals I am not worthy (οὐκ εἰμὶ ἱκανὸς) to stoop down and untie. (Mark 1:7)

> For I am the least of the apostles; I am not worthy (οὐκ εἰμὶ ἱκανὸς) to be called an apostle, because I persecuted the church of God. (1 Cor 15:9)

The 1 Corinthians passage is the same one that contains the "last will be first" and "least will be greatest" theme, which as I showed earlier is another way that Mark alludes to Paul.²⁰⁷

It is also significant that Jesus explicitly defends John's authority in Mark, and that he does this right after he cleanses the temple so that it can become a place of prayer for "the

---

²⁰⁴ Mark 1:4; Gal 2:2; 5:11; Rom 10:8; 1 Cor 1:23; 15:11-12; 2 Cor 4:5; 11:4. In Mark, John is also presented as a new Elijah, and Tarazi (*Paul and Mark*, 192) points out some parallels between Elijah and Paul.

²⁰⁵ Mark 1:4; Rom 2:4; 6:4; 2 Cor 7:9-10; Eph 4:5; Col 2:12. Of course, there is a difference in that John actually does the baptizing, while Paul says "Christ did not send me to baptize but to preach." (1 Cor 1:17).

²⁰⁶ Mark 1:4; Gal 1:16-17. See Tarazi, *Paul and Mark*, 136-38.

²⁰⁷ See **The Irony of the Cross** in chapter 5.

nations." In fact, Mark makes sure that the passage about John's authority begins in a way that directly ties it to the temple cleansing:

> And they came again to Jerusalem. And as he was walking in the temple, the chief priests and the scribes and the elders came to him, and they said to him, "By what authority are you doing these things, or who gave you this authority to do them?" Jesus said to them, "I will ask you a question; answer me, and I will tell you by what authority I do these things. Was the baptism of John from heaven or from men? Answer me." And they argued with one another, "If we say, 'From heaven,' he will say, 'Why then did you not believe him?' But shall we say, 'From men'?" – they were afraid of the people, for all held that John was a real prophet. So they answered Jesus, "We do not know." And Jesus said to them, "Neither will I tell you by what authority I do these things." (Mark 11:27-33)[208]

The dilemma of the "the chief priests and the scribes and the elders" is the same as that of the "pillars" of the church in Jerusalem: if Paul's authority did not come from God, why did they make an agreement with him (Gal 2:1-10)? And then if Paul's authority did come from God, why did they renege on that agreement with him (Gal 2:11-14)?

Modeling Jesus' Life after Paul's

On the other hand, much of what I've already presented amounts to suggesting that Mark deliberately created a literary Jesus whose words and actions parallel the words and actions of Paul. Mark's Jesus defends the Gentile mission before the fact, in the face of opposition from his disciples, just as Paul defended his Gentile mission in the face of opposition from the "pillars,"

---

[208] See also Tarazi, *Paul and Mark*, 204-6.

some of whom were reputed to have been among those disciples. To make this connection Mark portrayed Jesus leading reluctant disciples to Galilee, visiting other Gentile lands, interacting positively with individual Gentiles, performing miracles of feeding for mixed Jewish-Gentile crowds, insisting that recalcitrant disciples stop preventing children from reaching him, narrating parables, and so forth. There are also parallels to the core content of the gospel that Paul preached: the outline of Jesus' life is a veritable image of the "Christ crucified" that was so central to Paul's proclamation. These are thematic parallels, but I've also pointed out some parallels to specific events in Paul's life – such as Jesus' rebuke of Peter for rejecting the cross, which parallels Paul's rebuke of Peter for implicitly rejecting what the cross meant in practice in Paul's Gentile community.

The Pauline source for these Jesus versus Peter stories is Galatians 2:1-12, and there is another equally striking case in which Mark's inspiration appears to have come from the same text. In Mark 3:22, scribes who "came down from Jerusalem" accuse Jesus of demon possession.

> And the scribes who came down from Jerusalem said, "He is possessed by Beelzebul, and by the prince of demons he casts out the demons." And he called them to him, and said to them in parables, "How can Satan cast out Satan? . . . Truly, I say to you, all sins will be forgiven the sons of men, and whatever blasphemies they utter; but whoever blasphemes against the Holy Spirit never has forgiveness, but is guilty of an eternal sin" – for they had said, "He has an unclean spirit." (Mark 3:22-30)

These "scribes who had come from Jerusalem" appear again in 7:1. They criticize Jesus' disciples for eating without washing their hands, and this leads up to Jesus' proclamation that what one eats does not matter, it's how one speaks and behaves that matters.

> Now when the Pharisees gathered together to him, with some of the scribes, who had come from Jerusalem, they saw that some of his disciples ate with hands defiled, that is, unwashed. (For the Pharisees, and all the Jews, do not eat unless they wash their hands, observing the tradition of the elders . . .) And the Pharisees and the scribes asked him, "Why do your disciples not live according to the tradition of the elders, but eat with hands defiled?" And he said to them, "Well did Isaiah prophesy of you hypocrites, as it is written, 'This people honors me with their lips, but their heart is far from me; in vain do they worship me, teaching as doctrines the precepts of men.' You leave the commandment of God, and hold fast the tradition of men." And he said to them, "You have a fine way of rejecting the commandment of God, in order to keep your tradition! . . . And when he had entered the house, and left the people, his disciples asked him about the parable. And he said to them, "Then are you also without understanding? Do you not see that whatever goes into a man from outside cannot defile him, since it enters, not his heart but his stomach, and so passes on?" (Thus he declared all foods clean.) And he said, "What comes out of a man is what defiles a man. For from within, out of the heart of man, come evil thoughts, fornication, theft, murder, adultery, coveting, wickedness, deceit, licentiousness, envy, slander, pride, foolishness. All these evil things come from within, and they defile a man." (Mark 7:1-23)

The parallels between Mark chapter 7 and Galatians 2:11-14 are too dense to be coincidental. In Mark, the scribes come "from Jerusalem"; in Galatians, the men who cause the strife come "from James," who is based in Jerusalem. In Mark, Jesus' opponents attack him for engaging in table fellowship with men who are ritually unclean; in Galatians, Paul's opponents convince

Jews to stop table fellowship with Gentiles, who are considered ritually unclean. In Mark, Jesus calls the scribes "hypocrites" (ὑποκριτῶν, the only use of that word in Mark); in Galatians, Paul accuses Peter and the Jews who also quit eating with Gentiles of acting hypocritically (συνυπεκρίθησαν . . . ὑποκρίσει). In Mark, "the commandment of God" or "the word of God" contrasts with something variously called "the tradition of the elders," "the precepts of men," "the traditions of men," and "your tradition"; in Galatians the gospel that is "not man's gospel" contrasts with "the traditions of my fathers" that Paul was zealous for before he began preaching the gospel.[209] In Mark, Jesus criticizes the scribes for "nullifying" (ἀθετεῖτε) and "annulling" (ἀκυροῦντες) God's commandment; in Galatians, Paul warns that the Law cannot nullify (ἀθετεῖ, 3:15) or "annul" (ἀκυροῖ, 3:17) God's promises to Abraham. In Mark, the story leads to the conclusion that what matters is how one speaks and acts, and ends with a catalog of evils; in Galatians the epistle leads to the conclusion that the Law boils down to "love for the neighbor," followed by a catalog of evils.[210]

This story and the ones about Jesus versus Peter clearly hark back to Paul's confrontation with the "pillars" in Galatians 2:1-12, which means the Galatians text was prominent in Mark's mind as he wrote his gospel. Other parallels point in the same direction. As I pointed out, Mark chapter 7 picks up a thread that began in 3:22-30. The chapter 3 story in turn is sandwiched inside one about Jesus' family setting out to abduct him because

---

[209] In Mark: τὴν παράδοσιν τῶν πρεσβυτέρων, (ἐντάλματα ἀνθρώπων, τὴν παράδοσιν τῶν ἀνθρώπων, and τὴν παράδοσιν ὑμῶν. In Galatians: τῶν πατρικῶν μου παραδόσεων.
[210] These parallels are discussed in Tarazi, *Paul and Mark*, 177-8. See also Goulder, *Five Stones*, 96.

they think he's gone mad; in 3:20-21 they set out, and in 3:31-35 they arrive:

> And the crowd came together again, so that they could not even eat. And when his family heard it, they went out to seize him, for people were saying, "He is beside himself." (Mark 3:20-21)

> And his mother and his brothers came; and standing outside they sent to him and called him. And a crowd was sitting about him; and they said to him, "Your mother and your brothers are outside, asking for you." And he replied, "Who are my mother and my brothers?" And looking around on those who sat about him, he said, "Here are my mother and my brothers! Whoever does the will of God is my brother, and sister, and mother." (Mark 3:31-35)

In the middle part of the sandwich (3:22-30), the scribes who "came down from Jerusalem" in order to attack Jesus and question his authority parallel the men from James in Galatians (Gal 2:11-14). The visit of Jesus' relatives in Mark parallels the visit of the men from James in Galatians. In Mark the scribes say that "by the prince of demons he casts out the demons," and in response Jesus points out that a house divided cannot stand. This image of a split within a community parallels the split that resulted in Paul's community when Peter's actions caused the Jews to separate themselves from the Gentiles. The whole scene, in which the accusers are themselves guilty parallels that of Galatians, which starts with an allusion to accusations against Paul (Gal 1:8-10; cf. 5:11), and ends with the proclamation that Paul's opponents are "severed from Christ ... fallen away from grace" (Gal 5:4; cf. 1:8-9). The finality of those last two phrases sounds like Jesus' proclamation that "whoever blasphemes against the Holy Spirit never has forgiveness, but is guilty of an eternal sin." (Mark 3:29).

The outer parts of the sandwich are related. In Mark we read about Jesus' mother and brothers; in Galatians we read about Jesus' brother James. In Mark we find an allusion to the special status of a family relationship; in Galatians we find an allusion to the special status of Peter, James, and John who are "reputed to be pillars." In Mark we hear that special status rejected; in Galatians we hear that special status rejected. Jesus' words in Mark are functionally identical to Paul's assertion in Galatians that "what they [the so-called pillars] were makes no difference to me; God shows no partiality":

> And he replied, "Who are my mother and my brothers?" And looking around on those who sat about him, he said, "Here are my mother and my brothers! Whoever does the will of God is my brother, and sister, and mother." (Mark 3:33-35)

Like the internal part of the sandwich in Mark, this external part also carries the same theme of the accusers being guilty themselves. In the first part, the word that implies that Jesus' relatives think he's gone mad is ἐξέστη, which literally means "to stand outside."[211] Then when they arrive, they are the ones who stand "outside" (ἔξω) asking about Jesus. As I explained earlier, the whole idea of being "outside" carries special significance as a bad place to be in this part of Mark, since it surfaces again just a few verses later in the famous conclusion to the sower parable:

> And he said to them, "To you has been given the secret of the kingdom of God, but for those outside (ἐκείνοις δὲ τοῖς ἔξω) everything is in parables; so that they may indeed see but not perceive, and may indeed hear but not understand; lest they should turn again, and be forgiven." (Mark 4:11-12)

---

[211] There is also an interesting link here to 2 Cor 5:13, where Paul reports that he is sometimes subjected to the same accusation: "For if we are beside ourselves (ἐξέστημεν), it is for God; if we are in our right mind, it is for you."

In Galatians, people who want to force Gentiles to obey the Jewish Law accuse Paul of hypocrisy and consider non-Law-observant Gentiles to be standing outside the pale of the Messianic community. Their side is led by James the Lord's brother, who in a face-to-face meeting acknowledges Paul's authority but later undercuts Paul by urging Peter to disassociate himself from non-Law-observant Gentiles. In Galatians, Paul proclaims the frightening verdict that anyone who takes this stand is outside the pale of the Messianic community, outside of grace, cut off from Christ. Here too Mark's narrative parallels Galatians. The Lord's brothers and mother believe he is "standing outside" the pale of the Jewish community and come to take corrective action. In doing so it turns out that it is actually they who are "outside." And in 4:11-12, it turns out that those who stand "outside" are destined to be deaf and blind to the gospel word, with the frightening verdict that they will not be forgiven. That verdict sounds very much like Paul's dire warning, "You have been severed from Christ, you who are seeking to be justified by law; you have fallen from grace" (Gal 5:4).[212]

All of this evidence makes a very strong case that Mark was drawing on the scenario described in Galatians 2:1-12. In other instances similar evidence is present but less overwhelming.[213] One example is the way Mark repeatedly has Jesus expounding his teachings to the disciples "privately" (κατ' ἰδίαν):

> . . . he did not speak to them without a parable, but privately (κατ' ἰδίαν) to his own disciples he explained everything. (Mark 4:34)

---

[212] For more on the parallels between these texts, see Tarazi, *Paul and Mark*, 154-57.
[213] See also Tarazi's exposition of parallels to Gal 2:1-12 in Mark 2:1-17; see pp.146-148.

> And after six days Jesus took with him Peter and James and John, and led them up a high mountain apart by themselves (κατ' ἰδίαν); and he was transfigured before them . . . (Mark 9:2)

> And as he sat on the Mount of Olives opposite the temple, Peter and James and John and Andrew asked him privately (κατ' ἰδίαν), "Tell us, when will this be, and what will be the sign when these things are all to be accomplished?" (Mark 13:3-4)

This imagery of the teacher privately laying out his teaching to a select group of leaders of his community is precisely what Paul does in Galatians:

> I went up by revelation; and I laid before them (but privately [κατ' ἰδίαν] before those who were of repute) the gospel which I preach among the Gentiles . . . (Gal 2:2)

"Those who were of repute" in Galatians are Peter, James, and John, the same three named in Mark 9:2 and the same ones with the addition of Andrew in Mark 13:3-4.[214]

If the narrative reworks events from Paul's epistles into events in Jesus' life, it stands to reason that it might rework other elements from Paul's epistles into the narrative. For example, there may be a Pauline source for Mark's identification of Jesus' as a τέκτων in 6:3. That word is often translated "carpenter" but it means more generally "builder," and that is the meaning typically ascribed to it in 1 Corinthians 3:10, where Paul likens himself to an ἀρχιτέκτων, often translated "master builder." The words are the same except for the prefix in 1 Corinthians.

---

[214] Tarazi argues that the occurrences of κατ' ἰδίαν in 6:31 and 7:33 also parallel Gal 2:1-14. "Thus, all occurrences of the expression 'privately' can be accounted for on the basis of its use in Gal 2:2." (*Paul and Mark*, 163)

Appropriating Paul's Language and Example 157

> Is not this the carpenter (τέκτων), the son of Mary and brother of James and Joses and Judas and Simon, and are not his sisters here with us?" And they took offense at him. (Mark 6:3)

> According to the grace of God given to me, like a skilled master builder (ἀρχιτέκτων) I laid a foundation, and another man is building upon it. Let each man take care how he builds upon it. (1 Cor 3:10)

By itself this could be a coincidence, but considering all the other clear cases where Mark used 1 Corinthians and adapted Pauline material to make it into Jesus material, there seems a good chance that this is not just a coincidence.[215]

---

[215] Tarazi also points out that these are the only places in the New Testament where the root τέκτων appears, besides the parallel in Matt 13:55.

Part III

The Genre of Mark

9
Why Genre Matters

Many modern readers of scripture find it difficult to accept the idea that Mark wrote his Gospel by recasting material he found in the Old Testament, Paul's epistles, and the Homeric epics into a story about Jesus. However, the reason for their difficulty is not inherent in the idea of a written gospel; it is shared only by modern readers who classify a gospel as an instance of the modern literary genre of nonfiction. Those who classify a gospel as a work of fiction have no difficulty accepting any sources of inspiration for Mark's creativity. Most people today fall into one of these two groups, yet neither classification is appropriate. Mark wrote his Gospel before anyone had conceived of our present system of fiction and non-fiction as top-level genres.

The question of genre is thus more than an academic classification scheme; it has a bearing on how we interpret the text. Many biblical scholars do try to determine the gospels' genre, but the way they answer the question typically has little or no impact on how they interpret the text, which shows that they are treating genre as no more than an academic classification scheme. This state of affairs results from a fundamental error in methodology. The root of the problem is that the way biblical scholars typically ascertain the gospels' genre does not reflect the way in which real authors and readers determine genre in the real world. The result is that scholars typically pay lip service to the idea of *genre as key to interpretation* while in reality they assume that *interpretation is the key to genre*. Applying a more realistic methodology leads to an understanding of the gospels' genre that makes sense of Mark's use of Paul's epistles to write a story about Jesus.

If most people today tend not to take the question of genre very seriously, it is because whenever they pick up a book to read it they take for granted their knowledge of its genre and what that entails. They don't think about it explicitly, but it's there in the background profoundly molding their interpretation of what they read. It's like the air we breathe, which constantly moves into and out of us without notice until and unless that movement is restricted, at which point our utter reliance upon air suddenly takes center stage in our conscious attention. In like manner, assumptions about genre become evident only when we meet a book that contradicts those assumptions, and then they make themselves known with surprising force.

Contemporary Americans are accustomed to taking for granted the broad generic distinction between fiction and nonfiction. The depth of this belief is evident in the fact that the most controversial book to be published in America in the relatively recent past excited passions because it straddled this generic boundary. Many books on the fringes and extremes of various political and religious spectrums have been published over the last few decades, but none of them excited such nation-wide anger and alarm as Edmund Morris's *Dutch: A Memoir of Ronald Reagan*.[216] Although marketed as Ronald Reagan's official biography, and written in corresponding nonfiction style complete with footnotes, *Dutch* is suffused with fictional elements throughout. The author writes from the viewpoint of a fictional character who was a contemporary of Reagan's and participated in the events of his life. Morris not only injected his

---

[216] Random House, 1999.

fictional persona into real events but also made up conversations and documents, and even footnoted some of the imaginary documents. A reader of the book would be alerted to the genre mix-up on the dust cover blurb, but within the book's text nothing gives a clue to the fictional character of the author's persona and much of his narrative. It was not just the general public that saw this mix of genres as sacrilege – many historians were just as incensed at the book's blatant transgression against the norms of one of their own genres. One professor, aghast at the thought that someday a reader might pick up the book without the dust jacket and never realize that this nonfiction text included fiction, exclaimed in outrage: "Let's call it biofiction or biofantasy or bioimaginings, but not biography, which has a venerable tradition."[217]

Consider the contrasting reception experienced by another book identical in form insofar as the text reads like nonfiction and comes complete with footnotes, many of which cite imaginary sources: Michael Crichton's *Eaters of the Dead*, which later was made into the movie, *The 13th Warrior*. The text of Crichton's novel claims to be an actual manuscript written in the tenth century as the memoirs of an Arab traveler to the Vikings, published and annotated by modern scholars. No controversy attended this book's debut; indeed it was met with widespread critical approval although it, like *Dutch*, mixes fiction and nonfiction without informing the reader which is which. The difference in reception between these two books illustrates a fundamental presupposition that people today apply to the modern genres of fiction and nonfiction: in the genre of fiction, nonfictional material can freely mix with the fictional material,

---

[217] Joyce Appleby, quoted by Kate Masur in *Perspectives*, December 1999. Online: http://www.historians.org/perspectives/issues/1999/9912/9912new1.cfm.

but in the genre of nonfiction, no fictional material at all is allowed unless it is explicitly marked as such.[218] If Morris's book had been marketed as fiction, it would not have generated a controversy. The nonfiction versus fiction generic distinction is a deeply ingrained expectation that profoundly influences how people interpret what they read, though the ways in which this expectation operate are rarely thought about explicitly.

The first century knew nothing of our distinction between fiction and nonfiction as genres, but ancient authors and readers had just as deeply entrenched yet unspoken beliefs about the genres of their own culture. If our understanding of *Dutch* is so profoundly affected by our view of it as fiction or nonfiction, it stands to reason that ancient readers' understanding of the gospels, and the way the evangelists went about writing them, was profoundly affected by the way they saw these texts fit into their own culture's system of genres. And since the Gospel of Mark is generally seen as the earliest gospel, Dennis MacDonald does not exaggerate when he calls the search for Mark's genre "the elusive Holy Grail of gospel studies."[219]

Biblical Scholarship on the Gospels' Genre

Modern scholars generally assume that the genre of a text can be determined by comparing its form and content to genres current in that text's contemporary culture. Since nothing quite like a gospel existed before the first gospel was written, different

---

[218] The difference in the way the Morris and the Crichton books were received is also, of course, because few people really care that much about getting right what happened in the tenth century, but even medieval historians didn't object to Crichton's book. No one objected because mixing nonfiction and fiction in a fictional narrative is deemed to be normal.

[219] Dennis R. MacDonald, *The Homeric Epics and the Gospel of Mark* (New Haven, Conn.: Yale UP, 2000), 3.

Why Genre Matters 165

ways of looking at form and content lead in different directions. Before the late twentieth century, scholars generally saw the gospels as an essentially new genre. Later came recognition that this stand is untenable: new genres can develop out of existing ones, but no author can create a genre from scratch, as if he were writing in a generic vacuum. As Michael Vines puts it, "Genre functions as a conventional bridge between author and reader, therefore an utterly new genre would be either incomprehensible, or at least seriously prone to misinterpretation."[220]

Once recognition of this fact of literary life took hold, the search was on for the genre or genres that most likely gave birth to the gospel genre. Depending on which aspects of the text's form and content any given scholar considers most important, a wide variety of genres from contemporary Greco-Roman and Jewish culture have been advanced as candidates, including aretalogy, encomium, memorabilia, Socratic dialogue, Greek tragedy, Homeric epic, apocalyptic Jewish Novel, and Greco-Roman biography.[221]

Over the last couple of decades, the last of these – Greco-Roman biography – seems to have become the majority view. That view is vigorously championed by Richard Burridge, and

---

[220] Michael E. Vines, *The Problem of Markan Genre: the Gospel of Mark and the Jewish Novel* (Atlanta: Society of Biblical Literature, 2002), 8. Richard Burridge states this more strongly: "any idea of the gospels as unique, *sui generis* works is a nonsense: authors cannot create, and readers cannot interpret, a total novelty." (*What are the Gospels? A Comparison with Graeco-Roman Biography* [Grand Rapids: Eerdmans, 2004], 247) See also Tolbert, *Sowing*, 50.

[221] For an excellent survey of scholarly literature on the subject, see Vines, *Markan Genre*, 1-31. Some in-depth examinations of the gospels' genre include Burridge, *What are the Gospels*, Tolbert, *Sowing the Gospel*, 50-60; Collins, *Is Mark's Gospel a Life of Jesus* and Collins, "Genre and the Gospels," Journal of Religion 75 (1995): 239-246.

for him it leads to the conclusion that the gospels must have been intended to be historically accurate in the same sense that we today think of historical accuracy:

> So we may conclude that the authors of the gospels were aware of the βίος nature of their work. Similarly, their audiences must have realized this; as Hengel says, "The ancient reader will probably have been well aware of the differences in style and education, say, between Mark and Xenophon; but he will also have noticed what the gospels had in common with the literature of biographical 'reminiscences' - and unlike the majority of German New Testament scholars today, he did not mind at all regarding the evangelists as authors of biographical reminiscences of Jesus which went back to the disciples of Jesus themselves."[222]

Another way of looking at Burridge's line of thought here is to recognize that he is essentially assigning the gospels to the modern genre of nonfiction, and he is applying to them the modern belief in the sacrosanct character of that genre as free from the contamination of fiction. Biography cannot mix with biofiction, biofantasy, or bioimaginings. Burridge's point of view is understandable, for the belief that the genre of biography is necessarily a sub-genre of nonfiction runs deep in modern readers' minds. Even an academic ostensibly trying to understand the ancient world on its own terms would find it hard to break free from this presupposition. However, seen in these terms, the revolution in scholarly thinking about the gospels' genre, in which the majority view made a transition from classifying the gospels as sui generis to classifying them as biography, turns out to be no revolution at all. In both cases, the vast majority of scholars implicitly interpret the gospels as if they are instances of the broad modern genre of nonfiction. This is

---

[222] Burridge, *What are the Gospels*, 246.

what governs their interpretation of the works, and this makes any interpretation of Mark that sees him reworking Pauline epistles into a narrative about Jesus unacceptable.[223]

The view of ancient biography as conforming to modern presuppositions about the nonfiction genre is itself questionable,[224] but that is not what I want to address here. Nor do I intend to cover in detail the great mass of evidence that has been adduced by Burridge and others in defense of their various conclusions about the gospels' genre. Instead, I will render most of that evidence irrelevant by calling into question key assumptions which have led scholars to look for evidence in the wrong places.[225]

How Authors and Readers Actually Determine Genre

What tends to be missing in modern biblical scholarship is a realistic consideration of how authors and readers actually determine genre. Burridge's approach is typical, insofar as his

---

[223] This is often implicit and sometimes even explicit as an unquestionable assumption. A symposium about intertextual relationships in the Bible, for example, introduces its subject with these words: "The exegete analyses texts which are demonstrably non-fictional, whereas the literary scholar only analyses fictional texts. Since biblical texts are non-fictional, it is only natural that questions both as to the context in which those texts originated and as to their history and origin should be crucial in biblical research. At the same time the question comes up what the biblical text has to do with the events that preceded it and led to the writing of it. These questions are not discussed in the same way in literary studies." (Sipke Draisma, ed., *Intertextuality in Biblical writings* [Kampen: Kok, 1989], 9)

[224] See the discussion in Vines, *Markan Genre*, 4.

[225] I will add, however, that even for those who share the assumption that the most important determinant of genre is a text's content and form, the conclusion that the gospels fit the genre of Greco-Roman biography is suspect; Burridge's is the most thoroughly developed version of these arguments, and for an excellent summary and critique of them see the blog by Neil Godfrey at http://vridar.wordpress.com (posts on 1/17, 1/20, and 1/29/2011). The author is not a scriptural scholar per se but is a thorough researcher and a trenchant critic of the scholarly literature he reviews.

argument is based exclusively on characteristics of the text, and often on characteristics that require statistical analysis to see their significance. The data cited by Burridge include such things as the percentage of sentences that have Jesus as the subject of the verb,[226] the relative amount of the text that is focused on Jesus, the relative number of settings in the narrative which follow Jesus, similarities to popular literature in the language style, and so forth. Mary Ann Tolbert reaches a different conclusion but bases her analysis on the same kinds of evidence: she finds that the style and content of the Markan story is more similar to popular novels of the ancient world than it is to biographies.[227] Michael Vines divides his predecessors into those who focus on form and those who focus on content, while he asserts that he looks at both, but he too focuses on internal characteristics of the text, for his argument is that what matters most is the apocalyptic understanding of history expressed in the text.

The list could be extended with any number of additional examples, and the problem with all of them is that the form and content of a text is not the primary determinant of genre. In other words, *the typical approach to this question in modern scholarly literature doesn't reflect the actual processes by which either authors or readers determine the genre of a work.* The typical approach taken by scholars implicitly assumes that the reader of

---

[226] An appendix in Burridge's book presents a long series of computer-generated pie charts tallying the percentage of times verbs refer to various subjects in various ancient works of literature. (Burridge, *What are the Gospels,* 308-21)

[227] Phrases like "popular literature" or "popular novel" are inherently misleading. As Gamble has pointed out, there really was no such thing as popular literature in anything remotely like the sense we think of today when we use such terms. The closest corollary in the ancient world was "light reading for the small minority who could read and those who also read the more serious literature available to them." (Harry Gamble, *Books and Readers in the Early Church* [New Haven: Yale UP, 1995], 39)

a literary work would have to read the entire text before figuring out what its genre is. It is as if that task could be done only by carefully analyzing the entire text for statistically significant differences and similarities compared to other works whose genre was already known.

One way to gain some insight into why this is problematic is to think carefully about your own experience with literary genre. There are two fundamentally different perspectives to consider: that of the author and that of the reader. If you are the writer, you typically decide upon the genre before you begin writing: you know right at the start if you're writing an email or a novel, a greeting card or a technical support web page.[228] Genre is a function of your intention. While writing, you would typically follow the conventions associated with the chosen genre – most of the time you don't sprinkle smileys in the technical support page text, and in an email you use informal language that would be inappropriate in an academic article.

If you are the reader – and this is where the typical scholarly analysis of the gospels departs from real life – you likewise determine genre before you begin. When you select a text to read, you generally have a reason to read it; you know something about it before you begin, and part of what you know is its genre. When you read an email you know it's an email. When you pick up a book from the nonfiction book stacks of the library, you know it's a nonfiction book. When you open the

---

[228] As with all general rules there are exceptions. You could, for example, start writing a blog post and turn it into an academic article or a novel later, but then when you made the change you would be aware of what you were doing. It would be a very rare situation for someone else to publish your blog post as a novel without your knowledge and consent and without revisions to make it suitable for the change in genre.

pages of a scholarly journal, you know you are going to read a scholarly article. You do not read through the whole text, thinking to yourself about all the ways in which the text is similar to or different from genres you know, and determine the genre only when you're done reading and have analyzed the data. If you find first-person and second-person informal style in an academic periodical, it might strike you as strange because that is contrary to academic article conventions in the discipline of biblical studies, but you do not as a result decide you're reading an email or a blog.

The point is that there is no such thing as a free-floating text, no such thing as letters and words floating through the ether without physical presentation, such that you can only determine genre by the character of the text itself. *It is the context in which a text is presented that is the primary determinant of generic expectations and assumptions.* What made the difference in the reception of *Dutch* and *Eaters of the Dead* is the way they were marketed and presented, not in the generic conventions of the text. If *Dutch* had been marketed as fiction there would have been little or no controversy. There is no evidence that this principle was any different in the ancient world than it is today. Relatively few scholars who examine the question of the gospels' genre recognize this. One biblical scholar who does acknowledge the importance of the way a text is presented is Harry Gamble:

> . . . genre is presupposed in the act of writing and in the act of reading, and though they may not correspond absolutely, the aims of writing and reading can meet only if recognizable generic signs are provided either in the text or in the situation where the text is received and read, or both. A sense of the genre of any particular

text is essential to its comprehension: the reader must be able to judge what sort of writing is being read.[229]

A few recognize not just the importance but the priority of evidence pertaining to "the situation where the text is received or read." K. L. Noll states plainly that "Social situation of reception is the primary consideration in the determination of a genre of communication."[230]

Applying Different Generic Criteria to the Gospels

Gamble asserts that scholars have generally not paid enough attention to the actual ancient manuscripts and their physical characteristics:

> The failure to consider the extent to which the physical medium of the written word contributes to its meaning – how its outward aspects inform the way a text is approached and read – perpetuates a largely abstract, often unhistorical, and even anachronistic conception of early Christian literature and its transmission.[231]

Just as today it makes a difference whether one finds a text on the nonfiction shelf of the library, in an email, or in a blog, the manner in which an ancient text was preserved and presented matters:

> All aspects of the production, distribution, and use of texts presuppose social functions and forces – functions and forces that

---

[229] Gamble, *Books and Readers*, 38.
[230] K. L Noll, "The Evolution of Genre in the Book of Kings: The Story of Sennacherib and Hezekiah as Example," in Patricia Kirkpatrick and Timothy Goltz, eds., *The Function of Ancient Historiography in Biblical and Cognate Studies* (T&T Clark, 2008), 30-56; here: 45 n.56. See also p.43.
[231] Gamble, *Books and Readers*, 42.

are given representation, or inscribed, in the design of the text as a concrete, physical object.²³²

Moreover, what we learn about the production and distribution of the text does tell us about the author's intention, for as Gamble points out, each of the gospel authors

> . . . was self-consciously engaged in literary composition and therefore sensible not only of his own compositional techniques and theological aims, but also of the prospects for the valuation, circulation, and use of his work.²³³

Therefore, a more realistic approach to the determination of genre would result in giving priority to a very different kind of evidence than the internal text characteristics that scholars typically analyze. The physical evidence of how the gospel texts were preserved should be central, not incidental, to the search for their genre.

To date, the most insightful investigation into aspects of the physical evidence that may have a bearing on genre is the one that David Trobisch presents in his book *The First Edition of the New Testament*.²³⁴ From a broad survey of the earliest manuscripts that preserve New Testament books, Trobisch concludes that a spontaneous and haphazard process could not have resulted in the uniformity of certain characteristics that we

---

²³² Ibid.
²³³ Gamble, *Books and Readers*, 101.
²³⁴ Oxford: Oxford UP, 2000. A German edition preceded the English edition: *Die Endredaktion des Neuen Testaments: Eine Untersuchung zur Entstehung der christlichen Bibel* (Göttingen: Vandenhoeck, 1996). For a summary of the evidence presented in this book, see my review article, "David Trobisch and David Parker on the Origin of the New Testament, the Historical Jesus, and How Manuscripts Can Reveal What Texts Conceal" in JOCABS 2(2009):1. Online: http://www.ocabs.org/journal/index.php/jocabs/article/view/41/16.

find in the manuscripts. This leads to the conclusion that the manuscripts derive from a single archetype, which in turn suggests that a single editor or publisher deliberately created the entire package at some very early date.[235] In other words, the earliest evidence we have that witnesses to how the New Testament texts were presented to their readers indicates that they were presented as scripture, in a New Testament counterpart to what was destined to become seen as the Old Testament. Trobisch's theory turns the entire field of canon history on its head: instead of a long history of independent writings gradually being assembled into a whole, the whole is promulgated at once, and there's a long history of ultimately failed attempts to dispute parts of it.

Such a wholesale rethinking of canon history has unsurprisingly failed to take the conservative world of biblical scholarship by storm, but the evidence is too strong to be dismissed out of hand. Since even the earliest surviving manuscripts of the gospels share the common characteristics that Trobisch cites,[236] in effect we have no clear evidence that any of them originally circulated independently before being assembled into the canonical collection we now know as the New Testament. Even if one chooses to reject the package-publication theory, the picture that best fits the actual physical evidence is of a unified church leadership that produced this literature and tightly controlled its propagation over an extended period of time.

---

[235] For a project of this scale multiple editors and copyists would most likely be involved, but I am using the words "editor" and "publisher" in the singular to reflect the idea that the project was led by one person or undertaken by a single team with a clearly-defined set of goals.

[236] This is not the place to present Trobisch's evidence in detail, but parts of it, the *nomina sacra* and codex format, are discussed below.

The nature of the physical evidence does not just indicate that a single group controlled the production and distribution of the gospels; it also indicates that these texts were specifically aimed at Christians, rather than being intended for broad evangelistic purposes. As Gamble observes, the system of abbreviations called the *nomina sacra* is found fully developed already in the earliest surviving manuscripts, and it witnesses to the intention that only readers familiar with the system would be reading the manuscripts:

> The system of nomina sacra, though not an esoteric code, stands out as an in-group convention that expressed a community consciousness and presumed a particular readership.[237]

In-group conventions in works whose production and distribution was carefully controlled suggests an intention to write and publish authoritative scripture, for scripture is aimed at a religious community, not at people outside that community.[238]

Another distinctive feature of the earliest surviving New Testament manuscripts compared to other works of literature is their codex (book) format which replaced the scroll format that was the universal standard at the time. As Gamble observes, this too could be indicative of an intent to publish the New Testament texts as scripture, since the scroll format for non-scriptural texts persisted for a period of time:

> The existence of a late second-century roll of Irenaeus's *Against Heresies* (P. Oxy. 405) could suggest that works of scholarship, as

---

[237] Gamble, *Books and Readers*, 75, 78.

[238] Outsiders might read it, but it would not be scripture to them and would not be aimed at them.

distinct from scriptural texts, persisted for a while in roll form in Christian scholastic circles.[239]

Against Heresies may be taken as a representative kind of text aimed at the Christian community yet not intending to function as authoritative scripture. Such texts characteristically identified their author and cited other individuals or texts as authorities for the theological points they tried to make. By contrast, the gospel texts do not identify their authors and do not appeal to any other authority than the Old Testament. In other words, they speak with an authoritative voice aimed at the Christian community, and this authority was bolstered by the editors who attached to these texts the names of individuals whose personal authority would be unimpeachable due to a direct connection to Jesus.

Once you understand that scripture is first of all authoritative, the content of the text itself confirms the conclusion you reach by examining the material evidence of how it was preserved. The text was written to be scripture because it was written to be authoritative, to substantiate a particular view of who and what is authoritative. As I pointed out earlier, Mark's Gospel was

---

[239] Ibid., 80. Elsewhere Gamble notes that "There is no justification in bibliographic terms, for example, for an a priori discrimination between scriptural and nonscriptural texts, not only because the scriptural canon had not yet been determined, but also because the methods of producing and circulating texts were the same for all texts." (p.94) The words "scriptural" and "canonical" are not interchangeable, and the statement on p.94 does not necessarily contradict the statement on p.80. A work may well have been intended as scripture, and received by some for a while as scripture, without necessarily making it into the final form of the canon. Indeed, even if Trobisch's theory is correct and the New Testament was a unitary publication by a single church leadership group, that does not preclude there being other groups who endeavored to produce and get acceptance for their own scriptural works. For another study that shows that early Christians differentiated between scriptural and nonscriptural texts and preferred the scroll for scriptural texts, see Larry W. Hurtado, *The Earliest Christian Artifacts: Manuscripts and Christian Origins* (Grand Rapids: Eerdmans, 2006).

written as a treatise on authority, not to convey any special teaching of Jesus, which is conspicuous by its absence. Even the teaching *about* Jesus that Mark conveys – that is, the centrality of the crucified Christ over the resurrected Christ – is about authority insofar as it, like everything else, is oriented toward backing up Paul's authority in this view of what Jesus was all about.

In addition, the text of Mark explicitly identifies itself as "the beginning of the gospel." For the Pauline churches, "the gospel" meant not only Paul's preaching but Christ himself as well, so a claim like that could only be authoritative or sacrilegious.

As Tarazi points out, Mark's authoritative status can also be detected in a unique address to "the reader" in chapter 13:

> Another indication that Mark intended to write a "scripture" is the remark ". . . let the reader understand . . ." in 13:14. That reference to *one* reader is telling. Nowadays, being children of the post-printing press era, our understanding of the meaning of "books" and even "reading" is quite different from that of the first century A.D. At that time, copies of any given manuscript were very few and their "reading" was done usually in gatherings. This is borne out by the meaning of the Hebrew verb *qara'* and the corresponding Greek *anaginsoko*; both meant 'to read *aloud*," and not just for oneself, as we understand it today. Thus, the very notion of reading implied that it would be done aloud by one person, the "reader," in an official gathering at which the others present were the "hearers." Rev 1:3 offers another witness to this: "Blessed is *he who reads aloud* the words of the prophecy, and blessed are *those who hear*, and who keep what is written therein; for the time is near." Two things in this text are especially significant: a) the RSV translates the same Greek word once without and once with "aloud": b) the original Greek of Revelation has "Blessed is *the reader* and *the hearers* of the words of

Why Genre Matters

the prophecy." Therefore, if Mark was addressed to one reader, that person was "*the* official, public reader" of the gathered community. And since scripture was read and commented upon at these gatherings, the reader or commentator is the one who had to understand the text, in order to explain it to the others.[240]

On the basis of internal evidence alone Tarazi concludes that

> . . . in Mark we have a "story" intended to be read in the Pauline gatherings as a prophecy would, a "story" being offered as a "word," and more specifically as the "word of God." This is exactly how the "stories" of the Patriarchs, the exodus, and the kingdoms of Israel and Judah, are handled in the Old Testament. In other words, Mark was conceived as scripture.[241]

Therefore, both internal and external evidence suggests that the genre originally intended by the authors, editors, and publishers, and the genre indicated by the way in which the texts were presented, and thus the genre as received by the original audience, was that of authoritative scripture.

---

[240] Tarazi, *Paul and Mark*, 125-26.
[241] Ibid., 126.

10
Scripture as a Genre

Most scholars are looking for finer-grained literary categories when they use the word "genre," but scripture versus non-scripture is just as important a generic starting point for the first-century Christian community as fiction versus nonfiction is for present-day Americans. It is true that when the gospels were written, the New Testament canon had not yet been fixed, but this has no bearing on whether any individual work was intended by its author to function as scripture or was received by its original audience as scripture. Different communities could have differing views about which specific writings should be considered scripture, while agreeing on the essential characteristics of scripture per se.

What is clear from the use of the word γραφή within the earliest Christian texts is that scripture is a class of literature that is invested with divine authority by those who see it as scripture. The essential characteristic of scripture is its authoritative voice. Scripture is not read simply so that the reader might become more knowledgeable about something, or to learn the truth about something in order to satisfy curiosity; it is read with a view to finding out how God decrees that one should think and behave.

A given work might or might not be written with express intent that it function as scripture. In some cases (such as, perhaps, some of the Psalms), a work written for other purposes might be appropriated by a community as scripture. However, when an author consciously writes scripture, the primary purpose would not be to inform or entertain but to influence, with intent to use scriptural authority to shape a community in some way.

Paul's epistles clearly fit this description, and they were apparently received as scripture from the beginning,[242] which means they were most likely intended to function as scripture from the beginning. Regardless of who wrote them, their authoritative status depended on the personal authority of the apostle who was credited with authoring them. Because the authors of these letters could depend on the name of Paul for authority, they were free to adapt a non-scriptural genre (that of literary epistle) to the exigencies of the early Christian community's situation. But the text of Mark is anonymous, and an author setting out to create scripture without the benefit of an authoritative name would be in a different situation. An author composing a new work in such a situation would not break out in a totally new literary direction but would follow the precedent of what worked in similar situations in the past. Such precedents would be readily found in the Old Testament, which provided examples of what worked in the past and which dominated the literary world of early Christianity, as Harry Gamble notes:

> The force of Christian dependence on Jewish scripture for the question of the literary culture of early Christianity is not much appreciated, and its implications have been neglected under the influence of form criticism's preoccupation with oral tradition.[243]

---

[242] As discussed earlier, the manuscripts of the epistles and those of the gospels share the same characteristics. See also 2 Peter 3:16, in which Paul's epistles are classified as scripture.

[243] Gamble, *Books and Readers*, 23. See also my conclusion below, which points out that viewing the gospels as a scriptural genre undermines the foundations of oral tradition theory and form criticism methodology.

Scripture as a Genre 181

Within the genre of scripture as represented by the Old Testament, there was a limited range of sub-genres, such as historical narrative (comprising the Torah, the Former Prophets, and works such as Chronicles), prophetic oracles (the great prophets and the twelve), psalms, and wisdom literature. Of these sub-genres, the gospels best fit into the historical narrative category.

More specifically, insofar as the gospel narrative constitutes a story about the origin of the Christian faith, the closest parallel is to the Torah and to the Former Prophets (Joshua, Judges, and the books of Samuel and Kings). The latter are often called "historical" books while the Torah is not, but this distinction is the result of modern generic sensibilities. Genesis is sometimes seen to be more myth or legend than history, but in fact the texts themselves present the whole story starting with creation as a single continuous historical story. Within this body of literature are sections that parallel in many ways what we find in the gospels, most notably the Elijah-Elisha cycle of stories, which, as will be seen later, may have been a model for the gospels.

Some scholars do recognize the gospels' character as historical narrative, and categorize them generically within a broad genre of historiography rather than biography. Eve-Marie Becker categorizes Mark as historiography[244] but observes that while the

---

[244] "The framework within which the Gospel literature is situated can be referred to as 'historiography' in the broader sense: the Gospel of Mark reports the Ἀρχὴ τοῦ εὐαγγελίου [Beginning of the gospel] by way of a narrative of the events (ereignisgeschichtlich) at the beginning of the proclamation of the Gospel. In the frame of the macro-genre of Hellenistic historiography the Gospels represent a special early Christian form of literature (εὐαγγέλιον) closely related to 'historical monography.'" (Eve-Marie Becker, "The Gospel of Mark in the Context of Ancient Historiography," in Patricia Kirkpatrick and Timothy Goltz, eds., *The Function of Ancient Historiography in Biblical and Cognate Studies* [T&T Clark., 2008], 124-134,

evangelist can be compared to historians he isn't one because he "does not give any explicit references concerning his authorship nor concerning his methodology in working with literary sources."[245] This is a problem only if Mark is judged by the standards of non-scriptural historiography. Other scholars who opt to view Mark as creating a new "gospel" sub-genre of "historiography" acknowledge that there is no need to look to Greco-Roman models. In their commentary on Mark, John Donahue and Daniel Harrington observe that Mark's only pre-texts are the Hebrew scriptures – the earliest gospel contains no quotation from any Greco-Roman author and no significant public figure is even mentioned except Herod and Pilate. Therefore they conclude that the secular Greco-Roman literature is really irrelevant:

> Although study of the proposed Greco-Roman models is intrinsically interesting and helpful for a broader understanding of the world that may have been confronted by early Christian preaching, it is more fruitful to view Mark as a 'gospel,' not a unique but at least a *distinctive* genre of literature, which presents the Pauline Christ-event (also called "gospel") in a narrative form, and which weaves together diverse traditions (including the Old Testament) to create a unified story of saving significance of the public life, death, and raising up of Jesus of Nazareth.[246]

Donahue and Harrington propose that the genre one needs to know when one reads Mark in order to interpret it as intended is simply biblical narrative:

---

here: 127) Adela Yarbro Collins takes a similar line (*Is Mark's Gospel a Life of Jesus*, 28-29).
[245] Becker, "Gospel of Mark," 130.
[246] John R. Donahue and Daniel J. Harrington, *The Gospel of Mark* (Collegeville, Minn.: Liturgical Press, 2002), 16.

If awareness of genre is a necessary entrée to proper interpretation, then potential readers of Mark may be lost in the welter of proposals. Even if there may have been no single model that Mark followed, his work is most at home in the realm of biblical narrative.[247]

An understanding of the character of historical narrative in the Old Testament texts is thus critical to understanding the gospels.[248]

Fiction versus Nonfiction in Scriptural Historiography

As noted earlier, few generic assumptions are more powerful in our own culture than those underlying the modern conceptions of fiction and nonfiction. Consequently, few scholars can resist the temptation to fit ancient literature into that system. One of the best ways to see why that does not work in the case of scriptural historiography is to observe the dispute between biblical scholars Robert Alter and Meir Sternberg over whether scriptural historiography is fiction, fictional history, historical fiction, or history.

---

[247] Ibid.

[248] Some scholars caution against assuming that all of the gospels are the same genre; see, for example: Willi Marxsen, *Mark the Evangelist: Studies on the Redaction-History of the Gospel* (New York: Abingdon, 1968), 212, and Vines, *Markan Genre*, 25. However as a practical matter the other gospels are not different in their "social situation of reception," and not sufficiently different in their form or content to reach a significantly different conclusion about their genre. As for their form and content, each shows evidence of having been modeled after Mark (or vice versa if one considers Mark to be later), and having been modeled after Old Testament scriptural historiography. The warning about considering the possibility of different genres applies only to genre at the level of an academic classification scheme, a level that the original author was not interested in, had no impact on the original audience, and is outside the scope of this book.

For Robert Alter,[249] the Bible (to both of these scholars, "the Bible" means what Christians call the Old Testament) is a mix of fiction and history, with the parts set in earlier times more like historicized fiction, and the parts covering relatively recent periods more like fictionalized history.

> Under scrutiny, biblical narrative generally proves to be either fiction laying claim to a place in the chain of causation and the realm of moral consequentiality that belong to history, as in the primeval history, the tales of the Patriarchs, and much of the Exodus story, and the account of the early conquest, or history given the imaginative definition of fiction, as in most of the narratives from the period of the Judges onward.[250]

How does one know that biblical narrative is fiction? For Alter, one indicator is the fact that the authors write as though they know things no historian could know:

> What a close reading of the text does suggest ... is that the writer could manipulate his inherited materials with sufficient freedom and sufficient firmness of authorial purpose to define motives, relations, and unfolding themes, even in a primeval history, with the kind of subtle cogency we associate with the conscious artistry of the narrative mode designated prose fiction.[251]

Narratives set in more recent times do the same thing with a slightly more historical base. King David did exist, says Alter, but no historian would know what the author of the David stories purports to know:

> . . . these stories are not, strictly speaking, historiography, but rather the imaginative reenactment of history by a gifted writer . . .

---

[249] Robert Alter, *The Art of Biblical Narrative* (San Francisco: Basic, 1981).
[250] Ibid., 32-33.
[251] Ibid., 32.

> He feels entirely free … to invent interior monologue for his characters; to ascribe feeling, intention, or motive to them when he chooses; to supply verbatim dialogue (and he is one of literature's masters of dialogue) for occasions when no one but the actors themselves could have had knowledge of exactly what was said.[252]

> Biblical narrative in fact offers a particularly instructive instance of the birth of fiction because it often exhibits the most arresting transitions from generalized statement, genealogical lists, mere summaries of character and acts, to defined scene and concrete interaction between personages. Through the sudden specifications of narrative detail and the invention of dialogue that individualizes the characters and focuses their relations, the biblical writers give the events they report a fictional time and place.[253]

The biblical author is thus neither more nor less a historian than Shakespeare:

> The author of the David stories stands in basically the same relation to Israelite history as Shakespeare stands to English history in his history plays. Shakespeare was obviously not free to have Henry V lose the battle of Agincourt, or to allow someone else to lead the English forces there, but, working from the hints of historical tradition, he could invent a kind of Bildungsroman for the young prince Hal; surround him with invented characters that would serve as foils, mirrors, obstacles, aids in his development; create a language and a psychology for the king which are the writer's own achievement, making out of the stuff of history a powerful projection of human possibility. That is essentially what the author of the David cycle does for David, Saul, Abner, Joab,

---

[252] Ibid., 35.
[253] Ibid., 42.

Jonathan, Absalom, Michal, Abigail, and a host of other characters.[254]

Everything Alter says fits the facts we know about the biblical narratives, and it is not difficult to see that everything he says about Old Testament historiography applies equally to the gospels.

However, Meir Sternberg[255] has what he thinks is a radically different viewpoint. He argues that in fact there is no fiction at all in biblical historical narrative. That doesn't mean he thinks it is all factually accurate. No "historical" work is completely accurate, and no "fictional" work is completely imaginary. Sternberg asserts that you label a literary work's genre based on what the author's intention is, not on its degree of accuracy. History is "a discourse that claims to be a record of fact." Fiction is "a discourse that claims freedom of invention."

> . . . what makes fictional and breaks historical writing is not the presence of invented material — inevitable in both — but the privilege and at will the flaunting of free invention.[256]

Thus, even if the account of David is shown to be a product of the author's imagination, that does not affect its genre; it may still be nonfiction. Indeed, in the case of the Bible, the authors by no means intended the narrative to be read as fiction:

> Were the narrative written or read as fiction, then God would turn from the lord of history into a creature of the imagination, with the most disastrous results. The shape of time, the rationale of monotheism, the foundations of conduct, the national sense of

---

[254] Ibid., 35-36.
[255] Meir Sternberg, *The Poetics of Biblical Narrative: Ideological Literature and the Drama of Reading* (Bloomington: Indiana UP, 1987).
[256] Ibid., 29.

identity, the very right to the land of Israel and the hope of deliverance to come: all hang in the generic balance. . . . [The Bible] claims not just the status of history but, as Erich Auerbach rightly maintains, of the history — the one and only truth that, like God himself, brooks no rival.[257]

Suppose, Sternberg wonders, someone were to tell the biblical narrator that the Babylonians have a different story that's just as valid. The response is easy to guess:

> Would the biblical narrator just shrug his shoulders, as any self-respecting novelist would do? ... This way madness lies — and I mean interpretive, teleological, as well as theological madness.[258]

In other words, the biblical author did not intend the text to be received as fiction. As for Alter's assertion that the omniscience of the biblical narrator is a mark of fiction, Sternberg counters that the claim of inspiration explains this feature of the narrative:

> . . . the narrator's claim to omniscience dovetails rather than conflicts with his claim to historicity. It is no accident that the narrative books from Joshua to Kings fall under the rubric of Former Prophets. ... But if as seekers for the truth, professional or amateur, we can take or leave the truth claim of inspiration, then as readers we simply must take it — just like any other biblical premise or convention, from the existence of God to the sense borne by specific words — or else invent our own text. And to take it means to read the Bible on its own historiographic terms, suspending all the 'how do you know?' questions one would automatically address to a historical narrative playing by documentary rules.[259]

---

[257] Ibid., 32.
[258] Ibid., 32.
[259] Ibid., 33-34.

Yes, of course, agrees Sternberg, there is made-up stuff in the Bible, but that does not mean it's fiction or that the writers were deceivers. The Bible comes from an ancient world where different conventions ruled.

> But if it is convention that renders Jane Austen immune from all charges of fallacy and falsity, it is convention that likewise puts the Bible's art of narrative beyond their reach. . . . Herein lies one of the Bible's unique rules: under the aegis of ideology, convention transmutes even invention into the stuff of history, or rather obliterates the line dividing fact from fancy in communication. So every word is God's word. The product is neither fiction nor historicized fiction nor fictionalized history, but historiography pure and uncompromising.[260]

Therefore, Alter's use of the word "fiction" is simply wrong, dead wrong.

> . . . it is doubly surprising to find him in the camp of fiction. This line having once been adopted, however, it is not at all surprising that he comes to grief. The case has never been stated so well, and the parts abound in shrewd observation, but the whole suffers from the same fatal flaw as all the previous arguments for the Bible's fictionality.[261]

Both Alter and Sternberg are brilliant scholars, and neither suffers from the common tendency to religious bias that colors much if not most biblical scholarship. But both have stumbled over the rock of modern generic assumptions, and their attempt to understand an ancient culture ends up in a quibble over the meaning of emotion-charged words.

---

[260] Ibid., 34-35.
[261] Ibid., 24.

Both agree that much of the content of scriptural historiography is, pure and simple, made up, the product of the authors' imagination. Both agree that the authors' intent, however, was to link their message to historical reality. Neither asserts that readers were meant to think of the content of the narrative as just the imaginary world created by a novelist. Essentially the scholars differ only in the language they use.

Alter uses the terms "fiction" and "historiography" with the meanings that they have today – he is classifying "historiography" as a sub-genre of nonfiction. Sternberg uses the same terms but assigns to them the meanings that he imagines they would have had at the time the Bible was written. Of the two approaches, Sternberg's is certainly more artificial since people did not use terms like fiction or nonfiction in the ancient world. What he accomplishes by using them in this artificial manner is to assert what Alter never disputes: the biblical writers intended to write an absolutely authoritative narrative, unlike modern fiction which the reader can take or leave as one likes. Both agree that in writing this authoritative narrative that purports to present history, the authors felt under little constraint to "stick to the facts."

History versus Myth in Scriptural Historiography

The Alter versus Sternberg impasse is resolved by recognizing that "scriptural historiography" is a genre of ancient literature that simply does not fit in the present-day generic system of "fiction" and "nonfiction." Calling the genre of biblical narrative "historical narrative" or "historiography" creates similar problems. Here again, reviewing some of the debates among scholars can help clarify not only the terminology but the character of the Old Testament genre.

K. L. Noll can serve as an example of one who refuses to apply the word "history" to biblical narrative because of what the word implies in modern culture, like Sternberg rejecting the word "fiction" for similar reasons. Noll correctly observes that the word "history" carries different connotations in ancient cultures than it does in our own:

> In common modern parlance (whether we like it or not), a "history" is a factual account and balanced interpretation of real events, a definition that will apply to very few ancient narratives. (Not even every passage in Thucydides will pass muster.)[262]

For some scholars, the Torah is the prime example of scriptural historiography par excellence,[263] but for Noll it is not historiography at all because it was not written in order to accurately represent the past:

> The narrative [of Deuteronomy] is a deliberate lie cleverly rationalized (and sometimes even willfully believed), a strategy especially motivated by the need for a past that fits present formulations of identity. Occasionally, the narrative goes beyond this to a full-fledged myth, a religiously constructed moral universe that parallels and replaces the mundane physical universe.[264]

For Noll, this contravenes the generic standards of what we today call historiography so drastically that we should not use the word to describe the biblical narrative: "To call a biblical narrative a history or historiography is to say nothing useful at all, because it implies nothing with respect to the text's function

---

[262] Noll, "Evolution of Genre," 32.
[263] John Van Seters, "The Pentateuch as Torah and History: In Defense of G. Von Rad," in Erhard Blum et al., eds., *Das Alte Testament: Ein Geschichtsbuch?* (Munich: Lit, 2005), 47-64; here: 51.
[264] Noll, "Evolution of Genre," 31.

in its ancient context."²⁶⁵ Biblical narrative should not even be called "malleable history" as Ehud Ben Zvi does with respect to the narrative about King David:

> Rarely does one encounter a scholar who seems to be aware of the anomaly that is created by positing an ancient scribe who both freely invented details and believed that, by doing so, he was presenting an accurate narrative about the past. . . . Therefore, if the genre is history as Ben Zvi assumes and if these narratives are the product of malleability one reasonable hypothesis would be that the authors were liars who knowingly falsified their account of the past. . . . I can see no alternative, given Ben Zvi's categories, but to conclude that the authors of the Kings account were religious fanatics incapable of distinguishing between fact and fantasy. If that fantasy is intended by its author to be received as an accurate account of a real event, the author is either a liar or delusional.²⁶⁶

The assumption here is that the label "historiography" necessarily assumes an intent to present "an accurate narrative

---

²⁶⁵ Ibid., 32.
²⁶⁶ Noll, "Evolution of Genre," 40-41. Noll wants to avoid calling the scriptural author a liar and finds a way out of this dilemma by arguing that the original intent was not to deceive, but over time the text was understood differently: "What began as self-consciously fictional narrative ended as a tale of origin or, to invoke the most common scholarly label, a *Heilsgeschichte*. This shift in genre was a shift in readers' response to the text, not something intended by the authors of that text, another representative example of the Darwinian process of generic evolution. . . . Since the tale was not circulated, there is no external evidence to indicate how readers received it. In fact, there is no evidence *that* readers received it. (The manuscript may have been preserved unread for several human generations at a time prior to the Hellenistic period.)" (ibid., 46-47) ". . . texts constructed for religious purposes often employ hyperbole without any indication that the text in question attempts to portray the real world. In short, the author of S-C/S-K [Sennacherib story in Chronicles, Sennacherib story in Kings] did not believe his narrative really happened, nor did he expect his reader to believe it, but he probably believed his narrative was true." (ibid., 51) This is also the case with Ps 2: "This is the realm of myth – it is true but not factual." (ibid., 50)

about the past."²⁶⁷ But that attributes to the word a technical meaning it does not necessarily always have even in the modern world. In fact, the word "historiography" does apply well to biblical narrative if a more basic meaning is applied to it, as is done by Eve-Marie Becker: ". . . historiography can be defined as a literary narrativization of at least partially historical material (traditions, motifs, etc.)."²⁶⁸

Baruch Halpern also wants to avoid applying the term "historiography" to biblical narrative, for a slightly different reason: he argues that if we use that term we would have to consider the biblical texts to be either "bad history" or "fraudulent history." He assumes no great difference in the meaning of the word "history" as used today and as used by the ancients:

> But it is a common property of histories throughout the ages that they claim to be true in detail, in specifics – they claim not to contain invented details or events, rather than reconstructed ones, except as metaphorical vehicles for the presentation of the uninvented details. . . . That is, a history lodges claims to trustworthiness – the contrast is to romance, which may sometimes lodge claims to trustworthiness at a moral level, but does so only during the reading at the level of specifics.²⁶⁹

Then and now, a history can fail to live up to the claim to be true in specifics and still be considered a history:

---

[267] Noll states this explicitly in his conclusion: "One text evolved through several species of literary genre. But at no point can this tale be described accurately as a work of history, for the story remembers a war in a radically inaccurate way, *and always was intended to do so*." (author's emphasis; ibid., 56)

[268] Becker, "Gospel of Mark," 127

[269] Baruch Halpern, "Biblical versus Greek Historiography: A Comparison," in Erhard Blum et al., eds., *Das Alte Testament: Ein Geschictsbuch?* (Munich: Lit., 2005), 101-128; here: 102.

Scripture as a Genre 193

There are serviceable histories, average histories, and bad histories. There are even fraudulent histories, whose authors know at some level that they are twisting the evidence from the past ... So, while accuracy is not a defining property of historiography, the reader's assumption that the author was attempting to be accurate is.[270]

By these standards, if biblical narrative is classified as historiography it must be either bad or fraudulent because it doesn't even try to be historically accurate.[271] He avoids that conclusion in part by the expedient of assuming that wherever authors wrote imaginary content into apparently historical texts, they weren't intending their texts to be received as history; they intended to write a different genre, such as poetry or "romance" (which for Halpern essentially means fiction). As examples of narratives that were written as romance and mistakenly read as history, he cites the book of Jonah and the Yahwist narrative:[272]

> Likewise, the J source seems to transpose into a vertical, or historical, dimension the relations among Israel sections (or, tribes), or among a larger group of populations with which its author was familiar, at least at second hand. Thus, it expresses certain relationships among Aramean peoples in terms of a network of eponymic kinship relations. In this respect, it is poetic rather than prosaic, analogical rather than historical. Later, it was

---

[270] Ibid., 103.

[271] It is a common thing, of course, not to want to label scripture as fraudulent, but it often ends up leading to theories that are strained at best. Adela Yarbro Collins, for example, accepts Mark's gospel as history but asserts that it's not fraudulent because Mark believed the miracle stories (*Is Mark's Gospel a Life of Jesus*, 45). This approach to solving the problem assumes that only miracles are ahistorical and discounts the possibility of the kind of authorial freedom that we know pervades biblical narrative. Later I will point out other ways to deal with this conundrum.

[272] The Yahist narrative is also called the J source and is one of several postulated sources that together became the books of Genesis through Kings in the Old Testament. Another of these sources is the P (Priestly) source.

taken to be historical, even by the redactor responsible for the combined text. That it originated as historiography, however, seems improbable.²⁷³

He offers no evidence to back up his assertion that it "seems improbable" the author intended the text to be received as historiography. One might reasonably suppose that things seem this way because for Halpern the only alternative is to accuse the scriptural author of perpetrating a fraud.

Another way Halpern exculpates the author of a narrative that would otherwise have to be considered fraudulent is to assume that the author was writing for an "insider" audience, and only "outsiders" were deceived:

> [The priestly source] P certainly represents a revisionist historical reconstruction, whether the vehicle of its presentation is history or romance. And it presents itself as authoritative about details in the past. So it may in places be regarded as a piece of bad or even fraudulent historiography, like Deuteronomy. More likely, however, its author will have argued to colleagues that the narrative was roughly, rather than specifically, accurate. The insider audience (see below) will not have taken it to be historiographic.²⁷⁴

The "insiders" in this conjectural scenario correspond to what in New Testament days one might refer to as the church leadership:

---

²⁷³ Ibid., 105. The same reasoning is applied to the Priestly source. Before introducing the outsider/insider dichotomy that I discuss next, Halpern writes: "Most of all, P is more a vehicle for delivering a corpus of law and doctrine than it is a work evincing serious antiquarian interest. So, assuming that the author himself invented some of the variants, the work is at best more historical romance than history, more a docudrama than a documentary."
²⁷⁴ Ibid., 108.

The insider audience hangs together in the Near East, and despite internal dissent presents a common face to the outsider audience. These are thus a canon elite, a group of people who mediate the interpretation of official texts to others, and who do so as a group. This is the basis on which Judaism, and Catholicism thereafter, became religions of tradition, rather than of individual reflection on the text.[275]

For the culture and age in which scripture was written, when few were literate and most depended on hearing scriptural texts read to them in a community gathering, such a conjecture carries a good deal of verisimilitude.[276] However, it skirts the issue insofar as the author and his insider audience are already in agreement and there is no need to write for the insiders. Halpern's own analogy to explain the insider versus outsider distinction makes this clear:

> The whole exercise was not very different from the formulation of government or other political press releases today, and the outsider audience was not very different from uncritical journalists who parrot government releases in the press.[277]

Government press releases are not written to influence the government insiders; if there were only insiders there would be no need for slanted press releases. Likewise, the scriptural author and his insider collaborators are writing for the "outsiders" in the sense of the entire religious community other than themselves. The purpose is to influence the behavior of the community, and

---

[275] Ibid., 113.
[276] See Gamble on literacy rates among early Christians. He notes that ". . . throughout the early centuries of the church only a small minority of Christians who were not clerics were literate." (*Books and Readers*, 10) and observes that ". . . it is difficult to imagine any Christian community where either no one could read or *no authority accrued to those who could*." (emphasis added; ibid., 9)
[277] Halpern, "Biblical versus Greek Historiography," 112.

thus it is really the "outsiders" *within the community* who are the intended audience. Therefore asserting that the "fraudulent" adjective does not apply because insiders knew what the author was doing is misleading and misrepresents what the authors were doing.

It is evident then, that there are some pitfalls to labeling the gospels' genre as "historiography." However, the phrase "scriptural historiography" indicates a very specific kind of historiography. The author's goal is not to present an accurate record of the past, and the reader's goal is not to learn an accurate record of the past. The author's goal in scripture is to influence the community. An audience that receives scripture as it was intended would be influenced by it, would internalize the author's vision of the past without trying to find – or without being influenced differently by – an alternative "accurate" vision of the past. The search for an "accurate" version of the past involves a completely different approach to the text than the conventions of the scriptural genre expect. Scriptural narratives are not written with intent to satisfy the reader's curiosity. This is why Halpern's concerns are misplaced and why Meir Sternberg can say that, "if it is convention that renders Jane Austen immune from all charges of fallacy and falsity, it is convention that likewise puts the Bible's art of narrative beyond their reach."[278] The purpose of scriptural historiography is well described by John Van Seters' remarks about the Deuteronomic historian:

> The past was used in many different ways and by means of many distinct forms to exercise an authority over institutions, customs, rights, and behavior. An expansive portrayal of the past, however, could embody the explanation and the legitimation of all of these

---

[278] Sternberg, *Poetics of Biblical Narrative*, 34.

in one complex genre. The prestige of a dynasty, the primacy of a temple and its priesthood, the question of territorial rights and boundaries, civil and religious laws – all could be integrated and supported by one 'history,' instead of using a variety of forms, such as king lists, temple legends, priestly genealogies, treaty 'histories,' and law codes. The genius of the Dtr [Deuteronomic] history is that it attempted such a wide-ranging integration of forms in order to set forth within one work the whole foundation of Israelite society.[279]

Scriptural historiography, then, is not quite like modern historiography, modern fiction, or modern non-fiction. Nor can it be equated with what moderns call "myth" although its purpose may be to do what myth is said to do: construct a moral universe. Unlike myth, the moral universe of scriptural historiography is anchored in historical reality: the word "myth" might apply to the book of Job, but it is misleading if applied to the historical narratives of the Torah and the Former Prophets.

Within the historical sections of the Old Testament, the Court History of King David in 2 Samuel is often celebrated as one of the finest instances of historiography from the ancient world. But upon closer examination, Van Seters determined that it was almost entirely composed from scratch centuries after the fact in the Persian era.[280] The author of that history was constrained by the name "David," but that might be the only thing in the narrative that anchors it to historical reality in the modern sense of historical reality.[281] Earlier biblical scholars who attributed

---

[279] John Van Seters, *In Search of History: Historiography in the Ancient World and the Origins of Biblical History* (New Haven: Yale UP, 1983), 357.
[280] John Van Seters, "Uses of the Past: The Story of David as a Test Case," in Kirkpatrick and Goltz, *Function of Ancient Historiography*, 18-29; here: 29.
[281] Another example is the story of Hezekiah and Sennacherib, in which the author was apparently constrained only by the names of the two kings and the fact that there was

historical reality to this narrative essentially found what they wanted to find:

> What must be avoided at all cost in such discussion is the danger of anachronism; for instance, the notion that ancient scribes could engage in archival research and retrieve ancient documents for their historical accounts, or that copious records were meticulously kept by scribes for future use by historians. Such notions about annals and official records stored in palace and temple archives were introduced into biblical studies in the seventeenth century for apologetic purposes and have persisted ever since.[282]

Van Seters concludes that the narrative "is a pseudo-history of David with a strong moral and political purpose, to discredit the institution of the monarchy and any messianic hope for the future."[283] This example illustrates the main points about scriptural historiography: the narrative is anchored to known historical facts, it is written to achieve a practical political or religious purpose, and in the furtherance of that purpose the author is free to invent whatever does not unreasonably transgress the bounds of plausibility.

Actually, the author of scriptural historiography is not just free to invent, he is compelled to invent whatever is necessary to achieve his purpose. He is not constrained by what can be established reliably or even by what he knows to be factually true. He is constrained by the necessity to get his message across to his readers without presenting to them something they would

---

a military campaign. See Ehud Ben Zvi, "Malleability and its Limits: Sennacherib's Campaign against Judah as a Case Study," in Lester L. Grabbe, ed., *"Like a bird in a cage": The Invasion of Sennacherib in 701 BCE* (Continuum International Publishing Group, 2003), 73-105.

[282] Van Seters, "Uses of the Past," 18. What happened with oral tradition theory and the New Testament is somewhat similar to this process.

[283] Ibid., 29.

recognize as patently false. Thus, in scriptural historiography, the veneer of historicity in the modern sense of that word may be exceedingly thin, and historical facts may be – must be – misrepresented if that is what it takes to get the intended message across.[284]

---

[284] This can be seen in the gospels, for example, by observing how stories adopted from Mark by later evangelists are manipulated to suit the purposes of the new situation in which the later evangelists were writing.

11
Mark as Scriptural Historiography

If, then, Mark and the other gospels were written and published with intent to function as scriptural historiography, we should not expect historical accuracy in details to have been particularly high on the evangelists' list of literary goals. Yet that is precisely what most scholars who study the gospels do assume, and such assumptions have a profound effect on which interpretations of the gospels gain broad acceptance in biblical scholarship.

The literary relationship between Mark and Paul's epistles that I have documented in Part 2 of this book, is but one example of relatively new approaches to intertextuality[285] in the gospels which have faced an uphill battle for acceptance partly because of unrealistic generic expectations. Traditionally, research on relationships between texts focused on a limited number of ways in which an author used earlier texts in the composition of a new one. These ways were typically categorized into a hierarchy consisting of quotations, allusions, and echoes. The first two terms mean for scholars what they do for everyone else: a quotation is a more or less word-for-word replication or paraphrase of part of an earlier text in a later text, while an allusion involves just enough similarity in wording or theme to show that the author of the later text meant to evoke part of an earlier text in the reader's mind. An "echo" is essentially a harder-to-identify form of allusion; the similarity between the

---

[285] At the end of this chapter I will discuss ways in which this word applies more broadly to my analysis of Mark than it does in many recent books about New Testament literary relationships.

earlier and the later text might be enough to imply that the author of the later text was familiar with the earlier one, but not enough to reliably indicate a conscious intention to evoke the earlier one.[286] More recently, the approach to intertextual relationships in the gospels has expanded dramatically in scope, with some scholars discovering patterns in all four gospels similar to what I am finding in Mark: whole episodes and major features of their overall literary structure were inspired by Old Testament texts, the Pauline epistles, and extra-biblical literature.

Among the pioneers in this relatively new approach to intertextuality in the gospels, sometimes called mimesis or narrative intertextuality, are Thomas Brodie, Dennis MacDonald, and Michael Goulder.[287] Brodie characterizes this

---

[286] "Intertextual echo" has been proposed as an umbrella term for all of these kinds of intertextual relationships. See Moyise, "Intertextuality," 419.
[287] See Thomas L. Brodie, *The Quest for the Origin of John's Gospel: A Source-Oriented Approach* (New York: Oxford UP, 1993); *The Crucial Bridge: The Elijah-Elisha Narrative as an Interpretive Synthesis of Genesis-Kings and a Literary Model for the Gospels* (Collegeville, Minn.: Liturgical Press, 2000); *The Birthing of the New Testament: The Intertextual Development of the New Testament Writings* (Sheffield: Sheffield Academic Press, 2004); *Proto-Luke: The Oldest Gospel Account: A Christ-Centered Synthesis of Old Testament History Modeled Especially on the Elijah-Elisha Narrative: Introduction, Text, and Old Testament Model* (Limerick: Dominican Biblical Institute, 2006); Brodie, MacDonald, Porter, *The Intertextuality of the Epistles*; MacDonald, *Homeric Epics*; Dennis R. MacDonald, ed., *Mimesis and Intertextuality in Antiquity and Christianity* (Harrisburg, Penn.: Trinity Press International., 2001); Dennis R MacDonald, *Does the New Testament Imitate Homer. Four Cases From the Acts of the Apostles* (New Haven, Conn.: Yale UP, 2003); Dennis R MacDonald, "My Turn"; Michael D. Goulder, *Luke: A New Paradigm* (Sheffield: Sheffield Academic Press, 1989); *St. Paul vs. St. Peter: A Tale of Two Missions* (Westminster John Knox Press, 1994); *Five Stones and a Sling: Memoirs of a Biblical Scholar* (Sheffield Phoenix Press Ltd., 2009).

kind of relationship by citing one of the most well-known intertextual relationships in the world of ancient literature:

> . . . the kernel of ancient writing was not in allusions; it was in taking hold of entire books and transforming them systematically. Virgil did not just *allude* to Homer; he swallowed him whole.[288]

Brodie observes that the case of the Aeneid mimicking the Odyssey was not an isolated example; the bulk of Roman literature was built upon Greek literature; within the Old Testament the books of Chronicles rework the material in Genesis through Kings; and within the New Testament each gospel reworks the contents of earlier gospels.[289] An author who was building upon or imitating earlier literature would not always do so in a way that would be easily recognizable today, that is, by borrowing words, phrases, or sentences. As MacDonald observes,

> Because imitative strategies in antiquity were protean, they resist tidy taxonomies and defy detection. Authors felt free to borrow whatever they wished from any models whatever and to transform what they borrowed as they saw fit.[290]
>
> In ancient narratives such imitations usually obtain to characterizations, motifs, and plot—seldom to wording."[291]

---

[288] Brodie, *Birthing of the New Testament*, 74. For details on the results of, and evidence for, this "swallowing whole" process, see Adam Winn, *Mark and the Elijah-Elisha Narrative: Considering the Practice of Greco-Roman Imitation in the Search for Markan Source Material* (Eugene, Ore.: Pickwick, 2010), chapter 1.

[289] See the lists of precedents in Thomas L. Brodie, "Towards Tracing the Gospels' Literary Indebtedness to the Epistles," in MacDonald, *Mimesis*, 104-116 (here: 107) and Brodie, *Birthing*, 23ff.

[290] MacDonald, *Homeric Epics*, 172.

[291] MacDonald, "My Turn," 1. A few of the typical patterns include elaboration (taking an idea from the source text and expanding on it); compression or synthesis

In fact, it is easier to define mimesis by what it is not than by how it is done:

> Simply stated, a mimesis critic assesses a text for literary influences that one might classify as imitations instead of citations, paraphrases, allusions, echoes, or redactions.[292]

Identifying such imitations is often difficult and requires a different methodology from the focus on wording similarity typically employed for the traditional approach to intertextual relationships. To use the Odyssey and the Aeneid again as an example, one cannot read portions of them and find direct allusions in the latter to the former; by reading the whole of both of them one can recognize that the latter was inspired by the former, but *proving* that would be a difficult enterprise indeed.

Nevertheless, several scholars have proposed objective criteria that might help in identifying instances of mimesis. Their approaches vary but boil down to an attempt to establish three things: availability, similarity, and intelligibility.[293]

(taking a section of the source text and shortening or altering it); fusion or conflation (combining elements from multiple sections of the source text into a different context); substitution of images (using different images or metaphors to express the same idea expressed in the source text); positivization (repeating a theme that the source text treats negatively but giving it a positive spin, or vice versa); internalization (change what is expressed as an external reality into an internal feeling or attitude); and form change (take content from one literary form such as an epistle, and express the same ideas in a new form such as historiography). This list is from Brodie, *Birthing*, 10-12. See also the longer list and survey of other scholars' lists in Brodie, *Intertextuality*, 288-292.

[292] MacDonald, "My Turn," 1.

[293] See Dennis R. MacDonald, "A Categorization of Antetextuality in the Gospels and Acts: A Case for Luke's Imitation of Plato and Xenophon to depict Paul as a Christian Socrates," in Brodie, *Intertextuality*, 211-25.

Establishing availability verifies that mimesis is plausible by showing the historical likelihood that the source text was available to the author who wrote the postulated imitation text. Plausibility is strengthened if it can be shown that other authors, ideally contemporaries of the one in question, also borrowed from the same source text.

Establishing similarity is the crux of the matter, of course, and no formula can guarantee success in this endeavor. The best that can be done here is to create a way to roughly gauge varying degrees of similarity. Thus, Dennis MacDonald cites the importance of determining the density and order of parallels between a text and its postulated source, with extra weight applying to distinctive traits. In other words, a large number of parallels (greater density) between two texts is more significant than one or two would be. A sequence of parallels that happens in the same order in both texts increases the probability that the source text was used. And if any given parallel with a source text involves textual characteristics that are so unique or distinctive as to rarely be found elsewhere, that can carry substantial weight by itself.

Establishing intelligibility is the final test: does it make sense that the author in question would borrow from the source text, and does his use of the source text make sense in the context of what we know he is trying to accomplish in his own text?

As an example of how the methodology works, consider Dennis MacDonald's proposal to view the transfiguration

---

212; MacDonald, *Homeric Epics*, 172ff.; Stanley E. Porter, "Further Comments on the Use of the Old Testament in the New Testament," in Brodie, *Intertextuality*, 98-110 (here: 103); Brodie, *Birthing*, 44-46; Brodie, *Intertextuality*, 292.

episode in Mark as an imitation of a transfiguration episode in the Odyssey. Availability is readily established. The Homeric epics were not only widely known in the ancient world, they were universally used in ancient Greek education, and consequently they were also widely used as literary examples to be followed. Similarity is also readily established, as the parallels to Mark are dense:

> The combination of motifs in Odyssey 16.172-303 and Mark 9:2-10 are too close to be accidental. In both a god transforms the hero into glory befitting a deity, including the transformation of clothing: a 'well-washed cloak' and 'clothes ... dazzling white, such as no fuller on earth could bleach them.' The transformation produces terror and the offering of gifts in order to appease the one who was transformed. The gifts offered in both accounts were refused, the recipients of both transfigurations were scolded for making mortals divine, and the heroes in both accounts insist on total secrecy.[294]

As for intelligibility, MacDonald argues that the Homeric "transfiguration" scene plays a role in a secrecy-revelation theme in the Odyssey just as the Markan transfiguration scene plays a role in Mark's "Messianic secret" theme.

The nature of the evidence does not permit certainty even where the methodology can be applied very effectively, as it can be in this example. On the other hand, the practice of mimesis was so widespread that it should not be ruled out when the evidence is weak. The infinitely varied patterns of mimesis "resist tidy taxonomies and defy detection," and it is quite possible that

---

[294] Dennis R MacDonald, "Secrecy and Recognitions in the Odyssey and Mark: Where Wrede Went Wrong," in Ronald F. Hock, et al., eds., *Ancient Fiction and Early Christian Narrative* (Atlanta: Scholars Press, 1998), 139-153; here: 152.

that mimesis did happen even where it is difficult or impossible to apply the established criteria.

Mimesis in Mark

In books published in 2000 and 2004,[295] Thomas Brodie presents his thesis that the main narrative model for Mark is the cycle of Elijah-Elisha stories in 1 Kings 17 through 2 Kings 13. Among the evidence he cites: parallels at the beginning, middle, and end of the two narratives; similar overall length; similar narrative character of short episodes at the start spiraling into longer ones later in the narrative; similar abrupt and enigmatic endings; and similar motifs, such as juxtaposition of north and south geographical references with symbolic meanings. He also finds parallel episodes, such as the healing of a leper which recalls the healing of the leper Naaman in 2 Kings 5 and the multiplication of loaves which recalls 2 Kings 4:42-44.[296]

More recently, others have developed this thesis at greater length: Wolfgang Roth in *Hebrew Gospel: Cracking the Code of Mark* (2009)[297] and Adam Winn in *Mark and the Elijah-Elisha Narrative* (2010).[298] Roth identifies John the Baptist and Jesus with Elijah and Elisha. Winn points out that the Elijah-Elisha

---

[295] *Crucial Bridge* and *Birthing*.
[296] Brodie, *Crucial Bridge*, 88ff. See also *Birthing*, 154-188, in which Brodie suggests that Mark used an early version of Luke that was modeled on the Elijah-Elisha narrative. He presents that thesis in a concise manner along with the proposed text of proto-Luke in *Proto-Luke: The Oldest Gospel Account: A Christ-Centered Synthesis of Old Testament History Modelled Especially on the Elijah-Elisha Narrative: Introduction, Text, and Old Testament Model* (Limerick: Dominican Biblical Institute, 2006).
[297] Wolfgang Roth, *Hebrew Gospel: Cracking the Code of Mark* (Wipf & Stock Publishers, 2009).
[298] Adam Winn, *Mark and the Elijah-Elisha Narrative: Considering the Practice of Greco-Roman Imitation in the Search for Markan Source Material* (Eugene, Ore.: Pickwick, 2010).

cycle is unique in the Old Testament in its density of miracle stories, which corresponds to what we find in Mark. In addition to the Elijah-Elisha parallels that Brodie cited for the healing of the leper in Mark 1:40-45 and the multiplication of loaves episodes, Winn finds a parallel between Jesus' journey to the Gentile areas of Tyre and Sidon (Mark 7:24-30) and 1 Kings 17:7-6, in which the Lord sends Elijah to Zarephath.[299]

What none of these authors have done, however, is advance a plausible reason for why Mark chose to model his Jesus narrative after the Elijah–Elisha narrative cycle. Thus, a reviewer of Winn's book laments:

> Finally, what is the purpose of the imitation? Winn does not say. Through this omission, the work proves ultimately unsatisfying, since the author refuses to deal with the issue of the significance of Mark's literary dependence upon the Elijah–Elisha cycle (60). However, the reader surely benefits from a review of the important interconnections between these two sections of scripture as well as through his critique of other works that consider Markan imitation.[300]

The interpretation of Mark's literary purpose that I have presented in this book solves this conundrum. In the Old Testament, Elijah and Elisha are the prophets that are sent outside Israel to minister to Gentiles: that narrative cycle was made to order for a narrative that would defend and promote

---

[299] Others have also noticed individual plot elements that may have come from the Elijah-Elisha cycle, such as the "withered hand" which appears in 1 Kings 13:4 and Mark 3:1-5. See K. Hanhart, "Son, Your Sins are Forgiven," in Frans Van Segbroeck, et al., eds., *The Four Gospels 1992: Festschrift Frans Neirynck* (Leuven: Leuven University Press, 1992), 997-1016; here: 1003.

[300] Dean Deppe, book review in *Review of Biblical Literature*, online: http://bookreviews.org/pdf/8056_8809.pdf.

Mark as Scriptural Historiography

Paul's Gentile mission.[301] Roth's interpretation of John the Baptist as corresponding to Elijah and Jesus as corresponding to Elisha also fits perfectly insofar as Elijah was in effect a forerunner to Elisha, who then completed the work begun by Elijah.[302]

Tarazi points out broader or more basic parallels between how the message and symbolism of the Old Testament deals with Gentiles or outsiders and how the message and symbolism of Mark takes on the same theme. An example is in the prologue to the centerpiece of Mark's narrative prior to the passion. A literal rendering of the Greek helps make this apparent:

> Again he began to teach beside the sea. And a very large crowd gathered toward (πρὸς) him, so that he got into a boat and sat in the sea (καθῆσθαι ἐν τῇ θαλάσσῃ); and the whole crowd was toward (πρὸς) the sea on the land. And he taught them many things in parables, and in his teaching he said to them . . . (Mark 4:1-2)

Tarazi asserts that the symbolism here sets the stage for a teaching that supports the Gentile mission, insofar as the Sea of Galilee represents the Mediterranean Sea, or the center of the Roman Empire at large:

> We have seen this terminology before (2:13; 3:23; 3:9), but this time Jesus sits in the sea and the people on the land turn toward him. That is to say, Jesus' new center from which he teaches his entire Messianic community has moved out of Jerusalem and into

---

[301] My thanks to Paul Tarazi for pointing this out to me. Once it is proposed it seems obvious, but until then it easily escapes notice.

[302] Winn objects that he sees some correspondences between Jesus and Elijah, but as Brodie and MacDonald have shown, no ancient author would feel constrained to always use the same literary model for any given character in a narrative. The pattern in this case is what matters.

the Roman empire at large; it is from there, and not Jerusalem that his teaching (4:2), which carries divine authority, originates. But this is just a new example of the New Testament following the pattern and example set by the Old: it was from the wilderness of Sinai that God's word in the *torah* was carried into Canaan, and it was from the foreign land of Babylonia that God's prophetic word was addressed to Jerusalem.[303]

Thus, Mark uses mimesis of Old Testament texts on many levels in support of Paul's Gentile mission.

At first glance, this picture is complicated by Dennis MacDonald's thesis that much if not most the Gospel of Mark is an artfully crafted reformulation of characters and themes from the Homeric epics:

> Mark seems to have borrowed from Homer the motifs of disguise, testing, signs, recognitions, disclosure, and silence, and, as in the Odyssey, the use of these motifs permits situational irony in which the reader, knowing the identity of the stranger, enjoys the narrative at a level inaccessible to the characters themselves.[304]

MacDonald's evidence fits the criteria for mimesis remarkably well. The Homeric epics were widely available and widely copied, the density of the parallels is often striking, and Mark's purposes in reworking Homeric material are intelligible.

It is not necessary to choose between Elijah-Elisha and Homeric epic as sources for Mark; in some cases, the evangelist may have drawn on both. From the fact that the multiplication of loaves episodes resemble both 2 Kings 4 and the feast of Nestor for 4,500 men at the shore of Pylos, MacDonald

---

[303] Tarazi, *Paul and Mark*, 157.
[304] The most complete exposition of this theory is in MacDonald, *Homeric Epics*. This summary statement is from MacDonald, "Secrecy," 153.

concludes that, "Like many ancient narratives, the earliest gospel was eclectic in its dependence on literary models; Mark was an equal-opportunity imitator. Nonetheless, the bulk of the narrative issues from emulation of Greek epic."[305]

As an "equal-opportunity imitator," Mark also had available to him another body of scripture to draw upon as his source: Paul's epistles. In Part II, I presented many instances of similarity and intelligibility. Other scholars have already made the case for availability, and Thomas Brodie summarizes a simple common-sense approach to this matter:

> It is a commonplace of New Testament research that many of the epistles were written almost a generation before the Gospels and Acts. It is a further commonplace that within the Roman Empire communications were good. If the evangelists were interested in gaining copies of some epistles they had ample time to do so. In fact, it is difficult to imagine a credible scenario in which no evangelist ever had access to a copy of an epistle.[306]

Those who doubt that Mark knew the epistles generally assume that various individual New Testament books or groups of books were produced by separate theological "schools." The only evidence for this is in apparent disagreements between the New Testament writings. But such evidence is inconclusive:

---

[305] MacDonald, *Homeric Epics*, 177-178, 189.
[306] Brodie, *Intertextuality*, 87. See also Brodie, "Towards Tracing the Gospels' Literary Indebtedness to the Epistles," in MacDonald, *Mimesis*, 104-116 (here: 108-109, 116); Brodie, *Birthing*, 21, 75, 132-146; Kealy, *History*, 2: 2: 404. Even Romaniuk, acknowledges the possibility ("Le Probléme des Paulinismes," 271). Not everyone agrees, of course; Bart Ehrman asserts that "There is little to suggest that the anonymous author of Mark's Gospel had actually read the writings of the apostle Paul . . . " (*God's Problem. How the Bible Fails to Answer Our Most Important Question – Why We Suffer* (New York: HarperOne, 2008), 86.

disagreements can exist within one school or group as well as between schools.

In the case of Mark versus Paul, any disagreements are relatively trivial while the agreements are fundamental. As Joel Marcus asserts, "Claiming that Mark is a Paulinist does not require that he agree with Paul about everything . . ."[307] Although this may seem to be self-evident, Martin Werner's entire book *Der Einfluss paulinischer Theologie im Markusevangelium* – which continues to be regarded by many as proof of Mark's anti-Pauline status – revolves around the assumption that anything less than complete agreement makes Mark non-Pauline.

For example, Werner cites vocabulary statistics to show Mark's language is not Pauline. The implicit assumption is that a disciple of Paul would necessarily write with the same vocabulary. But in fact, a disciple of Paul might have grown up in a different environment and have a different literary style, or adopt a different style for a different literary genre. And in many cases of direct borrowing Mark does use Pauline vocabulary that Werner missed.[308]

Werner also cites instances where Mark doesn't mention something from the epistles, such as Mark's omission of a reference to the non-divine source of the Law, which Paul asserts in Galatians 3:17.[309] The implicit assumption is that if Mark were a disciple of Paul he would carefully make sure he did not omit any detail from any Pauline epistle when writing his

---

[307] Marcus, "Mark," 473. He develops this further in 476-8.
[308] See chapter 8. See also Boismard and Benoit, *Synopse*, 24 and Tarazi, *Paul and Mark*, 111-236.
[309] Werner, *Der Einfluss*, 84, 203-9.

Gospel. But in fact, Mark will have borrowed only what he needed to accomplish his purpose and was under no compunction to take every little detail from every Pauline epistle.[310]

Moreover, even if it were possible to reliably establish the existence of independent schools, that would not mean such schools were unaware of writings produced by the others. The belief in an early Christianity separated into multiple hermetically sealed units that were unaware of what the others were doing does not fit what we know about travel and communication in Greco-Roman society in this period. Richard Bauckham and Michael Thompson have presented convincing arguments against the belief that early Christians lived in such hermetically sealed communities.[311]

All of the evidence that points to Mark's use of other texts to provide ideas for the creation of details in his own text makes sense when one sees Mark as an instance of scriptural historiography. Mark's approach to crafting an ostensibly historical story is similar to the approach taken by the author of the Court History of King David. In other words, judging from Mark's use of several sources including the Elijah-Elisha cycle, Homer, and Paul's epistles, Mark may have been in a similar

---

[310] If one were to apply Werner's methodology to a deutero-Pauline epistle, one might conclude that it too is not Pauline. Marcus implicitly chastises scholars who consider Mark to be Pauline but do not address Werner's arguments in detail, but if Werner's basic assumptions are invalid, the time and effort required for detailed refutation is not worthwhile.

[311] See Bauckham, "For Whom Were Gospels Written," in *The Gospels for all Christians: Rethinking the Gospel Audiences* (ed. Richard Bauckham: Grand Rapids: Eerdmans, 1998), 9-48 and Thompson, "The Holy Internet: Communication Between Churches in the First Christian Generation," in Bauckham, *Gospels for all Christians,* 49-70.

situation where he had little actual historical data to go on for creating a historical narrative. He may have had little more actual historical information than the names of some of the primary characters in the story. He used scriptural sources to come up with motifs and a framework for the story that would accomplish his literary purpose. In doing so, he borrowed from what we now call Old Testament scripture, from what we now call New Testament scripture (the epistles), and from what we might call secular Gentile scripture.

Homeric epic was used in Mark's day as a kind of secular scripture, forming the educational framework of his day. Borrowing motifs from Homeric epic was a way to make what Mark was writing more relevant as scripture to his Gentile audience who grew up with Homeric epic as the normative standard of Greek literature. In other words, all of the examples of mimesis in Mark substantiate the conclusion that Mark's genre is best labeled "scriptural historiography" and follows the standards and conventions of that genre as found in the Old Testament.

Mimesis in the Other Gospels

Mark does not stand alone in having been composed in this manner. The other gospels follow the same pattern. The *New Testament Introduction* series by Paul Tarazi is dedicated to showing that not only Mark but also the other three gospels made extensive use of Paul's epistles.[312] Brodie notes that Luke-Acts can be seen as an imitation of the entire Old Testament but finds that it too is more particularly based upon the Elijah-Elisha

---

[312] Vol. 2, Luke and Acts (Crestwood: SVS Press, 2001); vol. 3, *Johannine Writings* (Crestwood, SVS Press, 2004); vol. 4, *Matthew and the Canon* (St. Paul, Minn. OCABS Press, 2009).

cycle of stories. In Luke-Acts this extends to the literary structure: two balancing parts centered on the assumption into heaven of the central character of the first part, a structure unique in all of ancient literature.[313] Brodie also cites a number of specific parallels in Luke-Acts to literary techniques and episodes in the Elijah-Elisha stories, and concludes that "Luke's use of the Elijah-Elisha text is systematic, complete."[314] He goes on to say that the evangelist also used the entire book of Judges, and "As with the Elijah-Elisha narrative, Luke's transformation of Judges is systematic, complete, essentially non-repetitive, and maintaining aspects of the original order."[315] He also details somewhat less extensive use of other sources, such as the books of Chronicles.[316]

One of the best commentaries on Luke to have been written in modern scholarship is the two-volume *Luke: A New Paradigm* by Michael Goulder. One of Goulder's primary goals in the book was to substantiate the theory that Luke employed extensive authorial creativity in his crafting of the story about Jesus. Goulder concludes, for example, that Luke made up virtually all of the narrative in Lk 1:5-2:40, inspired by stories he found in the Torah and the Former Prophets.[317] Some seven years after the book was created, Mark Goodacre published his own critical examination of Goulder's arguments,[318] finding some of them convincing and some less so. What is interesting about this scholarly debate is the starting point that both begin from: they

---

[313] Brodie, *Crucial Bridge*, 83; see also Brodie, *Birthing*, 83-86.
[314] Brodie, *Birthing*, 86.
[315] Ibid., 86.
[316] Ibid., 87.
[317] See Goulder, *Luke*, 289.
[318] Mark S. Goodacre, *Goulder and the Gospels: An Examination of a New Paradigm* (Sheffield: Sheffield Academic Press, 1996).

assume that Luke is "innocent unless proven guilty" of inventing stories for his narrative. However, for a work of scriptural historiography the assumption should be the opposite: Luke should be considered "innocent unless proven guilty" of trying to create a literally accurate history as a modern historian might. In other words, the burden of proof should fall on those who would argue against extensive authorial creativity. If one were to approach the subject from this standpoint, that is, from a realistic assessment of the generic models for Luke, more of Goulder's evidence would have been evaluated positively.

Goulder's arguments for Lucan creativity are largely based on distinctive features of the author's style, and he draws similar conclusions from distinctive features in the other gospels as well. In his memoir *Five Stones and a Sling*, Goulder recalls coming to the realization that each of the synoptic gospels had its own character of parables:

> Mark's parables were mostly agricultural: the Sower, the Seed Growing Secretly, and Mustard Seed. This was rather in line with Old Testament parables, which are said often to be about trees, "from the cedar in Lebanon to the hyssop that grows out of the wall." Matthew's parables are about people, mostly kings or wealthy merchants. Luke's parables, on the other hand, are about more down-to-earth characters: a prodigal son, an unjust steward, a widow, a beggar, a Samaritan. . . . I therefore had a theme ready made for my Oxford seminar: the parables in the Gospels were not the parables of Jesus, as was assumed by almost everyone . . . rather they were the creation of the evangelists, each of whom has produced instances in his own style. So I went well armed to Oxford, and as I hoped the paper was a great success. . . . I had noticed a whole row of things which other scholars had missed, because they had assumed that the parables were Jesus' own

handiwork, and had not thought of attributing them to secondary figures.[319]

Goulder continued to follow up on this discovery and noticed that these unique characteristics were not limited to parables:

> For instance, the Gospels contain a number of double animal images: "Be ye wise as serpents and harmless as doves"; "You strain out a gnat but swallow a camel"; "Give not that which is holy to the dogs and cast not your pearls before swine." There are ten of these double animal images in the Gospels, and all of them are in Matthew; this seems cogent evidence that they were created, not by Jesus, but by Matthew himself.[320]

This sort of authorial freedom is precisely what one would expect of the scriptural historiography genre, and it is surprising and difficult to accept only when one imposes on the text presuppositions borrowed from the modern genres of nonfiction, history, or biography.

The evidence of intertextual relationships in Matthew lead in the same direction as what we find in Mark and Luke. Aside from Mark as a source, Brodie finds that Romans was the source for much of the material in Matthew 1-17: "Matthew has taken

---

[319] Goulder, *Five Stones*, 58-59.
[320] Ibid., 62. For an extended analysis of Goulder's arguments for the evangelists' creativity especially in the case of Luke, see Goulder, *Luke*; and for an analysis of those arguments, see Goodacre, *Goulder and the Gospels*. In general, Goodacre expresses some agreement with Goulder: "Goulder has successfully isolated several Lucan features, the pervasiveness of which suggests that in L material Luke is particularly creative. This is Lucan creativity on the kind of scale which would necessitate the abandonment of any theory on which the evangelist draws conservatively on a written L text. Goulder has not, however, given adequate attention to the possibility that Luke has creatively written up stories which he received from oral traditions; much of the data he presents makes best sense on such a view." (Goodacre, *Goulder and the Gospels*, 291)

the difficult text of Romans and in chapters 1-17 of his Gospel has rendered it into a form that is vivid, positive, and practical."[321]

As for the fourth gospel, in *The Quest for the Origin of John's Gospel: A Source-Oriented Approach*, Brodie proposed that John's sources were the synoptic gospels and Ephesians.[322] Here too, part of the reason why this view has not won over the majority of biblical scholars has to do with assumptions about genre – particularly the assumption that an evangelist would feel constrained to keep as close to his sources as possible. A more realistic understanding of scriptural historiography would lead to a realization that John would not have felt bound to slavishly copy any sources he had at hand but could freely manipulate them to suit his purposes. In that case, John can readily be seen as having been inspired by and modeled loosely after the synoptics.

Goulder observes of Matthew and John that "Their methods are in each case the same: to follow the thread from the Torah where it leads, weaving in threads from the prophets and writings as they suggest themselves, and filling in the remaining gaps from their imagination."[323]

This picture fits perfectly the literary character of scriptural historiography. Following the example of the writers of the Old Testament scripture before them, the evangelists had little need for "biographical reminiscences."[324] Their primary aim was to

---

[321] Brodie, *Birthing*, 204-253. He also finds that sections of Deuteronomy are behind much of the material in Matthew 17:22-28.
[322] In *Birthing* (254-257), he suggests the Lucan source for John was the postulated Proto-Luke rather than the canonical Luke-Acts.
[323] Cited in Goodacre, *Goulder and the Gospels*, 19.
[324] Contra Burridge; see *What are the Gospels*, 246.

influence a religious community by telling a story; the story had to tie in to the community's perception of its own history but once the tie was established the structure and details of the story depended more on its rhetorical purpose than on a perceived need for what we today would call historical accuracy.

A Broader View of Intertextuality in Mark

In Mark's case the rhetorical purpose was to influence the community's perception not just of its history, but of another body of literature – the Pauline epistles. In this book I have mainly focused on the ways in which the Pauline literature influenced Mark's Gospel, but the relationship between them is a two-way street. A term that captures the multi-faceted character of this literary relationship is "intertextuality." Scholars of literature ascribe a broad range of meanings to this term, most of which fit along a spectrum that has a focus on authorial intention at one end and reader reception at the other end. In other words, different texts are related to one another either because authors have other texts in mind when composing a text, or because readers have other texts in mind when reading a text.[325] There can be a vast difference between the ends of the

---

[325] This is a simplified explanation. In much recent scholarship that revolves around the word intertextuality, the word "text" itself is redefined so broadly that it means anything at all in human culture that can carry some kind of meaning. See Steve Moyise, "Intertextuality and Biblical Studies: A Review," *Verbum et Ecclesia* 23: 2: 418-31; Draisma, *Intertextuality*; and Richard Hays, Stefan Alkier, and Leroy Andrew Huizenga, eds., *Reading the Bible Intertextually* (Waco, Texas: Baylor UP., 2009). Some scholars go so far as to take umbrage against other scholars who would dare to use "intertextuality" in the more narrow sense of an author using prior texts while composing a text; see, for example, Thomas R. Hatina, "Intertextuality and Historical Criticism in New Testament Studies: Is there a Relationship?" *Biblical Interpretation* 1:28-43.

spectrum, since any given text might call to a reader's mind other texts that the author didn't even know about.

In the case of Mark and the Pauline epistles, both ends of the spectrum apply. On the one hand, Mark knew the Pauline epistles and reworked material from them into his own text. On the other hand, the epistle authors had no knowledge of Mark's Gospel, but after Mark's Gospel was created, it profoundly influenced the readers' understanding of the epistles. In effect, Mark canonized the Pauline epistles. This too reflects a common function of scripture in general: what Mark does for Paul the New Testament as a whole does for the Old Testament.

In the case of the New Testament and the Old Testament the relationship is clearly between a later body of literature and an earlier one. However, some of the Pauline epistles were written or edited after Mark was written. In that case we might expect to find in the epistles allusions to a person named Mark, allusions that would be intended to confirm the relationship between the Gospel of Mark and the epistles. That is indeed what we find in Col 4:10; 2 Tim 4:11; and Philemon 1:24.[326] These references reinforce the canonization process by making it circular: Mark canonizes the epistles, and the epistles canonize Mark by confirming the role of a person named Mark among Paul's disciples. In some cases the references to Mark may have been added by the epistle's author who was writing in Paul's name, and in other cases Mark's name may have been added by an editor.

---

[326] See also 1 Peter 5:13 and the repeated references in Acts, all of which serve the same function. On this use of names in the New Testament see also Trobisch, *First Edition*, 48-51 and Tarazi, *Colossians and Philemon*, 101-102.

Part IV

The Historical Jesus in Mark

12
Conservatism and Curiosity

Scholars who have assumed a position over many years do not quickly recant it and publicly admit their error; nor can a novel hypothesis expect to carry the day at once in a conservative profession. It may be particularly difficult to shift opinion over texts which are fundamental to the faith of the critic. With time scholars came to treat sympathetically my arguments for the evangelists' creativity: their freedom to create Nativity stories out of Old Testament types, and their ability to create or develop parables in line with their own stylistic and doctrinal concerns. They have been less willing to accept Matthew and Luke as embroiderers of earlier Gospel traditions, because there is a hankering after putative lost sources and oral traditions which would take us back to the historical Jesus. . . . I believe that in the long run the arguments which I have advanced will persuade a new generation of scholars. But this will take time.
    Michael Goulder[327]

A Homeric-mimetic reading of the Gospels is a seismic paradigm shift with enormous implications. As is the case with all paradigm shifts, one must expect resistance from those who have benefited from business as usual. I no longer expect scholars of my generation to accept my work with open arms; if acceptance occurs at all, it will come from future generations.
    Dennis MacDonald[328]

If Mark built his narrative mainly by reworking traditions from the Old Testament, Homer, and the Pauline epistles, the historical Jesus is even more out of reach than many scholars

---

[327] Goulder, *Five stones and a Sling*, 134-35.
[328] MacDonald, "My Turn," 23.

have supposed. Goulder alludes to Mark when he speaks of Matthew and Luke as "embroiderers of earlier Gospel traditions," and in that case even the "earlier traditions" themselves for the most part do not go back to the historical Jesus. For many scholars as well as rank and file Christian believers, this view of the Gospel is difficult or impossible to accept.

Goulder refers to three impediments to recognition of the gospels' character as scriptural historiography: conservatism of professional scholars, conservatism of religious belief, and curiosity about "the historical Jesus." As far as academic conservatism is concerned, paradigm shifts come about slowly and with great reluctance in all fields of scholarship. This is true even in the hard sciences where obvious and irrefutable proof can often be marshaled by the leaders of change.[329] In a delightful essay, Mark Twain asserts that accepting scholarly consensus as the final word on something is the mark of youth and inexperience:

> I wish I could be as young as that again. Although I seem so old, now, I was once as young as that. I remember, as if it were but thirty or forty years ago, how a paralyzing Consensus of Opinion accumulated from Experts a-setting around, about brother experts who had patiently and laboriously cold-chiseled their way into one or another of nature's safe-deposit vaults and were reporting that they had found something valuable was a plenty for me. It settled it.
>
> But it isn't so now – no. Because, in the drift of the years I by and by found out that a Consensus examines a new thing with its feelings rather oftener than with its mind. You know, yourself,

---

[329] The most well-known treatment of this phenomenon is Thomas Kuhn's *Structure of Scientific Revolutions* (Chicago: University of Chicago Press, 1962).

that that is so. Do those people examine with feelings that are friendly to evidence? You know they don't. It is the other way about. They do the examining by the light of their prejudices – now isn't that true?[330]

A consensus among scholars is even more resistant to change than one that petrifies among the general public because of a phenomenon that Goulder laments: a field's "professors have made their reputations by assuming and extending it, and will not lightly abandon it." That is why "[s]hifts of paradigm do not come from professors; they come from young men, and from those on the margin of the subject."[331] And that is why those who are most prominent in a given field and most forcefully defend its established views may be the least in tune with reality, as Dean Koontz laments about another field of science:

> Scientists and animal behaviorists have written libraries full of nonsense about the emotions of dogs, suggesting that they do not have emotions as we know them, or that their exhibitions that appear to be emotionally based do not mean what we interpret them to mean in our sentimental determination to see a fellowship between humanity and canines. Like too many specialists in every field, they are educated not out of their ignorance but *into* ignorance, because they are raised to an imagined state of enlightenment – which is actually dogmatism – where they no longer experience the light of intuition and the fierce brightness of common sense. They see the world through cloudy windows of theory and ideology, which obscure reality.[332]

---

[330] Mark Twain, "Dr. Loeb's Incredible Discovery," in *The Complete Essays of Mark Twain* (ed. Charles Neider; Da Capo Press, 1991), 590-593; here: 590.
[331] Goulder 1989, *Luke: A New Paradigm*, 4.
[332] Dean Koontz, *A Big Little Life: A Memoir of a Joyful Dog* (New York: Hyperion, 2009), 81. Although his assessment here is of specialists in dogs, it applies, as he says, to specialists in every field.

Dennis MacDonald's thesis that Mark created some of his narrative by adapting stories from the Homeric epics offers a case study of how scholars tend to react to an attempt to introduce a new paradigm.[333] MacDonald is an accomplished biblical scholar; his thesis is well argued; he established a set of objective criteria for identifying literary relationships; and he amassed a wealth of evidence that admirably support those criteria. And yet, at least two of the most comprehensive commentaries on Mark to appear in recent years reject his thesis out of hand, one by ignoring it altogether and one by writing it off as "purely gratuitous."[334] That leading scholars who specialize in Mark's Gospel could treat one of their distinguished colleagues so dismissively reflects more on their own prejudices than it does on the validity of MacDonald's evidence and arguments.

Nevertheless, paradigms can change, and eventually "those on the margin of the subject" who can make a case get heard. Generations have passed since ideas about the evangelists' authorial creativity were first proposed, and acceptance of the idea has been gradually building over that time. Goulder wrote the selection at the head of this chapter just 23 years ago, and MacDonald wrote his comments just 6 years ago, and already the landscape of scholarship has shifted in their direction. It is

---

[333] *The Homeric Epics and the Gospel of Mark* (New Haven: Yale UP, 2000).

[334] Camille Focant, *L'évangile selon Marc* (Paris: Cerf, 2007), 30. The other is Joel Marcus, *Mark 8-16* (New Haven: Yale UP, 2009). Marcus mentions one trivial point from MacDonald's book but never even alludes to the thesis that point was intended to support (763). See also Adela Yarbro Collins, *Mark: A Commentary* (Minneapolis: Fortress Press, 2007), which does not mention MacDonald at all. Biblical scholarship is a vast field and things can be overlooked; however, MacDonald's was truly a landmark book that evoked much debate, and Collins' commentary appeared seven years after it.

just a matter of time before the shift Telford tentatively predicted 13 years ago becomes a reality:

> With the development . . . of narrative-critical tools and an increasing sensitivity on the part of scholars to the nuances of narrative theology, Volkmar's original suggestion that Mark's Gospel is an allegorical presentation of Pauline teaching in the form of a narrative may be due, therefore, for a comeback.[335]

Goulder also alludes to the conservatism of religious faith, a force that is even stronger for many people than the desire to preserve and advance reputation is for scholars. Ironically, this conservatism stems from unsupportable presuppositions about the character of God and the nature of truth in the Christian tradition. On the one hand, the Christian tradition – especially Eastern Orthodox tradition – insists that God cannot be described or circumscribed: you can say what God is *not*, but it is beyond human powers of understanding and comprehension to definitively say what he *is*. On the other hand, many individual Christians implicitly circumscribe God by assuming that he would only communicate his will by means of literally true rather than metaphorically true scripture. On the one hand, Christian tradition insists that Jesus Christ is himself "the way, the truth, and the light," which means that Christian "truth" is not a simple matter of accurately representing what is physically going on around us in the world. On the other hand, many individual Christians assume that scripture must be true in just that way, an accurate record of what actual people saw and heard physically going on around them in the world. A "conservative" view of scriptural interpretation is in reality out of tune with the essence of Christian tradition. A view of Mark as an author creatively using available sources to convey a message in a work

---

[335] Telford, *Theology of Mark*, 169.

of literature is fully compatible with a view of God as free to act through human beings however he sees fit. And such a view of Mark is fully compatible with a view of "truth" as something that scripture defines. Actually, if for people today knowledge of Jesus and what it means for him to "be" truth is preserved in Christian scripture, it is all the more important to set aside preconceived notions and find out what the authors of scripture really meant their original readers to understand. In other words, viewing Mark as a narrativization of the Pauline gospel is fully compatible with genuine Christian faith, while rejecting that view a priori is incompatible with genuine Christian faith.

The third impediment to shifting the reigning paradigm in gospel interpretation is curiosity about the historical Jesus. Since Mark is generally seen as the earliest gospel, it is naturally the focus of such curiosity. There are, however, many things in history which we are curious about and will never get an answer to, and this is one of them.

13
Historical Implausibilities

The implausible stage management testifies to the artificiality of the scene. . . . it is suspicious that, throughout this section of the Gospel, whenever Jesus is doing something a bit questionable, the Pharisees and/or their allies the scribes always seem to conveniently turn up, even in very unlikely places.
　　Joel Marcus[336]

The extraordinarily unrealistic settings of many of the conflict stories should be realized: Pharisees did not organize themselves into groups to spend their Sabbaths in Galilean cornfields in the hope of catching someone transgressing.
　　E. Sanders[337]

Those who want to find a historical record in Mark face an even greater obstacle than the ambiguous evidence for Mark's literary borrowing of non-Jesus material to create Jesus stories. This obstacle is the fact that *if Jesus' earthly ministry actually happened as Mark portrays it, the history of Paul's Gentile mission and the opposition it encountered would be incomprehensible.* How could it be that neither Paul nor anyone who worked with him, nor his opponents, knew about Jesus' determined endorsement of a mixed community sharing table fellowship together? How is it that everyone somehow forgot that Jesus explicitly "declared all foods clean" (7:19)? In the pitched battles Paul waged against his Judaizing opponents in his epistles, any one of the many stories about Jesus' conflicts over

---

[336] Marcus, *Mark 1-8*, 227; see also 240, 260.
[337] E. P. Sanders, *Jesus and Judaism* (Philadelphia: Fortress Press, 1985), 265.

Law observance would have been devastating evidence of the rightness of Paul's side, yet none are ever mentioned.

It's as if before Mark was written, nobody had ever heard of any of Jesus' sayings or parables, *even those directly related to the very controversies that Christian leaders were grappling with*. Why? As Goulder puts it: "The obvious answer is, They had not been made up yet."[338]

Even scholars who desperately want to believe that Mark has a historical core acknowledge how unrealistic many of the stories in Mark are. Some of the most blatant "artificiality," "implausible stage management," and "extraordinarily unrealistic settings" occur in stories that bear remarkable resemblances to Paul's experiences as recounted in Galatians.[339] A common interpretive strategy that conservative scholars engage in is to suggest that yes, there may have been some exaggeration here and there, but there's a historical core. Here's an example of this line of reasoning as it occurs in Jerome Murphy O'Connor's book, *Jesus and Paul: Parallel Lives*:

> The moneychangers can plausibly be located in the basilica at the south end of Herod's vast enclosure. The animals and birds for sale as sacrificial victims must have been at the opposite end; the north wall of the Temple had the only gate communicating with the open countryside . . . How could Jesus get away with disturbances at two such widely separated parts of the Temple? Why did the Temple police not intervene at the first and so block the second? Moreover, it is inconceivable that one man could expel the hundreds of people in the basilica, or that a single

---

[338] Goulder, "Pauline," 874. See also Heikki Raisanen, *Jesus, Paul, and Torah: Collected Essays* (JSNTSup 43: Sheffield: Sheffield Academic., 1992), 127-48; Telford, *Theology*, 151.
[339] See chapter 8.

individual could herd a mass of frightened animals. All of this, however, is but an example of *the condensation and hyperbole integral to a good story.* [340]

Why should we assume that an author would engage in "hyperbole" but not outright invention? In fact, as I have endeavored to show throughout this book, much of Mark's gospel can be identified as having been adapted from non-Jesus sources or made up or manipulated to accomplish the author's literary purpose. And this fact begs the question: would an author who in some places chooses to write allegory rather than "history" necessarily feel bound to strive for "historical accuracy" everywhere else? In other words, if Mark consciously wrote allegorical text anywhere, why should we assume that he would not do it everywhere? Why should the temple cleansing story not be an outright fiction rather than "condensation and hyperbole"?[341]

There is no dearth of evidence that whatever Mark's literary purposes were, reporting on what the actual historical Jesus said and did was not very high on the list. He appears to have reworked Old Testament stories into Jesus stories.[342] His

---

[340] Jerome Murphy-O'Connor, *Jesus and Paul: Parallel Lives* (Collegeville, Minn.: Liturgical Press, 2007), 44-45.

[341] Or as Michael Goulder puts the same thought in a slightly different context, "If so, a less modern attitude to historical accuracy is already conceded, and it seems arbitrary to allow Lucan creativity in ch. 1 and to deny it in ch. 7 or 15 *a priori*" (*Luke: A New Paradigm*, 78).

[342] See, for example, Farrer, *Mark and Matthew*, 14-15; Van Iersel, *Mark*, 40, 62, 66; Kermode, *Genesis*, 60-61; Brodie, *Birthing*. Even Collins, who generally adopts the position that Mark is a conduit of traditions, doubts the historicity of Judas, citing, for example, the language and actions of betrayal by a friend as a scriptural theme (*Mark*, 224). Marcus links the temptation story to the biblical story of Adam ("Mark," 475). Mark may also have reworked Homeric stories into Jesus stories; see MacDonald, *Homeric Epics*; MacDonald, "Imitations of Greek epic in the Gospel," in Levine et al., *Historical Jesus*, 372-375.

geographical references reflect the logic of symbolism, not of geographical reality.[343] His scenarios where Jesus disputes with Jewish authorities often simply do not make sense historically.[344] His constantly recurring doublets call into question how many times he found one story in his sources and duplicated it.[345] And if his authorial method would permit him to create the second of a pair, it hardly seems likely that it would prevent him from creating both parts.[346] The evidence is sufficient to make this not just possible but likely. Ultimately, one can say of every chapter

---

[343] Willi Marxsen was the first to point this out. Malbon notes that "Historical critics have searched in vain for a mountain in Galilee" but those who know scripture know the mountain is where God meets his people. ("Narrative Criticism," 37) The "sea" of Galilee symbolizes the Mediterranean but is just a lake; as Marcus observes, sleeping on a boat through a storm on the Sea of Galilee is "not at all credible." (*Mark 1-8*, 337) The improbable detour through the Decapolis reflects an intention to show Jesus in Gentile lands. (Focant, "Doublets," 1049; Marcus, *Mark 1-8*, 492; Tarazi, *Paul and Mark*, 165, 179)

[344] How and why did antagonistic scribes get into a little house that was so packed that a crowd formed around the door and four men had to climb in through the roof; and how is it that they found room to sit down there? (2:1-17)

[345] On the function of repetition in Mark, the classic text is Frans Neirynck, *Duality in Mark. Contributions to the Study of the Markan Redaction. Revised Edition with Supplementary Notes* (Leuven: Leuven University Press, 1988). See also Alter, *Art*, 181 on the use of repetition in general in scripture.

[346] A prime example is the two feedings of the thousands. If they so effectively symbolize a progression from an exclusive community to an inclusive community, it is hardly necessary to assume that they must have been modeled on some actual historical event. Even those who assume Mark mainly reports earlier traditions observe that the similarities in this case are too striking for Mark to have simply "juxtaposed two traditions." See Focant, "Doublets." Repetition applies even to the passion narrative, for scholars have also noted the striking parallels between Paul's martyrdom and that of Jesus. Farrer observes that the episode of Barabbas "is thrown into a form which is historically puzzling and it constitutes the very point in the passion of Christ where the parallel with John's martyrdom is most striking." He concludes one cannot know which story influenced the other (*Mark and Matthew*, 15). Tolbert also comments about how John's death anticipates Jesus' death, and how Herod's behavior anticipates that of the disciples (*Sowing*, 196).

in the book of Mark something similar to what Goulder says of chapter 13:

> The only section of the chapter which does not have a lot of Daniel and Thessalonians behind it is the persecution paragraph, 13:9-13; and here the details are strongly reminiscent of Paul and his friends. . . . The cumulative effect of these parallels is to suggest strongly that Mark has little or no tradition of what Jesus actually said about the future. He has a tradition, and it is the Pauline tradition . . .[347]

---

[347] Goulder, *Paul vs. Peter*, 88.

14
Historical Plausibilities

If the historical picture in Mark is implausible, how can a plausible one be constructed? It is possible to do so by starting with the picture of two Christian missions as described in Part I. The Gentile Christian mission was established not by various disconnected groups but by a single school in the sense of a network of leaders probably led at first by a charismatic leader. The leader and school came to be known by the name Paul. Their mission could not make progress if Gentiles were forced to follow Jewish traditions, especially circumcision. But they came up against opposition from people who wanted just such traditions followed and who could claim authority for their views by referring to personal or family relationships with Jesus.

Paul's school could write epistles in his name even if he were no longer able to lead this effort, but they would eventually realize that such letters were weapons with limited effectiveness. Opponents of Paul who could cite personal or family ties to Jesus, or links to the holy city of Jerusalem or the temple, could still claim higher authority than Paul, and some in Paul's communities might be inclined to follow their lead (as is evident already from the epistle to the Galatians). What was needed was a higher authority than Paul who would support Paul's version of the gospel against that of his rivals. The only higher human authority would be Jesus, and so the idea of a narrative about Jesus arose, though so far as we can tell, Paul's school knew virtually nothing about him other than the crucifixion and resurrection.

Such a narrative had to present its message with some subtlety. If written by a known partisan of Paul – and it seems likely that a person or persons with the literary skill to put together a book like Mark would be well known – such a text would have to be anonymous or it would lose authority among its most important target audience: people potentially influenced by Paul's opponents.[348] There may have been other reasons for concealing the connection to Paul also. Through his apparently arrogant behavior Paul made his own name odious in many quarters. Jerome Murphy-O'Connor has described the apostle to the Gentiles in terms that help explain why he inspired so much opposition: Paul "had few scruples about the way he attacked those who disagreed with him"; he was "less than honest" when it came to presenting his credentials in the most forceful way to others, and his "lack of empathy" for other people caused him to attribute "the most uncharitable explanation" for any opposition to him. His "tunnel vision" and "self-absorption" were so intense that he did not care about anyone or anything peripheral to his central vision. He showed "contempt" for those who disagreed with him and in fighting them wrote "brutal slashes," threw "tantrums," displayed "childishness," was "manipulative," employed "moral blackmail," and engaged at times in a "cruel intellectual game," "cruel laughter," and "sarcasm."[349]

A new narrative about Jesus also had to have basic verisimilitude, so the author could not have Jesus openly initiating a Gentile mission that everyone knew Paul had created. The disciples could not be completely discredited for it was known that they retained leadership positions. But their

---

[348] Sternberg (*Poetics*, 33) notes another reason for anonymity: "Anonymity in ancient narrative validates supernatural powers of narration . . ."
[349] *Paul. His Story* (Oxford: Oxford UP, 2004), 59, 110, 136, 145, 146, 151, 166, 167, 180, 185, 220. See also Goulder, *Paul vs. Peter*, 9, 184.

understanding of what Jesus was actually all about could be questioned, their aura of spiritual authority that came from mere membership in "the twelve" could be undermined, and their continued authority could be made contingent on their acceptance of Paul's approach to the conversion of Gentiles.

In the absence of information about what Jesus actually said and did, the natural sources for the framework and contents of such a narrative would be the framework and contents of the scripture already venerated by the Gentile mission: the Old Testament and Paul's epistles. And a Greek author would be thoroughly familiar with the Homeric epics and would have been raised in an environment where it was customary to imitate them.

In creating a mostly allegorical yet ostensibly historical story, Mark was following the pattern set by the scripture he already knew so well, for this is the pattern followed by the Old Testament. As the prophets before him knew, a message that cannot be effectively delivered in straightforward language has to be couched in allegorical language.[350] And as I showed in Part III, that is what they were typically doing in narrative texts.

A cautionary note is in order regarding this historical reconstruction, however. The scenario is plausible based on the assumption that the Pauline epistles are themselves more or less historical, but that assumption is itself not necessarily a safe one. In his examinations of the epistles, Thomas Brodie finds as much evidence that they are essentially reworking of earlier scriptures as he finds in the gospels. This leads him to ask the question, "To what extent, if any, is the historical Paul distant from the Pauline corpus as the historical Moses is from the

---

[350] Kelber, *Oral and Written Gospel*, 64.

Pentateuch?"[351] This raises the question of whether the historical situations we find in the epistles are themselves real. In some cases they may be, but maybe not as much as commonly assumed.

> The need to think twice in assessing the epistles is particularly well illustrated in Paul's autobiographical passages. These texts appear to be thoroughly spontaneous and realistic, springing directly from his personal experience, prime material for reconstructing history. But comparison with other ancient authors shows that Pauline autobiography is part of a larger literary practice and that the epistles deliberately use material which appears autobiographical for pedagogical purposes.[352]

Brodie quotes a book by George Lyons about the character of Pauline autobiography:

> Since we have only Paul's autobiographical remarks and not his opponents' accusations, which the consensus assumes provoked them, it is necessary to exercise restraint in asserting too confidently that specific charges actually existed, much less what they may have been. Even the existence of 'opponents' in the usual sense of the word is far from certain . . . What he says is determined by his rhetorical approach and not by his opponents' reproaches.[353]

In this book I have suggested that much of Mark is a reworking of Galatians, but much of Galatians is in turn a reworking of Genesis. Paul doesn't explicitly cite Genesis in

---

[351] Thomas L. Brodie, "The Triple Intertextuality of the Epistles: An Introduction" in Thomas L. Brodie, Dennis Ronald MacDonald, and Stanley E. Porter, eds., *The Intertextuality of the Epistles: Explorations of Theory and Practice* (Sheffield: Sheffield Phoenix Press, 2006), 71-89; here: 72.
[352] Ibid., 74.
[353] Ibid., 75. The quotation is from George Lyons, *Pauline Autobiography: Towards a New Understanding*.

Historical Plausibilities

chapters 1 or 2, but "the story of Abraham is a remarkable parallel at its earliest point to Paul's own story and to the pattern which the Galatians have followed and to which Paul writes to exhort them to remain constant."[354] So even the "historical" aspects of Galatians start to look like rhetorical strategy:

> The conclusion regarding Galatians is similar to that of Hays concerning Romans: while engaging a specific audience Paul is also engaging specific writings. Furthermore, it often appears difficult or even impossible to distinguish what is historical from what is scriptural. . . . The overall impression, from Romans to Jude, is that as a whole the New Testament epistles involve deliberate reworkings of the older Scriptures. They are not just occasional documents. In a basic, constitutive, way, their nature is scriptural – literary, in the most serious sense.[355]

---

[354] Ibid., 80, quoting Carol Stockhausen. Brodie also cites key terminology in chs.3 and 4 to show how the story of Abraham was in Paul's mind throughout Galatians.
[355] Ibid., 83.

Conclusion

. . . it seems likely to me that the historical authors of all four Gospels assumed that a literal acceptance of the historicity of the events they reported would be a prerequisite for appreciation of the metaphorical sense those events were intended to convey. It also seems likely that the first audiences for these Gospels did in fact read them in this way, accepting the literal historicity of the accounts in ways that assisted them in accepting the startling metaphorical claims. . . . [Therefore] the evangelists *were* lying or, at least, were passing on misinformation that they had foolishly come to believe themselves. Indeed they were spreading falsehood of a most insidious sort: they were encouraging people to make extreme commitments that could, and often did, cost them their honor, their families, or their lives and they were offering as surety for those commitments historical testimony regarding events that, in fact, had never occurred. . . .

We might even say that by grounding their theological claims about Christ in outlandish and unsustainable claims about history, they have laid the framework for a version of Christianity that is at least absurd and possibly fraudulent.
    Mark Allan Powell[356]

It is a commonplace in some circles to decry Paul as a perverter of the original purity of Christianity founded by Jesus. Yet Jesus in Mark offers no new teaching but rather points back to the Torah and the Old Testament scriptures, the same sources that Paul cites. And one of Mark's literary goals was to validate

---

[356] Mark Allan Powell, "Authorial Intent and Historical Reporting: Putting Spong's Literalization Thesis to the Test," *Journal for the Study of the Historical Jesus* 1,2:225-249; here: 243.

Paul as the premier apostle, and consequently Paul's epistles as the scripture in which the true gospel can be found. The author of Mark expects his readers to not only accept Paul's epistles as scripture but to go there in order to find the gospel teaching which is so obviously missing from the text of his Gospel.

But what about the perspective that Mark Allan Powell articulates so clearly in the above quotations? For Powell, the problem is not just that Mark's text contains some inadvertent historical inaccuracies. The problem is that the historical inaccuracies are extensive and are not "inadvertent." The common assumption that Mark was trying as much as possible to report literally true facts about Jesus simply cannot withstand a dispassionate review of the evidence. Not even the assumption that Mark himself believed what he was writing to be literally true stands up to the evidence.[357] Consequently, Powell asserts on the one hand that Mark's intentions were dishonorable and on the other hand that the result was necessarily evil. In his view, the gospels are "fraudulent" because they report things that did not happen as if they were historical; and a faith based on fraudulent reporting must be "absurd."

Powell correctly understands the facts, but his interpretation of them, and the appropriateness of his value judgment concerning them, is open to question. In effect he canonizes his own presuppositions about appropriate ways to guide a community, and then he judges Mark by that standard. But that standard is

---

[357] A fairly typical expression of this assumption is in Collins, *Question of Genre*, 45: "I would like to suggest that the primary intention of the author of Mark *was to write history*. . . . The presence of miracles and other mythic elements in the narrative do not refute the hypothesis since for the author of Mark these elements were simply true and real." See also Collins, *Mark*, 1. For a summary of where various scholars stand on this issue, see Kealy, *History*, 2:2:631.

foreign to Mark's own culture. As I clarified in Part III, Mark was immersed in a culture in which storytelling was the tried and tested and accepted way of guiding a community. He was faithfully following a centuries-long tradition. In his social environment, creating an extended parable-like story was the only way he could have gone about getting Jews and Gentiles to unite in a community with full acceptance of each other's differences.

Another possible reaction would be to condemn the aspect of Mark's culture which appears to promote an "end justifies the means" approach to influencing people. Certainly that principle has engendered much evil in the history of the world. But it's always a risky leap from general principle to specific application. Given a moment's reflection, any one of us can recall difficult situations when our options were limited and in order to accomplish something good we had to employ means that were not entirely harmless. We do not know all of the specific circumstances in which a culture developed or which each evangelist faced, and we are thus in no position to pass judgment on them or on the culture they lived in.

So Mark's intentions are in effect unimpeachable. As for whether the result of what he did was to lay a foundation for Christianity that is "at least absurd and possibly fraudulent," that depends on how you define Christianity. A Christian faith that demands literal truth from the gospel narratives is indeed like the proverbial house built on sand; sooner or later the rain will fall, and the floods will come, and the winds will blow, and the house will fall (Matt 7:27). A Christian faith that accepts scripture as the Word of God and seeks to understand its message without restricting that message to preconceived notions can adapt to cultural changes and find endless reservoirs of good in Christianity as a religious tradition.

2 Samuel chapters 11-12 relate a story about the prophet Nathan and King David. David had taken the wife of one of his military commanders and arranged military affairs so that the commander would be killed. The narrative explains that God brought the matter to David's attention by indirect means:

> And the Lord sent Nathan to David. He came to him, and said to him, "There were two men in a certain city, the one rich and the other poor. The rich man had very many flocks and herds; but the poor man had nothing but one little ewe lamb, which he had bought. And he brought it up, and it grew up with him and with his children; it used to eat of his morsel, and drink from his cup, and lie in his bosom, and it was like a daughter to him. Now there came a traveler to the rich man, and he was unwilling to take one of his own flock or herd to prepare for the wayfarer who had come to him, but he took the poor man's lamb, and prepared it for the man who had come to him." Then David's anger was greatly kindled against the man; and he said to Nathan, "As the Lord lives, the man who has done this deserves to die; and he shall restore the lamb fourfold, because he did this thing, and because he had no pity. Nathan said to David, "You are the man. Thus says the Lord, the God of Israel, ' . . . Why have you despised the word of the Lord, to do what is evil in his sight? . . .You have smitten Uriah the Hittite with the sword, and have taken his wife to be your wife, and have slain him with the sword of the Ammonites. Now therefore the sword shall never depart from your house, because you have despised me, and have taken the wife of Uriah the Hittite to be your wife.' . . . David said to Nathan, "I have sinned against the Lord." (2 Sam 12:1)

In this story, Nathan let David believe that he was telling him a literal truth, but in fact he was conveying to him a deeper truth.

Nathan's method of presenting his message was no accident – it was effective precisely because David at first took it to be literally true although it wasn't. After the parable's purpose was achieved, Nathan did not explicitly tell David that literally speaking there was no "lamb," but the king could easily have figured that out. By then, that fact made no difference either to Nathan or to David.

The story of Mark and his Gospel over the millennia of Christianity parallels the story of Nathan and David. Mark used a literary device to convey a deeper truth just as Nathan did in the story he told to David. Mark let his readers believe that he was telling them a literally true history, and his story was all the more effective for that reason.

The David and Nathan story is itself a parable – it's part of the Davidic Court History which was composed centuries after King David reigned in Judah, just as Mark was composed decades after Jesus preached in Galilee and Judea. Whether we conceive of Nathan as a parable teller or as a character within a parable, Mark continued that tradition of conveying a deeper truth by means of a story that does not necessarily have to be literally true to accomplish its purpose. Our relationship to Mark's Gospel is now similar to that of David's relationship to Nathan's parable after the purpose of the parable was revealed. The appropriate reaction for David was not to condemn Nathan for misleading him but to take to heart his intended message. The appropriate reaction to Mark for us is not to condemn what Mark did but to take to heart his intended message and to read the Pauline epistles to learn what the Christian gospel is all about.

Bibliography

Entries marked with an asterisk are especially recommended as sources to start with for further reading.

Journal name abbreviations follow Society of Biblical Literature standards.

Alkier, Stefan. "Intertextuality and the Semiotics of Biblical Texts." In Hays, Alkier, and Huizenga, *Reading the Bible Intertextually*, 3-21.

Allison, Dale C. "The Pauline Epistles and the Synoptic Gospels. The Pattern of the Parallels." *NTS* 28(1982):1-32.

*Alter, Robert. *The Art of Biblical Narrative*. San Francisco: Basic, 1981. Excellent discussion of "fiction" in scripture.

Alter, Robert, and F. Kermode, eds. *The Literary Guide to the Bible*. London: Fontana, 1997.

*Anderson, Janice Capel, and Stephen D. Moore. *Mark and Method: New Approaches in Biblical Studies*. Minneapolis: Fortress Press, 2008. A sampling of various methodological approaches to understanding the text of Mark.

Auerbach, Erich. *Mimesis: The Representation of Reality in Western Literature*. Introduction by Edward W. Said. Princeton: Princeton UP, 2003.

Aus, Roger David. *Feeding the Five Thousand: Studies in the Judaic Background of Mark 6:30-44 par. and John 6:1-15*. Lanham, Maryland: University Press of America, 2010.

Auwers, Jean-Marie, and Henk Jan de Jonge, eds. *The Biblical Canons*. Bibliotheca Ephemeridum Theologicarum Lovaniensium 163. Leuven: Peeters, 2003.

Avalos, Hector. *The End of Biblical Studies*. Amherst, N.Y.: Prometheus Books, 2007.

Bacon, Benjamin W. *The Gospel of Mark: Its Composition and Date*. New Haven: Yale UP, 1925.

Barnett, Paul. "The Existence of Jesus." *Quadrant* May, 2006:35-36.

Barrett, C. K. *The New Testament Background: Selected Documents*. New York: HarperCollins, 1987.

Bartholomew, Craig G., et al. *Canon and Biblical Interpretation*. Grand Rapids: Zondervan, 2006.

Bauckham, Richard. "For Whom Were Gospels Written." In Bauckham, Richard, *The Gospels for all Christians*, 9-48.

_____. *The Gospels for all Christians: Rethinking the Gospel Audiences*. Grand Rapids: Eerdmans, 1998.

_____. *The Jewish World Around the New Testament: Collected Essays 1*. Tübingen: Mohr Siebeck, 2008.

Becker, Eve-Marie. "The Gospel of Mark in the Context of Ancient Historiography." In Kirkpatrick and Goltz, *The Function of Ancient Historiography*, 124-134.

Ben Zvi, Ehud. "Malleability and its Limits: Sennacherib's Campaign against Judah as a Case Study." In Grabbe, *Like a bird in a cage*, 73-105.

*Best, Ernest. "Mark's Readers: A Profile." In Van Segbroeck, et al., *The Four Gospels 1992*, 839-858. An excellent survey of the evidence in Mark that indicates who its originally intended readers were.

_____. "The Role of the Disciples in Mark." *NTS* 23(1977):377-401.

Betz, Hans Dieter. *Galatians: A Commentary on Paul's Letter to the Churches in Galatia*. Philadelphia: Fortress Press, 1979.

Black, Clifton. "Christ Crucified in Paul and in Mark: Reflections on an Intracanonical Conversation." In Lovering and Sumney, *Theology and Ethics in Paul and His Interpreters*, 184-206.

_____. *Mark: Images of an Apostolic Interpreter*. Minneapolis: Fortress Press, 2001.

Black, David Alan, ed. *Perspectives on the Ending of Mark: Four Views*. B & H Academic, 2008.

Blum, Erhard, et al., eds. *Das Alte Testament: Ein Geschictsbuch?* Munich: Lit, 2005.

Boismard, M. E., and Paul Benoit. *Synopse des quatre Évangiles en français avec parallèles des Apocryphes et des Pères*. Paris: Cerf, 1972.

Borg, Marcus. *The Lost Gospel Q: The Original Sayings of Jesus*. Berkeley: Ulysses Press, 1996.

Boring, M. Eugene. *Mark: A Commentary*. New Testament Library. Westminster John Knox Press, 2006.

Boyarin, Daniel. *A Radical Jew: Paul and the Politics of Identity.* Berkeley: U. of California Press, 1994.

Breytenbach, C. "Vormarkinische Logientradition. Parallelen in der urchristlichen Briefliteratur." In Van Segbroeck et al., *The Four Gospels 1992,* 725-750.

Broadhead, Edwin K. *Prophet, Son, Messiah: Narrative Form and Function in Mark 14-16.* Sheffield Academic Press, 1994.

*Brodie, Thomas L. *The Birthing of the New Testament: The Intertextual Development of the New Testament Writings.* Sheffield: Sheffield Academic Press, 2004. Essential reading for anyone interested in understanding the New Testament. The amount of detailed literary analysis in the main body of this large book may be daunting for many readers, but the background material in the first nine chapters is very accessible and is itself worth the price of the book.

_____. *The Crucial Bridge: The Elijah-Elisha Narrative as an Interpretive Synthesis of Genesis-Kings and a Literary Model for the Gospels.* Collegeville, MN: Liturgical Press, 2000.

_____. "Greco-Roman Imitation of Texts as a Partial Guide to Luke's Use of Sources." In Talbert, *Luke-Acts,* 17-46.

_____. *Proto-Luke: The Oldest Gospel Account: A Christ-Centered Synthesis of Old Testament History Modelled Especially on the Elijah-Elisha Narrative: Introduction, Text, and Old Testament Model.* Bible as Dialogue, New Testament Series, 3A. Limerick: Dominican Biblical Institute, 2006.

_____. *The Quest for the Origin of John's Gospel: A Source-Oriented Approach.* New York: Oxford UP, 1993.

*_____. "Towards Tracing the Gospels' Literary Indebtedness to the Epistles." In MacDonald, *Mimesis and Intertextuality in Antiquity and Christianity*, 104-116. Concise exposition of some of the evidence for concluding that the evangelists read the epistles.

*_____. "The Triple Intertextuality of the Epistles: An Introduction." In Brodie, MacDonald, and Porter, *The Intertextuality of the Epistles*, 71-89. Presents the evidence for seeing the epistles as carefully crafted literary creations rather than occasional and spontaneous letters. See also Trobisch, *Paul's Letter Collection*.

*Brodie, Thomas L., Dennis Ronald MacDonald, and Stanley E. Porter, eds. *The Intertextuality of the Epistles: Explorations of Theory and Practice*. Sheffield: Sheffield Phoenix Press, 2006. One of the best symposia about literary relationships between texts of the New Testament.

Brooke, George John, and Thomas Romer, eds. *Ancient and Modern Scriptural Historiography*. Peeters, 2007.

Bryan, Christopher. *A Preface to Mark: Notes on the Gospel in its Literary and Cultural Settings*. Oxford: Oxford UP, 1993.

Burke, Trevor J., and J. K. Elliott, eds. *Paul and the Corinthians: Studies on a Community in Conflict: Essays in Honour of Margaret Thrall*. Supplements to Novum Testamentum, v.109. Leiden: E. J. Brill, 2003.

Burkett, Delbert. *The Son of Man Debate: A History and Evaluation*. Cambridge: Cambridge UP, 2000.

Burridge, Richard A. *What are the Gospels? A Comparison with Graeco-Roman Biography.* Foreword by Graham Stanton. Grand Rapids: Eerdmans, 2004.

Byrne, Brendan. *A Costly Freedom: A Theological Reading of Mark's Gospel.* Liturgical Press, 2008.

Cameron, Ron, and Merill E. Miller, eds. *Redescribing Christian Origins.* Atlanta: Society of Biblical Literature, 2004.

*Camery-Hoggatt, J. *Irony in Mark's Gospel: Text and Subtext.* SNTSMS, 72. Cambridge: Cambridge UP, 1992. In-depth analaysis of the use of irony in Mark.

Capes, David B., Rodney Reeves, and E. Randolph Richards. *Rediscovering Paul: An Introduction to His World, Letters, and Theology.* Downers Grove, Ill.: InterVarsity Press, 2007.

Casey, Maurice. *An Aramaic Approach to Q: Sources for the Gospels of Matthew and Luke.* New York: Cambridge UP, 2002.

Castelli, Elizabeth, and Hal Taussig. *Reimagining Christian Origins. A Colloquium Honoring Burton L. Mack.* Valley Forge, Penn.: Trinity Press International, 1997.

Castelli, Elizabeth. *Imitating Paul: A Discourse of Power.* Literary Currents in Biblical Interpretation. Louisville: Westminster John Knox Press, 1991.

Charlesworth, James H., and Lee Martin McDonald. *Jewish and Christian Scriptures: The Function of "Canonical" and "Non-Canonical" Religious Texts.* New York: T & T Clark, 2010.

Chilton, Bruce. *Rabbi Paul: An Intellectual Biography*. New York: Doubleday, 2004.

Chilton, Bruce, General Editor. *The Cambridge Companion to the Bible*. New York: Cambridge UP, 1997.

Clark, Timothy. "Recent Eastern Orthodox Interpretation of the New Testament." *CBR* 5(2007):3:322-340.

Cohen, Shaye J. D. *From the Maccabees to the Mishnah*. Library of Early Christianity. Wayne E. Meeks, General Editor. Louisville: Westminster John Knox Press, 2006.

Collins, Adela Yarbro. "Genre and the Gospels." *JR* 75(1995):2:239-246.

_____. *Is Mark's Gospel a Life of Jesus? A Question of Genre*. Marquette UP, 1990.

_____. *Mark: A Commentary*. Minneapolis: Fortress Press, 2007.

Collins, John J. *The Bible after Babel: Historical Criticism in a Postmodern Age*. Grand Rapids: Eerdmans, 2005.

_____. *Does the Bible Justify Violence?* Minneapolis: Fortress Press, 2004.

Conzelmann, Hans. *Die Mitte der Zeit. Studien zur Theologie des Lukas*. Tubingen: J.C. B. Mohr, 1954.

_____. *The Theology of St. Luke*. Trans. Geoffrey Buswell. New York: Harper and Row, 1960.

Craig, William Lane, and Bart D. Ehrman. *Is There Historical Evidence for the Resurrection of Jesus? A Debate between William*

Lane Craig and Bart D. Ehrman. Worcester: College of the Holy Cross, 2006.

Crossan, John Dominic. "Earliest Christianity in Counterfactual Focus." *BibInt* 8(2000):1/2:185-193.

_____. "Mark and the Relatives of Jesus." *NovT* 15(1973):81-113.

Crossan, John Dominic and Jonathan L. Reed. *Excavating Jesus. Beneath the Stones, Behind the Texts*. San Francisco: HarperCollins, 2001.

Crossley, James G., and Christian Karner, eds. *Writing History, Constructing Religion*. Ashgate, 2005.

*Culley, Robert C. "Oral Tradition and Biblical Studies." *Oral Tradition* 1(1986):1:30-65. A concise yet complete account of how the modern conception of oral tradition and form criticism developed.

DeLorem, Jean. *Intertextualities about Mark*. Draisma, Sipke, ed., *Intertextuality in Biblical Writings*, 35-42.

deSilva, David. *Honor, Patronage, Kinship, and Purity: Unlocking New Testament Culture*. Downers Grove: InterVarsity Press, 2000.

Diest, Ferdinand. *The Material Culture of the Bible: An Introduction*. Sheffield: Sheffield Academic Press, 2000.

Donahue, John R. "Jesus as the Parable of God in the Gospel of Mark." *Interpretation: A Journal of Bible and Theology* 32(1978):369-386.

Donahue, John R. *The Gospel in Parable: Metaphor, Narrative, and Theology in the Synoptic Gospels*. Philadelphia: Fortress Press, 1988.

Donahue, John R. "Windows and Mirrors: The Setting of Mark's Gospel." *CBQ* 57(1995):1-26.

Donahue, John R., and Daniel J. Harrington. *The Gospel of Mark*. Sacra Pagina series. Collegeville: Liturgical Press, 2002.

Draisma, Sipke, ed. *Intertextuality in Biblical writings*. Kampen: Kok, 1989.

Drury, John. "Understanding the Bread: Disruption and Aggregation, Secrecy and Revelation in Mark's Gospel." In Rosenblatt and Sitterson, *Not in Heaven*, 98-119.

Drury, John. "Mark." In Alter and Kermode, *The Literary Guide to the Bible*, 402-417.

Dungan, David L. *Constantine's Bible : politics and the making of the New Testament*. Minneapolis: Fortress Press, 2007.

_____. *A History of the Synoptic Problem: The Canon, the Text, the Composition, and the Interpretation of the Gospels*. New York: Doubleday, 1999.

Dunn, James D. G. "Altering the Default Setting: Re-envisaging the Early Transmission of the Jesus Tradition." *NTS* 49(2003):139-175.

_____. *The Cambridge Companion to Saint Paul*. New York: Cambridge UP, 2003.

_____. *Jesus, Paul, and the Law: Studies in Mark and Galatians*. London: SPCK, 1990.

Dunn, James D. G., and Scott McKnight, eds. *The Historical Jesus in Recent Research*. Winona Lake, Ind.: Eisenbrauns, 2005.

Duran, Nicole Wilkinson, Teresa Okure, and Daniel Patte, eds. *Mark*. Texts@contexts. Minneapolis: Fortress Press, 2011.

Dykstra, Tom E. "From Volkmar to Tarazi and Beyond: Mark as an Allegorical Presentation of the Pauline Gospel." *Forthcoming*.

_____. "The Gospels' Genre as Scriptural Historiography: Applying Lessons Learned from Ronald Reagan's Biography," *Journal of the Orthodox Center for the Advancement of Biblical Studies* (JOCABS), 4(2011):1:n.p.

_____. "'New, Unfounded, Unworkable, and Unnecessary': Thomas Brodie's Critique of Oral Tradition," JOCABS 3(2010):1:n.p.

Ehrman, Bart. D. *God's Problem. How the Bible Fails to Answer Our Most Important Question – Why We Suffer*. New York: HarperOne, 2008.

_____. *Jesus, Interrupted: Revealing the Hidden Contradictions in the Bible (and Why We Don't Know About Them)*. New York: HarperOne, 2009.

_____. *Peter, Paul, and Mary Magdalene. The Followers of Jesus in History and Legend*. New York: Oxford UP, 2006.

Elliott, J. K. *The Language and Style of the Gospel of Mark (Supplements to Novum Testamentum)*. Brill Academic Publishers, 1993.

Elliott, Neil. *Liberating Paul*. Augsburg Fortress Pub, 1994.

Ellis, Edward Earle. "The Date and Provenance of Mark's Gospel." In Van Segbroeck et al., *The Four Gospels 1992*, 801-816.

Evans, Craig A., and H. Daniel Zacharias, eds. *Early Christian Literature and Intertextuality*. London: T & T Clark, 2009.

Farrer, Austin. "Loaves and Thousands." *JTS* 4(1953):1-14.

_____. *St. Matthew and St. Mark*. London: Dacre, 1954.

Fenton, J. C. "Paul and Mark." In Nineham, Dennis E., ed, *Studies in the Gospels: Essays in Memory of R. H. Lightfoot*, 89-112.

Ferguson, Everett. *Backgrounds of Christianity*. Third edition. Grand Rapids: Eerdmans, 2003.

Fewell, Danna Nolan, ed. *Reading Between Texts: Intertextuality and the Hebrew Bible*. Louisville: Westminster John Knox Press, 1996.

*Focant, Camille. "Les Doublets dans la Section des Pains." In Van Segbroeck et al., *The Four Gospels 1992*, 1039-63. An in-depth examination of the symbolic significance behind the two feedings of the multitudes in Mark.

_____. *L'évangile selon Marc*. Commentaire biblique, Nouveau Testament, 2. Paris: Cerf, 2007.

_____. *Marc, un évangile étonnant : recueil d'essais*. Bibliotheca Ephemeridum theologicarum Lovaniensium, 194. Leuven: Leuven University Press, 2006.

Focant, Camille, and André Wénin, eds. *Analyse narrative et Bible: deuxième Colloque international d'analyse narrative des textes de la Bible, Louvain-la-Neuve, avril 2004.* Bibliotheca Ephemeridum theologicarum Lovaniensium, 191. Leuven: Leuven University Press, 2005.

Foster, Paul. "Is it Possible to Dispense with Q?" *NovT* 45(2003):4:313-37.

Fowler, Robert. "Reader-Response Criticism. Figuring Mark's Reader." In Anderson, Janice Capel, and Stephen D. Moore, *Mark and Method: New Approaches in Biblical Studies*, 59-93.

Fuller, Reginald H. "Baur Versus Hilgenfeld: A Forgotten Chapter in the Debate on the Synoptic Problem." *NTS* 24(1978):355-370

Furnish, Victor Paul. "The Jesus-Paul Debate: From Baur to Bultmann." In Wedderburn, A. J. M., ed, *Paul and Jesus: Collected Essays*, 17-50.

Gager, John G. *Reinventing Paul.* New York: Oxford UP, 2002.

*Gamble, Harry. *Books and Readers in the Early Church.* New Haven: Yale UP, 1995. Provides essential context for understanding the literary environment in which the scriptural authors worked and the physical evidence (manuscripts) that remains of what they produced. See also Parker, *An Introduction to the New Testament Manuscripts and their Texts.*

Garcia, Martinez, F. *The Dead Sea Scrolls Translated.* Leiden: E. J. Brill, 1994.

Gasque, W. Ward, and Ralph P. Martin, eds. *Apostolic History and the Gospel. Biblical and Historical Essays Presented to F. F. Bruce*. Exeter: The Paternoster Press, 1970.

*Giblin, C. H. "The Beginning of the Ongoing Gospel (Mk 1:2-16:8)." In Van Segbroeck et al., *The Four Gospels 1992*, 975-986. Proposes that the first verse of Mark indicates that the book as a whole is an account of how oral tradition about Jesus began.

Gillmayr-Bucher, Susanne. "Intertextuality: Between Literary Theory and Text Analysis." In Brodie, MacDonald, and Porter, *The Intertextuality of the Epistles*, 13-23.

*Goodacre, Mark. *The Case Against Q: Studies in Markan Priority and the Synoptic Problem*. Harrisburg, Penn.: Trinity Press International, 2002. One of a few books especially important for presenting the case for doubting the existence of Q.

*_____. *Goulder and the Gospels: An Examination of a New Paradigm*. JSNT 133. Sheffield, England: Sheffield Academic Press, 1996. Detailed examination of the arguments in Goulder's *Luke: A New Paradigm*. Neither book is easy reading but worth the effort for anyone looking for an in-depth analysis of Luke and its literary relationship to Mark.

*_____. *The Synoptic Problem: A Way Through the Maze (Understanding the Bible and its World)*. Sheffield Academic Press, 2001. Excellent introduction to the study of the relationships between the synoptic gospels. The entire text is available online at http://www.markgoodacre.org/maze.

*Goodacre, Mark, and Nicholas Perrin, eds. *Questioning Q: A Multidimensional Critique.* Downers Grove: InterVarsity Press, 2004. Another book that should be read by anyone tempted to accept Q as a working hypothesis.

*Goulder, Michael D. *Five Stones and a Sling: Memoirs of a Biblical Scholar.* Sheffield Phoenix Press Ltd, 2009. Worth reading as an enjoyable memoir written with a sense of humor. Especially valuable for what it reveals about the character of modern biblical scholarship. Essential reading for anyone who reads books produced by modern biblical scholars.

*_____. "Jesus' Resurrection and Christian Origins: A Response to N. T. Wright." *Journal for the Study of the Historical Jesus* 3(2005):187-195. Part of a series in which biblical scholars debate the historicity of Jesus' resurrection.

*_____. *Luke: A New Paradigm.* JSNTSup. 20. Sheffield: Sheffield Academic Press, 1989. An in-depth examination of Luke and its literary relationship to other scriptural books including Mark. See also Goodacre, *Goulder and the Gospels.*

_____. "Mark XVI.1-8 and Parallels." *NTS* 24(1978):235-40.

*_____. "Those Outside (Mk. 4.10-12)." *NovT* 33(1991):289-302. Argues that the phrase "those outside" in Mark 4:10-12 refers to Jesus' family.

_____. "A Pauline in a Jacobite Church." In Van Segbroeck et al., *The Four Gospels 1992*, 859-76.

*_____. *St. Paul vs. St. Peter: A Tale of Two Missions.* Westminster John Knox Press, 1994. Presents Goulder's thesis that the early church was divided between two main factions, one following Paul and one following Peter.

_____. *Type and History in Acts*. London: S.P.C.K, 1964.

_____. "Visions and Revelations of the Lord." In Burke and Elliott, *Paul and the Corinthians*, 303-12.

Gowler, David B. "The *Chreia*." In Levine, Allison, and Crossan, *The Historical Jesus in Context*, 132-148.

Grabbe, Lester L., ed. *"Like a bird in a cage": The Invasion of Sennacherib in 701 BCE*. Volume 363 of Journal for the Study of the Old Testament: Supplement Series. Continuum International Publishing Group, 2003.

Gray, Timothy C. *The Temple in the Gospel of Mark: A Study in Its Narrative Role*. Grand Rapids: Baker Book House, 2010.

Griffith-Jones, Robin. *The Gospel According to Paul: The Creative Genius who Brought Jesus to the World*. HarperOne, 2005.

Gundry, R. H. *Mark: A commentary on his Apology for the Cross*. Grand Rapids: Eerdmans, 1993.

Halpern, Baruch. "Biblical versus Greek Historiography: A Comparison." In Blum et al., *Das Alte Testament: Ein Geschictsbuch*, 101-128.

Hanhart, K. "Son, Your Sins are Forgiven." In Van Segbroeck et al., *The Four Gospels 1992*, 997-1016.

Hanson, K. C., and Douglas Oakman. *Palestine in the Time of Jesus: Social Structures and Social Conflicts*. Minneapolis: Fortress Press, 1998.

*Harrington, Daniel J. *What are they Saying About Mark?* Second edition. New York: Paulist Press, 2004. A good survey of what "reputable biblical scholars" have written about Mark.

Harris, H. *The Tübingen School.* Oxford: Oxford UP, 1975.

*Hatina, Thomas R. "Intertextuality and Historical Criticism in New Testament Studies: Is there a Relationship?" *BibInt* 1(1999):28-43. The word "intertextuality" is controversial in biblical scholarship, and this article explains some of the reasons why.

Hays, Richard. *Echoes of Scripture in the Letters of Paul.* New Haven: Yale UP, 1989.

Hays, Richard, Stefan Alkier, and Leroy Andrew Huizenga. *Reading the Bible Intertextually.* Waco, Texas: Baylor UP, 2009.

Helmer, Christine, and Christof Landmesser, eds. *One Scripture or Many? Canon from Biblical, Theological and Philosophical Perspectives.* Oxford: Oxford UP, 2004.

Helms, Randel. *Gospel Fictions.* Buffalo: Prometheus Books, 1989.

_____. *Who Wrote the Gospels?* Altadena, CA: Millennium Press, 1996.

Hengel, Martin. *The Zealots: Investigations into the Jewish Freedom Movement in the Period from Herod I until 70 A.D.* Edinburgh: T & T Clark, 1989.

Hengel, Martin. *The Four Gospels and the One Gospel of Jesus Christ.* Harrisburg, PA: Trinity Press International, 2000.

_____. *The Pre-Christian Paul.* Trinity Press International, 1991.

Hock, Ronald F., et al., eds. *Ancient Fiction and Early Christian Narrative.* Atlanta: Scholars Press, 1998.

Hoffmann, Paul, John S. Kloppenborg, and James M. Robinson, eds. *The Critical Edition of Q: A Synopsis Including the Gospels of Matthew and Luke, Mark, and Thomas with English, German, and French Translations of Q and Thomas.* Minneapolis: Fortress Press, 2000.

Hooker, Morna D. *The Gospel According to Saint Mark.* Black's New Testament Commentary. Hendrickson Publishers, 2009.

Horsley, Richard A. *Archeology, History, and Society in Galilee: The Social Context of Jesus and the Rabbis.* Harrisburg: Trinity Press International, 1996.

_____. *Jesus and the Spiral of Violence: Popular Jewish Resistance in Roman Palestine.* San Francisco: Harper and Row, 1987.

Horsley, Richard A., with J. S. Hanson. *Bandits, Prophets, and Messiahs: Popular Movements in the Time of Jesus.* New York: Seabury Press, 1985.

Huggins, R. V. "Matthean Posteriority: A Preliminary Proposal." *NovT* 34(1992):1-22.

Hurtado, Larry W. *The Earliest Christian Artifacts: Manuscripts and Christian Origins.* Grand Rapids: Eerdmans, 2006.

Kealy, Sean P. *A History of the Interpretation of the Gospel of Mark.* Lewiston: Edwin Mellen Press, 2007.

Kee, Howard Clark *The Beginnings of Christianity. Context and Controversy.* T&T Clark, 2005.

Kelber, Werner H. *Mark's Story of Jesus.* Philadelphia: Fortress Press, 1979.

———. *The Oral and the Written Gospel: The Hermeneutics of Speaking and Writing in the Synoptic Tradition, Mark, Paul, and Q.* Indiana UP, 1997.

———. *The Passion in Mark. Studies on Mark 14-16.* Minneapolis: Fortress Press, 1976.

Kenyon, Frederic G. *Books and Readers in Ancient Greece and Rome.* Oxford: Clarendon Press, 1932.

Kermode, Frank. *The Genesis of Secrecy: On the Interpretation of Narrative.* Cambridge: Harvard UP, 2006.

Kim, Seyoon. *Christ and Caesar: The Gospel and the Roman Empire in the Writings of Paul and Luke.* Grand Rapids: Eerdmans, 2008.

Kirkpatrick, Patricia, and Timothy Goltz, eds. *The Function of Ancient Historiography in Biblical and Cognate Studies.* T&T Clark, 2008.

Kloppenborg Verbin, John. *Excavating Q: The History and Setting of the Sayings Gospel.* Minneapolis: Fortress Press, 2000.

Koester, Helmut. *Paul and His World: Interpreting the New Testament in its Context.* Minneapolis: Fortress Press, 2007.

Koontz, Dean. *A Big Little Life: A Memoir of a Joyful Dog.* New York: Hyperion, 2009.

Kugel, James. *How to Read the Bible: A Guide to Scripture, Then and Now*. New York: Free Press, 2007.

Kuhn, Thomas. *The Structure of Scientific Revolutions*. Chicago: University of Chicago Press, 1962.

Leidner, Harold. *The Fabrication of the Christ Myth*. Tampa: Survey Books, 1999.

Levine, Amy-Jill, Dale C. Allison, and John Dominic Crossan, eds. *The Historical Jesus in Context*. Princeton: Princeton UP, 2006.

Lewis, David H. "Escaping the Gravitational Pull of the Gospels." *Quadrant* May, 2005:54-57.

Lindemann, Andreas. "Paulus im ältesten Christentum: Das Bild des Apostels und die Rezeption der paulinischen Theologie in der früh-christlichen Literatur bis Marcion." *BHT* 58(1979):151-4.

Loisy, A. *L'Évangile selon Marc*. Paris, 1912.

Lovering, Eugene H., Jr., and Jerry L. Sumney, eds. *Theology and Ethics in Paul and His Interpreters. Essays in Honor of Victor Paul Furnish*. Nashville: Abingdon Press, 1996.

Maccoby, Hyam. *The Mythmaker. Paul and the Invention of Christianity*. New York: Barnes & Noble, 1986.

MacDonald, Dennis R. "A Categorization of Antetextuality in the Gospels and Acts: A Case for Luke's Imitation of Plato and Xenophon to depict Paul as a Christian Socrates." In Brodie, MacDonald, and Porter, *The Intertextuality of the Epistles*, 211-25.

_____. *Does the New Testament Imitate Homer. Four Cases From the Acts of the Apostles.* New Haven, Conn.: Yale UP, 2003.

*_____. *The Homeric Epics and the Gospel of Mark.* New Haven, Conn.: Yale UP, 2000. Presents evidence that some of the stories in Mark were composed by imitating stories in the Homeric epics.

*_____. "My Turn. A Critique of Critics of 'Mimesis Criticism'" 2006. Online at http://iac.cgu.edu/drm/My_Turn.pdf. A response to critics of MaDonald's book *The Homeric Epics and the Gospel of Mark.* Like Goulder's *Memoir*, an important text for understanding the state of biblical scholarship.

_____. "Secrecy and Recognitions in the Odyssey and Mark: Where Wrede Went Wrong." In Hock, Ronald F., et al., eds, *Ancient Fiction and Early Christian Narrative*, 139-153.

MacDonald, Dennis R., ed. *Mimesis and Intertextuality in Antiquity and Christianity.* Harrisburg, PA: Trinity Press International, 2001.

Mack, Burton L. *The Christian Myth: Origins, Logic, and Legacy.* Continuum, 2003.

_____. *The Lost Gospel. The Book of Q and Christian Origins.* San Francisco: HarperCollins, 1993.

_____. *A Myth of Innocence: Mark and Christian Origins.* Philadelphia: Fortress Press, 1991.

Malbon, Elizabeth Struthers. "Narrative Criticism. How Does the Story Mean?" In Anderson, Janice Capel, and Stephen D. Moore, *Mark and Method: New Approaches in Biblical Studies*, 29-57.

Malet, Andre. *The Thought of Rudolf Bultmann*. Trans. Richard Strachan. Preface by Rudolf Bultmann. Shannon: Irish University Press, 1969.

Malina, Bruce J. *Christian Origins and Cultural Anthropology: Practical Models for Biblical Interpretation*. Atlanta: John Knox Press, 1986.

_____. "Jesus People: Scholars Search for the Early Church." *ChrCent* 120:15:28.

_____. *Windows on the World of Jesus: Time Travel to Ancient Judea*. Louisville: Westminster John Knox Press, 1993.

Malina, Bruce, and John J. Pilch. *Social-Science Commentary on the Letters of Paul*. Minneapolis: Fortress Press, 2006.

*Marcus, Joel. "Mark, Interpreter of Paul." *NTS* 46(2000):4:473-487. Ways in which Mark can be seen as Pauline. Not entirely superseded by the later commentary.

*Marcus, Joel. *Mark 1-8*. The Anchor Bible. New Haven: Yale UP, 2002. For a verse-by-verse commentary of Mark, this one and the second volume by the same author, *Mark 8-16*, is a good place to start.

*Marcus, Joel. *Mark 8-16*. The Anchor Yale Bible. New Haven: Yale UP, 2009.

Marguerat, Daniel, and Adrian Curtis. *Intertextualités: La Bible en échos*. Geneva: Labor et Fides, 2000.

Marxsen, Willi. *Mark the Evangelist: Studies on the Redaction-History of the Gospel*. Trans. James Boyce et al. New York: Abingdon, 1968.

Mason, Steve. *Josephus and the New Testament*. Peabody: Hendrickson Publishers, 1992.

_____. *Josephus, Judea, and Christian Origins: Methods and Categories*. Peabody: Hendrickson Publishers, 2009.

Mattill, A. J. *The Jesus-Paul Parallels and the Purpose of Luke-Acts: H. H. Evans Reconsidered*. NovT, 1975.

_____. "The Purpose of Acts: Schneckenburger Reconsidered." In Gasque, Ward, and Martin, *Apostolic History and the Gospel*, 108-122.

McDonald, Lee M. *The Formation of the Christian Biblical Canon*. Foreword by Helmut Koester. Peabody: Hendrickson Publishers, 1995.

McDonald, Lee Martin, and James A. Sanders, eds. *The Canon Debate*. Peabody: Hendrickson Publishers, 2002.

McNicol, Allan J., ed. *Beyond the Q Impasse: Luke's Use of Matthew: A Demonstration by the Research Team of the International Institute for Gospel Studies*. With David L. Dungan and David B. Peabody. Valley Forge: Trinity Press International, 1996.

Meier, John P. *A Marginal Jew: Rethinking the Historical Jesus*. Anchor Bible Reference Library. New York: Doubleday, 1991, 1994, 2001.

Meijboom, Hajo Uden. *A History and Critique of the Origin of the Marcan Hypothesis, 1835-1866. A contemporary Report Rediscovered, a Translation with Introduction and Notes*. John J. Kiewiet, trans. and ed. Mercer UP, 1993.

Mettinger, T. *The Riddle of the Resurrection: "Dying and Rising" Gods in the Ancient Near East.* Coniectanea Biblica 59. Stockholm: Almqvist & Wiksell, 2000.

Metzger, Bruce M. *The Canon of the New Testament. Its Origin, Development, and Significance.* New York: Clarendon, 1987.

Miller, John W. *How the Bible Came to Be.* New York: Paulist Press, 2004.

———. *The Origins of the Bible.* New York: Paulist Press, 1994.

Mitchell, M. M. "Homer in the New Testament?" *JR* 83(2003):2:244.

Montefiore, C. G. *The Synoptic Gospels Edited With an Introduction and a Commentary.* London: MacMillan, 1927.

Moreland, Milton C., managing ed. *The Critical Edition of Q: Synopsis Including the Gospels of Matthew and Luke, Mark and Thomas with English, German, and French Translations of Q and Thomas.* Ed. James M. Robinson, Paul Hoffmann, and John S. Kloppenborg. Leuven: Peeters, 2000.

Morgan, Robert. "Can the Critical Study of Scripture Provide a Doctrinal Norm?" *JR* 76(1996):2:206-232.

*Moyise, Steve. "Intertextuality and Biblical Studies: A Review." *Verbum et Ecclesia* 23:2:418-31. This and the following two articles by Moyise provide an excellent introduction to the history of the study of intertextuality and its application to biblical studies.

*_____. "Intertextuality and Historical Approaches to the use of Scripture." In Hays, Alkier, Huizenga, *Reading the Bible Intertextually*, 23-32.

*_____. "Intertextuality, Historical Criticism, and Deconstruction." In Brodie, MacDonald, and Porter, *The Intertextuality of the Epistles*, 24-34.

Moyise, Steve, ed. *The Old Testament in the New Testament: Essays in Honour of J. L. North*. Sheffield: Sheffield Academic Press, 2000.

Murphy-O'Connor, Jerome. *Jesus and Paul: Parallel Lives*. Collegeville, MN: Liturgical Press, 2007.

_____. *Paul. A Critical Life*. Oxford: Oxford UP, 1996.

_____. *Paul. His Story*. Oxford: Oxford UP, 2004.

Neirynck, Frans. *Duality in Mark. Contributions to the Study of the Markan Redaction. Revised Edition with Supplementary Notes*. Bibliotheca ephemeridum theologicarum Lovaniensium, 31. Leuven: Leuven University Press, 1988.

Neufeld, Dietmar, and Richard E. DeMaris, eds. *Understanding the Social World of the New Testament*. New York: Abingdon, 2010.

Nineham, Dennis E., ed. *Studies in the Gospels: Essays in Memory of R. H. Lightfoot*. Oxford: Basil Blackwell, 1955.

Noll, K. L. "The Evolution of Genre in the Book of Kings: The Story of Sennacherib and Hezekiah as Example." In Kirkpatrick and Goltz, *The Function of Ancient Historiography in Biblical and Cognate Studies*, 30-56.

Oden, Thomas C. and Christopher A. Hall. *Mark*. Ancient Christian Commentary on Scripture 2. Downers Grove, IL: InterVarsity Press, 1998.

*Orton, David E., comp. *The Synoptic Problem and Q: Selected Studies from Novum Testamentum*. Leiden: E. J. Brill, 1999. Several of the articles in this collection provide incisive critiques of the Q hypothesis.

Outler, Albert C. "The Gospel According to St. Mark." *PSTJ* 33(1980):3-90.

Pagels, Elaine. *The Gnostic Paul: Gnostic Exegesis of the Pauline Letters*. Philadelphia: Fortress Press, 1975.

Painter, John. *Mark's Gospel: Worlds in Conflict*. London: Routledge, 1997.

*Parker, D. C. *An Introduction to the New Testament Manuscripts and their Texts*. Cambridge: Cambridge UP, 2008. Aimed at scholars or university students rather than the general non-specialist reader, but should be one of the first books to read for anyone getting started in New Testament studies.

Parris, David P. "Imitating the Parables: Allegory, Narrative and the Role of Mimesis." *JSNT* 25(2002):1:33-53.

Patterson, Dilys Naomi. "Re-membering the Past: The Purpose of Historical Discourse in the Book of Judith." In Kirkpatrick and Goltz, *The Function of Ancient Historiography in Biblical and Cognate Studies*, 111-123.

Patterson, Stephen J. "Paul and the Jesus Tradition: It's Time for Another Look." *HTR* 84(1991):1:23-41.

Paulien, Jon. "Elusive Allusions in the Apocalypse: Two Decades of Research into John's Use of the Old Testament." In Brodie, MacDonald, and Porter, *The Intertextuality of the Epistles*, 61-68.

Perrin, Norman. *Jesus and the Language of the Kingdom: Symbol and Metaphor in New Testament Interpretation*. Philadelphia: Fortress Press, 1976.

Peterson, Norman. "Can One Speak of a Gospel Genre?" *Neotestamentica* 28:3:137-158.

Petrie, Stewart. "'Q' is Only What You Make It." Orton, *The Synoptic Problem and Q*, 1-6.

Porter, Stanley E. "Further Comments on the Use of the Old Testament in the New Testament." In Brodie, MacDonald, and Porter, *The Intertextuality of the Epistles: Explorations of Theory and Practice*, 98-110.

_____. *The Pauline Canon*. Leiden: E. J. Brill, 2004.

Powell, Evan. *The Myth of the Lost Gospel*. Las Vegas: Symposium Press, 2006.

*Powell, Mark Allan. "Authorial Intent and Historical Reporting: Putting Spong's Literalization Thesis to the Test." *Journal for the Study of the Historical Jesus* 1,2(2003):225-249. Although in my conclusion I question one aspect of Powell's argument, for the most part this is one of the most insightful articles available on the issue of historicity in the gospels.

_____. *What is Narrative Criticism? A New Approach to the Bible*. London: SPCK, 1993.

Price, Robert M. *Incredible Shrinking Son of Man: How Reliable Is the Gospel Tradition?* Prometheus Books, 2003.

Quesnell, Quentin. *Mind of Mark.* Loyola Press, 1969.

Raisanen, Heikki. *Jesus, Paul, and Torah: Collected Essays.* JSNTSup 43; Sheffield: Sheffield Academic, 1992.

Rau, G. *Das Markusevangelium: Komposition und Intention der ersten Darstellung christlicher Mission.* ANRW, 1985.

Reicke, Bo. *The New Testament Era; The World of the Bible from 500 B.C. to A.D. 100.* Trans. David Green. Philadelphia: Fortress Press, 1968.

_____. *Re-examining Paul's Letters: The History of the Pauline Correspondence.* Harrisburg: Trinity Press International, 2001.

Reventlow, Henning Graf, and William Farmer. *Biblical Studies and the Shifting of Paradigms, 1850-1914.* Sheffield Academic Press, 1995.

_____. *History of Biblical Interpretation.* Leiden: E. J. Brill, 2010.

Reynier, Chantal. *Saint Paul sur les routes du monde romain: Infrastructures, logistique, itinéraires.* Paris: Cerf, 2009.

Rhoads, David M., Joanna Dewey, and Donald Michie. *Mark as Story: An Introduction to the Narrative of a Gospel.* Second Edition. Minneapolis: Fortress Press, 1999.

Robbins, Vernon K. *Jesus the Teacher: A Socio-Rhetorical Interpretation of Mark.* Revised edition. Philadelphia: Fortress Press, 1992.

Robinson, James M. *Jesus: According to the Earliest Witness.* Minneapolis: Fortress Press, 2007.

Robinson, J., P. Hoffmann, and J. Koppenborg. *Documenta Q: Reconstructions of Q Through Two Centuries of Gospel Research: Excerpted, Sorted, and Evaluated.* Leuven: Peeters, 1996.

Rolland, Philippe. "Marc, lecteur de Pierre et de Paul." In Van Segbroeck et al., *The Four Gospels 1992*, 775-78.

Rollston, Christopher A., ed. *The Gospels According to Michael Goulder: A North American Response.* Trinity Press International, 2002.

Romaniuk, K. "Le Problème des Paulinismes dans l'Évangile de Marc." *NTS* 23(1977):266-274.

Rosenblatt, J. P., and J. C. Sitterson, eds. *"Not in Heaven:" Coherence and Complexity in Biblical Narrative.* Bloomington: Indiana UP, 1991.

Rubenstein, Jeffrey L., trans. *Rabbinic Stories.* Preface by Shaye D. Cohen. New York: Paulist Press, 2002.

Sanders, E. P. *Jesus and Judaism.* Philadelphia: Fortress Press, 1985.

Sanders, E. P., and Margaret Davies. *Studying the Synoptic Gospels.* Philadelphia: Trinity Press International, 1989.

Sandnes, Karl Olav. "Imitatio Homeri? An Appraisal of Dennis R. MacDonald's 'Mimesis Criticism.'" *JBL* 124:4:715-32.

Schenk, Wolfgang "Sekundare Jesuanisierungen von primaren Paulus-Aussagen bei Markus." In Van Segbroeck et al., *The Four Gospels 1992*, 877-904.

Schildgen, Brenda Deen. *Power and Prejudice: The Reception of the Gospel of Mark*. Detroit: Wayne State UP, 1999.

Schmithals, W. "Kritik der Formkritik." *ZTK* 77(1980):149-85.

Schnelle, Udo. *Apostle Paul: His Life and Theology*. Trans. Eugene Boring. Grand Rapids: Baker Book House, 2005.

Schweitzer, Albert. *The Quest of the Historical Jesus*. New York: MacMillan, 1910.

Sim, David C. "Matthew and the Pauline Corpus: A Preliminary Intertextual Study." *JSNT* 31(2009):4:401-422.

Smith, Stephen H. *A Lion with Wings: A Narrative-Critical Approach to Mark's Gospel*. Sheffield: Sheffield Academic Press, 1996.

Stanton, Graham. *Jesus and Gospel*. Cambridge: Cambridge UP, 2004.

Stegeman, Wolfgang, Bruce J. Malina, and Gerd Theissen. *The Social Setting of Jesus and the Gospels*. Minneapolis: Fortress Press, 2002.

Stegemann, Ekkehard, and Wolfgang Stegemann. *The Jesus Movement: A Social History of Its First Century*. Minneapolis: Fortress Press, 1995.

Stern, David. *Parables in Midrash: Narrative and Exegesis in Rabbinic Literature*. Cambridge: Harvard UP, 1991.

*Sternberg, Meir. *The Poetics of Biblical Narrative: Ideological Literature and the Drama of Reading*. Bloomington: Indiana UP, 1987. An interesting discussion of whether the word "fiction" can be applied to scriptural historiography.

Still, Todd D., ed. *Jesus and Paul Reconnected: Fresh Pathways into an Old Debate*. Grand Rapids: Eerdmans, 2007.

Stowers, Stanley. *Letter Writing in Greco-Roman Antiquity*. Library of Early Christianity. Westminster Press, 1986.

*Svartvik, Jesper. *Mark and Mission: Mk 7:1-23 in its Narrative and Historical Contexts*. Coniectanea Biblica New Testament Series, 32. Stockholm: Almqvist & Wiksell, 2000. Presents evidence for seeing Mark as a narrative presentation of the Pauline gospel.

Talbert, Charles H. *Literary Patterns, Theological Themes, and the Genre of Luke-Acts*. Society of Biblical Literature, 1975.

Talbert, Charles H., ed. *Luke-Acts: New Perspectives from the Society of Biblical Literature Seminar*. New York: Crossroad, 1984.

*Tarazi, Paul Nadim. *The New Testament : an Introduction. Vol. 1. Paul and Mark*. Crestwood: SVS Press, 1999. Presents Mark as a reworking of traditions from the Pauline epistles.

_____. *The New Testament: An Introduction. Vol. 2. Luke and Acts*. Crestwood: SVS Press, 2001.

_____. *The New Testament: An Introduction. Vol. 3. Johannine Writings*. Crestwood: SVS Press, 2004.

_____. *The New Testament: An Introduction. Vol. 4. Matthew and the Canon*. St. Paul: OCABS Press, 2009.

_____. *Colossians and Philemon: A Commentary*. The Chrysostom Bible. St. Paul: OCABS Press, 2010.

*_____. *Galatians. A Commentary.* Crestwood: SVS Press, 1994. Provides background for understanding the Pauline themes in Mark; see also *Romans* by the same author.

_____. *Romans: A Commentary.* The Chrysostom Bible. St. Paul: OCABS Press, 2010.

Taylor, Vincent. *The Gospel According to St. Mark.* Reprint of 1966 edition. Grand Rapids: Baker Book House, 1981.

Telford, William R. *The Theology of the Gospel of Mark.* Cambridge: Cambridge UP, 1999.

Theissen, Gerd. *The Gospels in Context: Social and Political History in the Synoptic Tradition.* Edinburgh: T & T Clark, 1992.

Thoma, Clemens, and Michael Wyschogrod. *Parable and Story in Judaism and Christianity.* New York: Paulist Press, 1989.

*Thompson, Michael B. "The Holy Internet: Communication Between Churches in the First Christian Generation." In Bauckham, *The Gospels for all Christians*, 49-70. Presents evidence that helps make the case for rejecting the view that the evangelists might have been unaware of the Pauline epistles.

Thompson, Thomas L. *The Messiah Myth: The Near Eastern Roots of Jesus and David.* New York: Basic Book, 2005.

*Tolbert, Mary Ann. *Sowing the Gospel: Mark's Work in Literary-Historical Perspective.* Augsburg Fortress, 1989. One of the most insightful works on Mark that has been produced by modern scholarship.

*Trobisch, David. *The First Edition of the New Testament*. New York: Oxford UP, 2000. Most scholars believe that many New Testament books were produced by independent Christian groups and were gathered into a single collection haphazardly over centuries. Trobisch presents evidence that a single publisher deliberately assembled and edited the New Testament books and published them as a cohesive literary whole. This is one of the foundational books that anyone who wants to understand the New Testament should read, along with Trobisch's *Paul's Letter Collection*.

*_____. *Paul's Letter Collection: Tracing the Origins*. Minneapolis: Fortress Press, 1994. Presents evidence that Paul's epistles are carefully crafted, edited, and published literary creations rather than occasional letters spontaneously written, collected, and preserved.

Trocmé, E. *The Formation of the Gospel According to Mark*. Philadelphia: Westminster Press, 1963.

Tull, Patricia. "Intertextuality and the Hebrew Scriptures." *CurBS* 8(2000):59-91.

Twain, Mark. *The Complete Essays of Mark Twain*. Ed. Charles Neider. Da Capo Press, 1991.

Tyson, J. B. "The Blindness of the Disciples in Mark." *JBL* 80(1983):261-268.

Van Iersel, Bas M. F. "Kai ethelen parelthein autous. Another Look at Mk 6:48d." In Van Segbroeck et al., *The Four Gospels 1992*, 1065-76.

_____. *Mark: A Reader-Response Commentary*. JSNTSup 164. Sheffield: Sheffield Academic Press, 1998.

Van Oyen, G. "Intercalation and Irony in the Gospel of Mark." In Van Segbroeck et al., *The Four Gospels 1992*, 949-974.

Van Segbroeck, Frans, et al., eds. *The Four Gospels 1992: Festschrift Frans Neirynck*. BETL 100. Leuven: Leuven University Press, 1992.

Van Seters, John. *In Search of History: Historiography in the Ancient World and the Origins of Biblical History*. New Haven: Yale UP, 1983.

_____. "The Pentateuch as Torah *and* History: In Defense of G. Von Rad." In Blum et al., *Das Alte Testament: Ein Geschictsbuch*, 47-64.

*_____. "Uses of the Past: The Story of David as a Test Case." In Kirkpatrick and Goltz, *The Function of Ancient Historiography in Biblical and Cognate Studies*, 18-29. On the Court History of David as composed in the Persian period. See also the earlier book *In Search of History*.

*Vines, Michael E. *The Problem of Markan Genre: the Gospel of Mark and the Jewish Novel*. Atlanta: Society of Biblical Literature, 2002. Although I am not convinced by the book's conclusion about Mark's genre, it is an excellent introduction to the subject.

Volkmar, Gustav. *Die Evangelien oder Marcus und die Synopsis der kanonischen und ausserkanonischen Evangelien nach dem altesten Text mit historisch-exegetischem Commentar*. Leipzig: Fues's, 1870.

_____. *Marcus und die Synopse der Evangelien nach dem urkundlichen Text und das Geschichtliche vom Leben Jesu*. Zurich: Schmidt, 1876. Available online

*_____. *Die Religion Jesu.* Leipzig: Brockhaus, 1857. The earliest scholarly text that interprets Mark as a narrative representation of the Pauline gospel. The theme is developed further in the author's later books.

Vorster, William. "Intertextuality and Redaktionsgeschichte." In, Sipke, *Intertextuality in Biblical writings*, 15-26.

Walter, Nikolaus. "Paul and the Early Christian Jesus-Tradition." In Wedderburn, *Paul and Jesus: Collected Essays*, 51-80.

Wedderburn, Alexander J. M. "Paul and Jesus: The Problem of Continuity." In Wedderburn, *Paul and Jesus: Collected Essays*, 99-115.

_____. "Paul and the Story of Jesus." In Wedderburn, *Paul and Jesus: Collected Essays*, 161-190.

Wedderburn, A. J. M., ed. *Paul and Jesus: Collected Essays.* Sheffield: JSOT Press, 1989.

Weeden, Theodore J. *Mark: Traditions in Conflict.* Philadelphia: Fortress Press, 1971.

Werner, Martin. *Der Einfluss paulinischer Theologie im Markusevangelium; eine Studie zur neutestamentlichen Theologie.* Giessen: Topelmann, 1923.

Wildemann, B. *Das Evangelium als Lehrpoesie. Leben und Werk Gustav Volkmars.* Kontexte, 1. Frankfurt: Peter Lang, 1983.

Wilder, Terry L. *Pseudonymity, the New Testament, and Deception: An Inquiry into Intention and Reception.* University Press of America, 2004.

Willits, Joel. "Presuppositions and Procedures in the Study of the 'Historical Jesus'. Or, Why I Decided Not to Be a 'Historical Jesus' Scholar." *Journal for the Study of the Historical Jesus* 3(2005):1:61-108.

Wills, Garry. *What Paul Meant.* New York: Viking, 2006.

Wills, Lawrence Mitchell. *The Quest of the Historical Gospel: Mark, John, and the Origins of the Gospel Genre.* New York: Routledge, 1997.

Winn, Adam. *Mark and the Elijah-Elisha Narrative: Considering the Practice of Greco-Roman Imitation in the Search for Markan Source Material.* Eugene, Ore.: Pickwick, 2010.

Winter, Paul. *On the Trial of Jesus.* 2nd ed. Berlin: Studia Judaica, Band I, 1974.

Witherington, Ben, III. *The Gospel of Mark: A Socio-Rhetorical Commentary.* Grand Rapids: Eerdmans, 2001.

_____. *The Jesus Quest: The Third Search for the Jew of Nazareth.* Downers Grove: InterVarsity Press, 1995.

Wrede, William. *The Messianic Secret.* Greenwood: Attic Press, 1971.

Zetterholm, Magnus. *Approaches to Paul: A Student's Guide to Recent Scholarship.* Minneapolis: Fortress Press, 2009.

www.ingramcontent.com/pod-product-compliance
Lightning Source LLC
Chambersburg PA
CBHW022108150426
43195CB00008B/311